Total Business Budgeting

A Step-by-Step Guide with Forms

SECOND EDITION

Total Business Budgeting

A Step-by-Step Guide with Forms

SECOND EDITION

Robert Rachlin

John Wiley & Sons, Inc.
New York • Chichester • Weinheim • Brisbane • Singapore • Toronto

This book is printed on acid-free paper. ∞

This publication is designed to provide accurate and authoritative information in regard to the subject matter covered. It is sold with the understanding that the publisher is not engaged in rendering legal, accounting, or other professional services. If legal advice or other expert assistance is required, the services of a competent professional person should be sought.

Library of Congress Cataloging-in-Publication Data:

Rachlin, Robert, 1937–
    Total business budgeting : a step-by-step guide with forms /
Robert Rachlin. — 2nd ed.
        p.   cm.
    Includes bibliographical references and index.
    ISBN 0-471-35103-2 (cloth : alk. paper)
    1. Budget in business—Handbooks, manuals, etc.   I. Title.
HG4028.B8R24   1999
658.15′4—dc21   99-30106

Printed in the United States of America.

10 9 8 7 6 5 4 3 2 1

Dedicated to Roseann, Melinda, Amy, Brian, Matthew, and Jeremy

Contents

Preface

Successful budgeting, resulting from the careful development and evaluation of all aspects of the budgeting process, can mean higher profits, company stability, industry leadership, and ultimately a well-managed and successful organization. *Total Business Budgeting: A Step-by-Step Guide with Forms*, second edition, demonstrates how a company can analyze outside influences, develop performance targets and budget segments, and organize and administer the budgeting process to make the crucial difference between success and failure of an organization. The second edition has been completely revised with new chapters on return on investment, shareholder value, leasing, and pricing.

The newly revised second edition presents complete budgeting techniques and applications for most business situations—from planning and control to implementation. Complete, detailed instructions, together with the forms, schedules, exhibits, examples, and formats provided throughout, take the reader through the myriad of details involved in developing all segments of the budgeting process. For ease of reference and use, a set of forms is also provided as an appendix. This is the only book you need to develop an effective budget.

Total Business Budgeting: A Step-by-Step Guide with Forms, second edition, is the only book on this topic that is written in step-by-step format and in nontechnical language. It is a must for all operating personnel who participate in or have responsibility for preparing part or all of the annual budget and how it fits into the overall strategic objectives of the company. Business executives in service industries, manufacturing companies, small to medium-size companies, and divisional operations of large companies can greatly benefit from this newly revised book, as well as those responsible for developing, directing, and using the budget process. This includes staff and line executives from operations, sales and marketing, business planners, strategists, project managers, manufacturing, finance, and other operational disciplines, such as presidents, senior members of management, controllers and assistants, general managers, plant managers, and budget directors and managers. Students of the subject of budgeting would also benefit from this book.

After reading *Total Business Budgeting: A Step-by-Step Guide with Forms,* second edition, you will know how to: analyze outside influences; develop a tailor-made budgeting system; make your budget reflect your long-term objectives and performance targets; learn how to use shareholder value and return on investment in applying these techniques to the budgeting process; utilize pricing and leasing in budget decisions; pinpoint budget variances; implement the budgeting process; add credibility to your budget proposal; help to reassess your company when you prepare budgets; develop meaningful and workable forms, policies, and procedures; consider the behavioral implications at play in setting up and controlling a budget; select a budgeting system to suit your company's specific needs; acquire the necessary budgeting data; develop budgets for all activities of the company; enhance your career through proper budget performance reports; define and understand budgeting costs; prepare all budget reports; organize and administer the budgeting process; and much more. In summary, you will fully grasp the whole process of budgeting and be able to achieve the goal of preparing successful budgets. I wish to thank my editor, Sheck Cho, for his assistance and guidance in publishing this book. Additional thanks are extended to the staff at John Wiley & Sons for assistance in making this book a reality.

Robert Rachlin
Plainview, New York
August 1999

CHAPTER ONE

Budgeting and the Management Process

A budget represents a company's formal expression of the plans and objectives of management, stated in terms of management's ideas about expectations for all the operational activities in a specified period. Although this may seem inordinately simple, the process and its execution still create frustrations in formulating accurate and meaningful budgets. Why?

The reason centers on the many variables needed to define the plans and objectives of the company. These variables are generated by both internal and external factors that affect the budgeting process in many ways. As one factor changes, others may be significantly affected throughout the preparation of the budget. Internal factors are mostly controllable by the company, whereas external factors are in most cases uncontrollable.

INTERNAL FACTORS

Internal factors can be placed in the following categories:

Risk Objectives. The attitude of management toward risk taking will dictate the amounts of monies and human resources that will be budgeted to specific segments of the company. For example, risk-taking organizations tend to be innovative in new products (high research and development expenses), expand into unknown markets (high marketing and sales expenses), invest in capital investments that assume higher risk (high capital investment expenditures), and incur higher than normal debt as a percentage of the company's total capitalization (high interest and principal payments).

Management Skills.   Management skills involve such basics as the ability of key executives to understand the business they are managing. Often, key executives are not totally familiar with all aspects of managing a specific business or functional area. These deficiencies usually arise when companies enter new markets through innovation, or the acquisition of companies or product lines unfamiliar to the executive. In addition, a key executive may have to deal with functional activities such as manufacturing, accounting, and legal problems that are unfamiliar due to the executive's background. Other management skills include the ability of managers who prepare budgets to interpret data, to follow ethical practices, and to understand the critical role of budgeting in managing a business.

Management Style.   Management style is often a function of aspects of the manager's background, such as experience in more than one industry, personal aspirations, aggressiveness or passivity, and the organizational structure to which the manager is accustomed or in which he or she is currently operating (decentralization versus centralization).

Product Innovation.   Management must be able to recognize the life cycle stage of a product, product line, or market (see Chapter 2 for further discussion). In addition, management must recognize the response time (fast or slow) in which competitors can enter the marketplace. When competitors need a longer time to enter the marketplace, a company has a longer time to dominate the market.

Operational Style.   How managers operate their budgetary segments will often determine how budgets are prepared. For example, someone who delegates authority may allow the budget to be built up from the bottom. A manager whose authoritarian style is not to delegate may prepare a departmental budget with little or no input from members of the department.

Attitudinal Differences.   Differences in attitude toward the budgeting process usually reflect the level of the individual within the organization. For example, the attitudes of chief executive officers differ from those of other managers in the following ways: Chief executive officers (CEOs) see the entire business, whereas other managers focus only on that part of the business that affects their authority; CEOs often measure results in nonquantitative terms, whereas other managers measure in quantitative terms; CEOs see competitors as adversaries, whereas other managers see them as part of doing business; CEOs are more concerned with longer time periods, whereas other managers are concerned with shorter periods; and CEOs develop total company performance commitments, whereas other managers are more concerned with specific performance standards for their own segments.

These internal factors determine how budgets are prepared, coordinated, and controlled and the extent to which they are used as a tool for measuring performance. These factors will become part of the entire process of preparing the company budget. Before the budgeting process begins, it is advisable to discuss the internal factors defined in this section and reach a consensus on each. Remember, most of these factors are controllable by management, and the decisions that are reached become a vital ingredient in the success or failure of an organization's budget. (External factors will be discussed in Chapter 2.)

FUNCTIONS OF BUDGETING

Business managers often ask, "Why do we go through this exercise of budgeting?" This is a fair question that can be answered by looking at what budgeting contributes to the management of an organization. Although some companies may have unique reasons for preparing budgets, a budget usually performs the following functions:

Timely Analysis.   Budgeting provides management with an accurate and timely analytical tool. It is the one set of documents that provides immediate analysis when compared to actual company performance on a reasonably timely basis.

Performance Prediction.   Although there are other methods of predicting performance, such as trend analysis, mathematical extrapolation, extension of past performance, and the like, budgeting predicts performance by bringing together all estimates under one function. Because most forecasts are related to other forecasts, continuity between budget estimates is always maintained. Therefore, individual and company predictions of performance are visibly displayed and readily understood by everyone within the organization.

Resource Allocation.   Budgeting provides an excellent tool for allocating an organization's resources. This process affords the opportunity to say "what if" about certain resource allocations and determine the impact of alternative allocations on a part of the organization or on the organization as a whole. Allocating resources in the budgeting process also provides a company with an early warning system for ongoing opportunities and anticipated threats.

Performance Control.   Budgeting provides the ability to control current performance and early warning signals of when and how certain forecasts are going to deviate from what was originally anticipated in the budget. Through the periodic monitoring of actual performance versus budgeted estimates, an organization is able to adjust to changes from budget by shifting resources to maximize results.

Managerial Instruction.   Budgeting provides useful instruction to managers by allowing them to learn from the mistakes they made in prior forecasts. Constant monitoring and analysis of performance results teaches managers where they made mistakes in judgment and how they can avoid future mistakes.

Consensus and Support.   Through the budgeting process, a consensus of ideas, strategies, and directions is developed. In addition, support for the total budget is generally agreed upon, and a unified direction is brought into focus for all budgeting department heads.

 Clearly, the advantages of budgeting outweigh the time and effort that go into the preparation of budgets. If used effectively, budgeting is a powerful tool for managing a business and provides the key to success as an organization.

WHY BUDGETS FAIL

The failure of budgets within an organization usually results from the following conditions:

Lack of Support.   Even though budgets may be formally presented and approved, many organizations give little or no support to the contents of the approved budget. This type of behavior adds significantly to budget failures.

Failure to Monitor the Correct Factors.   Too many managers are inept at distinguishing what parts of the budget to control. Many are concerned with too much detail and some with too little detail. A balance of control is necessary for those factors that have a significant impact on the operations under the control of the manager.

Failure to Use Sound Judgment.   Too often, managers attempt to substitute budgeting for sound judgment. Although judgment alone is inadequate, the use of judgment as a managerial tool in budgeting helps to promote innovation. Without innovation, budgets are usually doomed to fail.

Poor Understanding of Budgeting Role.   Failure to understand the role of budgeting is damaging. It is important to understand that budgeting is never "cast in

Exhibit 1.1   Relationship of Budgeting to the Planning Cycle

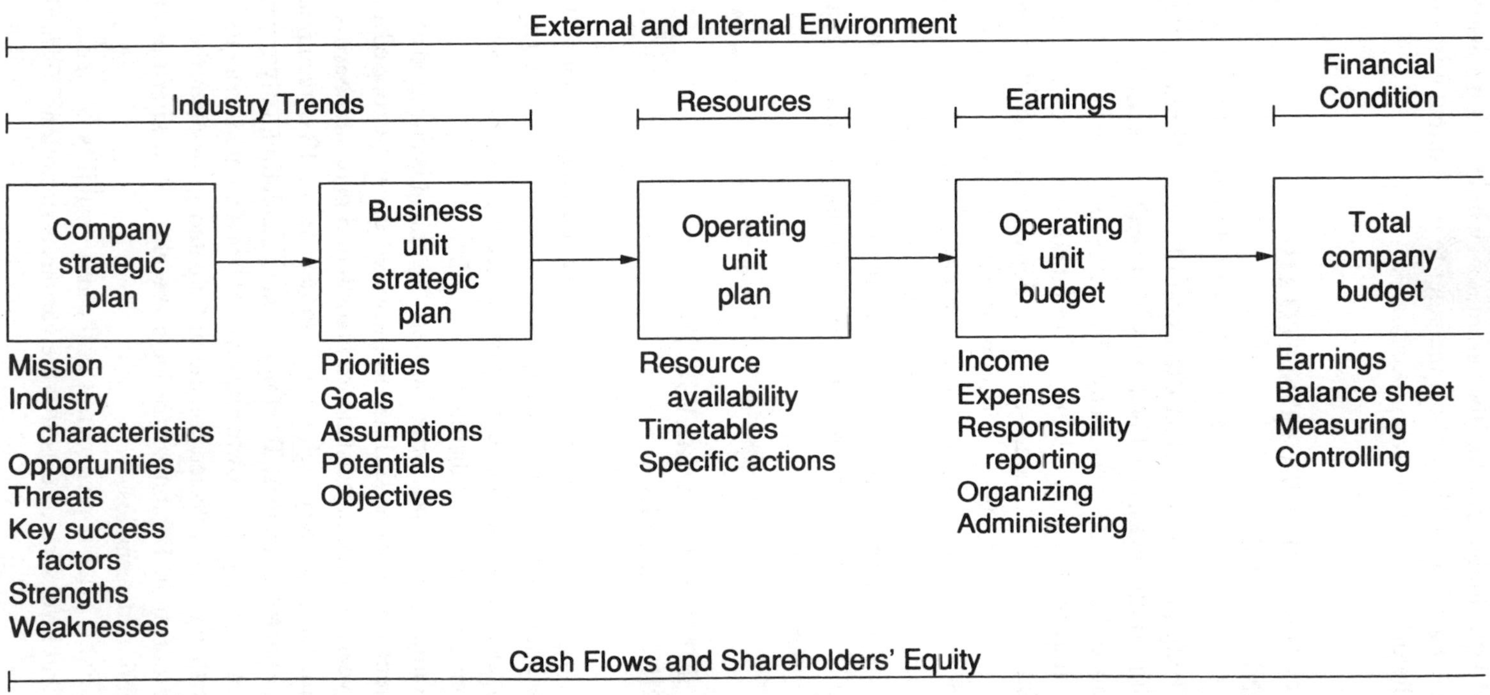

External and Internal Environment

Industry Trends | Resources | Earnings | Financial Condition

Company strategic plan → Business unit strategic plan → Operating unit plan → Operating unit budget → Total company budget

Company strategic plan:
Mission
Industry characteristics
Opportunities
Threats
Key success factors
Strengths
Weaknesses

Business unit strategic plan:
Priorities
Goals
Assumptions
Potentials
Objectives

Operating unit plan:
Resource availability
Timetables
Specific actions

Operating unit budget:
Income
Expenses
Responsibility reporting
Organizing
Administering

Total company budget:
Earnings
Balance sheet
Measuring
Controlling

Cash Flows and Shareholders' Equity

concrete." True, budgets outline the parameters within which a manager has to operate, but it is the responsibility of the manager to request that operational changes be made to the original budgets when necessary.

RELATIONSHIP OF BUDGETING TO THE PLANNING CYCLE

The budgeting process is a direct extension of the corporate strategic plans of the organization. Both the financial budgets—that is, (1) the activity forecasts that relate to the balance sheet and the company's financial condition and (2) the operating budgets, or estimates of activity relating to both income and expenses and to the components of the earnings statement—are reflections of the overall strategic plans of the company. For example, the preparation of the unit budget is dictated by the unit's operational plan, which is dictated by the strategic plan of the business unit, which in turn is generated by the overall corporate strategic plan. Exhibit 1.1 outlines the interrelationships of the plans and budgets at different levels within the organization. In addition, all aspects of the preparation of budgets and plans are affected by both external and internal factors.

USE OF SENSITIVITY ANALYSIS IN PREPARING BUDGETS

A simple "what if" scenario can be used to prepare budgets in an effort to determine alternative budgeting data. The "what if" technique, commonly referred to as sensitivity analysis, allows the budget preparer to see the consequences of using different assumptions and the impact thereof.

For example, once a pro forma earnings statement is prepared as shown in Exhibit 1.2, different assumptions such as no projected growth expected for the following budgeted year; an anticipated standard growth of 3 percent; above average growth of 6 percent; or an extremely high growth anticipated of 12 percent, can be developed with the projected outcomes. To simplify the calculation, only a yearly rate will be applied, but in reality, the growth rates would be calculated on a quarterly basis. Only sales growth will be reflected for the anticipated growth rate with all other costs remaining constant. Exhibit 1.3 reflects the change in after-tax profits using the above-mentioned scenarios.

Once Exhibit 1.3 is prepared, it is the responsibility of management to decide which budget level should be used at the various assumptions. To further enable man-

Exhibit 1.2   Budgeted Pro Forma Earnings Statement, Year Ended 20XX ($ in millions)

Net sales	$3,000
Less cost of goods sold (76%)	2,280
Gross profit	720
Less operating expenses:	
Selling expenses	190
Administrative expenses	160
Operating profit	370
Provision for income taxes (48%)	178
Net income	$ 192

agement to make this decision, additional calculations in the form of probabilities are necessary. What is the probability of net sales materializing at the various growth levels, that is, 3 percent, 6 percent, or 12 percent? Exhibit 1.4 illustrates a typical probability analysis using net sales levels only, and reflecting the results on net income. Using the sensitivity analysis approach, Exhibit 1.4 would be used as next year's earnings forecast.

Exhibit 1.3   Pro Forma Earnings Statement Using Various Assumptions, Year Ended 20XX ($ in millions)

	3%	*6%*	*12%*
Net sales	$3,090	$3,180	$3,360
Less cost of goods sold (76%)	2,348	2,417	2,554
Gross profit	742	763	806
Less operating expenses:			
Selling expenses	190	190	190
Administrative expenses	160	160	160
Operating profit	392	413	456
Provision for income taxes (48%)	188	198	219
Net income	204	215	237

Exhibit 1.4   Probability Analysis Using Net Sales, Year Ended 20XX ($ in millions)

		Probability Levels		
Level of Growth	3%	6%	12%	Total
Net sales	$3,090	$3,180	$3,360	
Probability levels	70%	20%	10%	
Revised net sales	2,163	636	336	$3,135
Less cost of goods sold (76%)				2,383
Gross profit				752
Less operating expenses:				
Selling expenses				190
Administrative expenses				160
Operating profit				402
Provision for income taxes (48%)				193
Net income				$209

CHAPTER TWO

Analyzing Outside Influences

Many outside influences affect the budgeting process by their impacts on various elements in both the earnings statement and the balance sheet. Any discussion of outside influences must consider major issues in the following areas:

- Business/industry
- U.S./world economics
- Politics
- Cultural demographics
- Technology
- Health/human resources
- Resource limitations

Each of these issues must be analyzed individually, those that affect the company must be reviewed, and the means by which they relate to the budgetary process must be identified. In addition, an estimate of the amount of risk that might be incurred must be identified. In addition, an estimate of the amount of risk that might be incurred must also be reviewed. To aid in this process, a worksheet is provided in Exhibit 2.1.

PREPARATION OF KEY OVERALL ISSUES WORKSHEET

Each of these major issues must be addressed and considered before the actual budgeting process begins. When difficulties in identification or response arise, it is recommended that only a limited amount of identifiable issues be addressed. It is further recommended that a company limit itself to no more than six key issues. For each key overall issue, prepare a separate worksheet according to the following instructions:

Company/Operating Unit.   Does the key issue relate to the overall company or to an autonomous operating unit that is part of a separate industry from that of the rest of the company?

Time Span.   Over what period should the data be used? For example, a key political issue may cover all budgets for the next three to four years depending on the terms of political office.

Preparer, Date Prepared, Relevant Budgeting Period, and Key Issue.   Self-explanatory.

Factors Concerning the Business.   Within the key issues, what factors affect the business? For example, for cultural/demographic issues, how will changes in national and/or local population mix influence markets and customer base?

How These Factors Will Become Part of the Budgeting Process.   Once the factors are determined, how are they going to be used as part of the budgeting process? For example, if population changes are anticipated, what considerations must be given to marketing, manufacturing, and servicing the customer?

Estimate of Risk.   Based on the specific factors, what element of risk can be expected? For example, what is the risk of the population change within the segment of the market that affects our business? The higher the risk factor, the quicker the payback that should be expected. Probabilities can become part of the calculation within the budgeting process.

ASSESSING THE ECONOMIC INPUTS

The issues identified in Exhibit 2.1 must now be analyzed to determine where and by how much they will affect the budgeting process. It is advisable to analyze only those economic factors about which information is known and not to take any wild guesses.

Exhibit 2.1   Key Overall Issues

Company/Operating Unit

Time Span

Preparer:

Date Prepared:

Used in What Budgeting Period:

KEY ISSUE:

Factors concerning the business:

How these factors will become part of the budgeting process:

Estimate of risk:

To assist in this exercise, a worksheet is provided in Exhibit 2.2. Note that the list of economic factors used in this worksheet is merely a sampling—each company and/or operating unit must determine its own economic factors.

It is interesting to note that most external factors are uncontrollable in the short, intermediate, and long term. However, several external factors are controllable in the long term, such as industry sales, types of industries in which a company wants to compete, and types of product lines it will sell. However, most internal factors are controllable in the short, intermediate, and long term. Some exceptions include quality of employees, pricing, and production methods. These factors usually extend beyond the short-range period, but are controllable within the intermediate and long-range period.

Once the estimates have been developed, they become part of the budgeting process and should be included in the estimates for the next budget period. To illustrate how economic factors affect the budget projections, let us focus on two examples, namely, inflation and seasonality index.

Impact of Inflation

The impact of inflation on a business is often misunderstood. Most successful businesses employ new ways of doing business in familiar markets with familiar products. Or, to put it more simply, they concentrate their strengths against their competitors' relative weaknesses.

Problems caused by inflation include inadequate depreciation, cash erosion, inflated inventories, pressures on working capital, high cost and limited availability of capital, inadequate pricing, poor productivity, and internal decision-making problems. Let us briefly review what happens in each of these areas during an inflationary period.

- *Inadequate Depreciation.* Depreciation charges are usually insufficient to recover the initial capital investment because depreciation represents part of the cash flow of a company.

- *Cash Erosion.* There are frequently reductions in the availability of cash to effectively operate the business.

- *Inflated Inventories.* Inventories are inflated by higher costs of materials, labor, and other factors. Therefore, inventories that are sold must be replaced at higher costs.

- *Pressures on Working Capital.* Working funds are greatly reduced, thus potentially slowing a company's growth.

- *High Cost and Limited Availability of Capital.* A heavy demand on capital usually exists, with limited availability of funds and at higher interest costs.

- *Pricing.* Noncompetitive prices result.

Exhibit 2.2   Financial Impact Profile

Company/Operating unit					Financial Impact Profile					Budget period
Impact on Earnings Statement					Economic Factors	Impact on Balance Sheet				
Volume	Sales $	Price	Operating Expenses	Earnings		Working Capital	Capital Structure	EPS	ROI	Capital Expenditure
					Interest rate fluctuations					
					Changes in currency values					
					Inflation rate					
					Governmental legislation					
					Declining productivity					
					Technology					
					Political unrest					
					Mergers and acquisitions					
					Natural disaster					
					Competitive reactions					
					Strikes					
					Supplier capacity					
					Unemployment					
					Market collapse					
					Social changes					
					High labor and material costs					
					Energy shortages					
					Industry growth					
					Demographic changes					
					Weather					
					Seasonal index					
					Material shortage					

Indicate (+) for positive results; (–) for negative results; (+ –) for both

Preparer _____   Date Prepared _____

- *Poor Productivity.* Productivity can be defined as increased output without a corresponding increase in input. It is important to understand that productivity applies not only to employees but to customers and stockholders. Worker or employee productivity exists when wages, salaries, and benefits increase at a rate greater than inflation so that employees experience an increase in real income. Customer productivity exists when average unit selling prices rise more slowly than consumer prices in general. And stockholder productivity exists when dividends, earnings, and return on equity increase faster than inflation. Productivity will generally decline unless a company can establish a level of standards acceptable for inflationary times.

- *Internal Factors.* Many areas of internal decision making are affected and therefore need to be part of the budgeting process during an inflationary period. They include cost, pricing, and financing policies; employee compensation, capital investment, and dividend policies; quality control standards; raw material resources; company and competitor sales growth; changing attitudes toward customers and competitors; and the overall ability of employees and management to be flexible during inflationary times.

Seasonality Index

The seasonality index relates to the seasonal activity patterns that affect most industries. For example, retailers generally have a high seasonal index during the more important holiday seasons such as Christmas, Easter, and the Fourth of July.

To determine your industry's seasonal index, develop historical data of seasonal indexes for the past two years from industry sources, and use these indexes to project estimated activity for any given period within the budget year. For example, Exhibit 2.3 is used to project averages for a given year. Based on year 20X1 and year 20X2, averages are calculated to arrive at the budget year projections. January is 86 (85 + 87)/2; February is 86.5 (87 + 86)/2; and so forth. These figures will indicate the expected increase or decrease in the marketplace and should be reflected in anticipated sales by month. A similar worksheet should be prepared for your company as illustrated in Exhibit 2.3.

USING PRODUCT LIFE CYCLES IN BUDGETING

Most product life cycle (PLC) curves are used to describe either a single product's sales growth or a life cycle for the total business. In either case, the PLC curve has been used principally to forecast a company's revenues. For example, most products

Exhibit 2.3 Seasonal Index Worksheet, Budget Year ____

	Year 20X1	*Year 20X2*	*Projected Budget Year*
January	85	87	86
February	87	86	86.5
March	90	92	91
April	115	117	116
May	101	100	100.5
June	90	88	89
July	106	108	107
August	92	95	93.5
September	90	93	91.5
October	85	84	84.5
November	98	99	98.5
December	125	129	127

have a very low sales growth during the introductory stage. As a company promotes the product through advertising and the buying public becomes aware of it and accepts it, the product begins to reflect substantial growth and enter into the growth stage. As competitors enter the marketplace, the product enters the maturity stage, and the amount of revenue it generates begins to level off. At this stage a product runs the risk of becoming obsolete and may eventually be replaced by other products (see Exhibit 2.4). In order to achieve steady growth, an organization must introduce new

Exhibit 2.4 Product Life Cycle

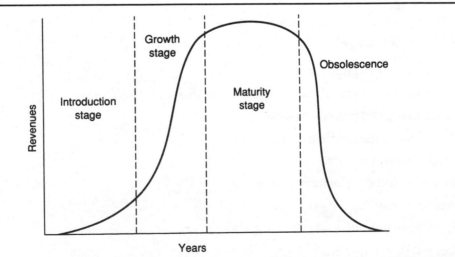

Exhibit 2.5   Business Life Cycle

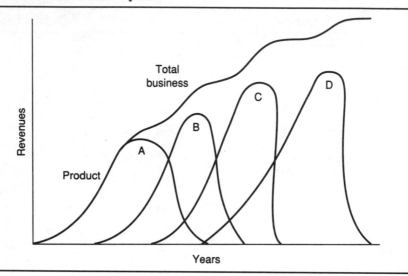

products as soon as the growth stage of older products begins to slow down (see Exhibit 2.5).

The life cycle concept can also be used to provide guidelines on budgeting revenues, expenses, balance sheet, and cash flow projections. For example, during the start-up or introduction stage, revenues are usually low: they rise during the growth stage, stabilize or reach their highest level during the maturity stage, and decline during the obsolescence stage.

The following list points out some exceptions to these rules. Although revenues are low, their items represent high levels of activity.

Introduction Stage

Direct labor—high per unit

Depreciation—high when accelerated depreciation is used

Advertising and promotion—high

Travel and entertainment—high

Market research—high

Research and development—high

Accounts payable—high

Long-term liabilities—high

Long-term debt—high

Growth Stage

Earnings per share—average

Sale of fixed assets—none

Dividends—very little

Debt repayment—none

Maturity Stage

Travel and entertainment—reduced

Research and development—reduced

Obsolescence Stage

Marketable securities—high

Taxes payable—high

Sales of fixed assets—high

These are but a few of the many guidelines that can be used to establish realistic standards in budget preparation. Keep in mind that the exceptions mentioned here are only a few of the exceptions possible in each stage. It is important to establish guidelines for each of the elements that constitute the financial statements: the earnings statement, the balance sheet, and the cash flow statement. Each product life cycle stage requires different standards based on due consideration of the exceptions identified.

CHAPTER THREE

Developing Performance Targets

The development of performance targets is an ongoing process that may be carried out in many ways. Performance targets may be developed on the basis of cost of capital, industry standards, key historical ratios, weighted industry averages, or established strategic plans of the company. Generally, the development of goals or performance targets start with the overall strategic goals of the company. These strategic goals are then translated into specific long-range goals, annual budget commitments, and finally operating budget plans for the current budget year.

PREPARING BUDGETING GOALS

To illustrate the process of preparing budgeting goals, a technique that allows the preparer to establish operating budget plans using strategic corporate goals as a base will be examined. Exhibit 3.1 is a worksheet designed to allow preparers to develop performance targets for their own companies. In addition, space is provided for an expected completion date for each of the four categories and, where possible, the names(s) of individual(s) who will be responsible for carrying out these goals. The goals to be detailed in the worksheet are examined further here.

Exhibit 3.1   Worksheet for Developing Performance Targets

_____ COMPANY NAME	Date Prepared: _____ Budget Period: _____ Preparer: _____

Strategic Corporate Goals:

(1) _____
(2) _____
(3) _____
(4) _____
(5) _____

Individual(s) Responsible:

(1) _____
(2) _____
(3) _____
(4) _____   Completion Date: _____

Specific Long-Range Goals:

(1) _____
(2) _____
(3) _____
(4) _____
(5) _____

Individual(s) Responsible:

(1) _____
(2) _____
(3) _____
(4) _____   Completion Date: _____

Annual Budget Commitments:

(1) _____
(2) _____
(3) _____
(4) _____
(5) _____

Individual(s) Responsible:

(1) _____
(2) _____
(3) _____
(4) _____   Completion Date: _____

Operating Budget Plans:

(1) _____
(2) _____
(3) _____
(4) _____
(5) _____

Individual(s) Responsible:

(1) _____
(2) _____
(3) _____
(4) _____   Completion Date: _____

Strategic Corporate Goals

The strategic goals of the company are established for the long term. They are based on the mission statement of the company, external and internal environments, strengths and weaknesses, and other pertinent data that established the company's long-term position in relation to the competitive and economic environment. For example, they may include such goals as the maintenance or improvement of the company's ability to attract capital; the expansion or maintenance of productivity and market share; and the increase in expected return on stockholders' equity. Although these are but a few of the strategic goals, they nevertheless give the preparer some insight as to what strategic goals are. These strategic corporate goals then become translated into long-range goals.

Specific Long-Range Goals

Based on the strategic goals that are established for the company, specific long-range goals can be established. Remember, these goals are based on the strategic goals and support the strategies outlined by the company for the long term. They include development of new markets and channels of distribution, market share expansion or contraction, development of new products and improvement of existing products, increase or effective maintenance of capacities in production, recommendations for new plant and equipment and/or expansion to reduce cost, development of human resource skills through both inside and outside training to meet the needs of the future; and the method by which capital is to be acquired, that is, debt versus equity. Upon completion of these specific long-range goals, annual budget commitments are developed.

Annual Budget Commitments

These commitments provide the basis for the preparation of the annual budget. They include such items as production quotas, productivity targets, pricing strategies, gross margin goals, capital investment limitations, and working capital goals. Annual budget commitments become the basis for the establishment of operating budget plans.

Operating Budget Plans

These budget plans are developed to support the daily, weekly, or monthly operating plans of the company. They include customer order delivery schedules, weekly and monthly production schedules, vendor delivery schedules, and other departmental work schedules.

ESTABLISHING PROFIT GOALS FOR SEGMENTS OR TOTAL COMPANY

Methods of establishing profit goals will depend on the philosophy of the company. In some cases, several methods may be used in conjunction to arrive at an overall average. Some of these techniques include the weighted industry average, weighted return on investment average, average weighted cost of capital, and other criteria such as corporate rate of return, past performance of the accountability center, corporate rate plus an additional percentage, risk of the accountability center, industry averages, and mandates by government regulations. Some of these methods are explored in this section.

Weighted Industry Average

This method is designed to develop an overall weighted average of return rates in dealing with more than one industry. Let us assume that a company is in five different industries: publishing, cosmetics, tobacco, electronics, and pharmaceuticals. Using industry return on assets rates (return on equity may also be used) and determining the percentage of the assets being used for each segment of the company, an average is developed as illustrated in Exhibit 3.2.

Based on the data provided in Exhibit 3.2, the average for the company in industries in which they participate is 17.8 percent. If these industry rates and percentage segments of the company's assets continue, the target or minimum rate should be 17.8 percent. Exhibit 3.3 provides a sample form for the preparer to use in applying this method.

Exhibit 3.2   Weighted Industry Average

Type of Industry	Current Industry Return on Asset Rates	Percentage Segments	Weighted Average
Publishing	15.9%	20%	.0318
Cosmetics	16.9	10	.0169
Tobacco	19.8	30	.0594
Electronics	16.2	10	.0162
Pharmaceuticals	17.9	30	.0537
Total		100%	.1780

Exhibit 3.3   Form for Determining Weighted Industry Average Return on Assets Rates

---

Weighted Industry Average Return On Assets Rates

Budget Period _____   Date Prepared _____

                                                                   Approval _____

Calculation

Industry Segments*	Current Industry ROA Rates	Percentage of Segments of Company's Assets	Weighted Average

---

Comments (state relationship of weighted average rate to overall corporate objectives).

---

*Should coincide as closely as possible with each industry for which company operates.

Weighted Return on Investment Average

To establish anticipated return on investment rates for the company, an analysis can be made of each operational division as a percentage of the total earnings. Based on the overall weighted average, changes can be made in the budget to reflect a higher budgeted return on investment rate.

In using the return on investment concept, there are many ways to develop the budget to increase the expected return on investment rate. They include:

- Merging operating divisions to eliminate duplication
- Eliminating operating divisions by selling parts of or all the divisions' assets to an outside buyer
- Effectively managing assets and controlling expenses
- Increasing the share of market
- Reevaluating the pricing structure in an effort to raise prices where feasible
- Changing the mix of products and/or divisions to bolster returns
- Raising the return on investment potentials by offering greater incentives (being cautious not to set an unattainable objective or foster mismanagement of assets)
- Acquiring other divisions and/or companies that would add to the potential base of the division. This technique is illustrated in Exhibit 3.4.

Based on the data provided in Exhibit 3.4, the budgeted weighted average for the entire company is 12.3 percent. This must be compared with the weighted average cost of capital to determine the feasibility of using this rate as an objective.

Weighted Average Cost of Capital[1]

This method takes all the components of capital that constitute a company's capital structure and assigns given values to each component in accordance with contractual and calculated rates in calculating a weighted average cost. These components of capital include both internal funds, such as retained earnings, and external funds, such as debt and preferred and common stock. Each of these components has a cost.

This cost belongs to the stockholders, because they invest in a company with the expectation of receiving some future benefits. These benefits induce them to pay the price for the stock in anticipation of future dividends and capital appreciation. Analysis of both benefits shows that they come from future earnings per share and are the principal factors affecting the price of the stock in the long run. Therefore, the stockholders' cost is measured by the inverse of the price-earnings ratio, or the earnings-price ratio.

The price-earnings ratio is a reflection of investor confidence. Investors react in different ways depending upon their outlook. For example, when investors are optimistic about increasing future profits, they bid the price of the stock upward, thus rais-

---

[1]Robert Rachlin, *Successful Techniques for Higher Profits* (New York: MARR Publications, 1981), pp. 25–29.

Exhibit 3.4   Illustration of Weighted Return on Investment Average

Division	Current ROI Potential	Divisional Earnings as % of Total	Weighted Average
A	7%	12%	.008
B	10	40	.040
C	11	28	.031
D	15	21	.032
E	20	6	.012
Corporate	—	(7)	—
		100%	.123

ing the multiple. Conversely, when they are pessimistic about the future of earnings, or when they find more attractive alternatives, they tend to stay out of the stock market, and falling prices reduce the price-earnings ratio.

A review of the components of capital will reveal the specific cost of most elements, such as debt and preferred stock. However, common equity presents a different problem and involves a different calculation. For example, earnings retained in the business have a cost because stockholders view retained earnings as an opportunity cost—that is, when these earnings are retained in the business, they cannot be used to earn money elsewhere. In theory, the retention of these funds is the same as if dividends were used to buy the company's stock. Therefore, the cost of common equity is part of the money that the stockholder has invested in the ownership of the company.

The cost of common equity is calculated as

$$\frac{\text{Anticipated earnings}}{\text{Net price per share}}$$

or as

$$\frac{\text{Dividends per share}}{\text{Net price per share}} + \text{Expected annual rate of growth of dividends}$$

The cost of equity is calculated to be 10 percent, given the following facts:

Anticipated earnings per share	$2
Net price per share	$20
Dividends per share	$1
Growth rate	5%

Thus

$$\frac{\$2}{\$20} = 10\%$$

or

$$\frac{\$1}{\$20} + 5\% = 10\%$$

The 10 percent cost of equity will be used in the overall calculation of the weighted cost of capital. Given the following facts, the weighted average cost of capital is calculated to be 8 percent, as shown in Exhibit 3.5:

Long-term debt	$250,000 at 10.2%
Preferred stockholders' equity	$100,000 at 8.2%
Common stockholders' equity	$350,000
Tax rate	50%

Note that the after-tax cost of long-term debt was 5.1 percent. Because interest costs are tax deductible, the tax rate of 50 percent (use current corporate tax rate) must be applied to this cost. All other costs are already after taxes, and no adjustments are necessary. In addition, each of the capital structure components are weighted as a percentage of the total capital structure of $700,000. This weight is multiplied by the after-tax cost to obtain an average weighted cost.

The average weighted cost of capital—in this case, 8.0 percent—is used as a base for determining the minimum required cutoff rate of return on new investments. In other words, in looking at our previous example, management should not approve any new investments that are expected to yield less than 8 percent. Anything that yields less than 8 percent will yield losses, and any investment yielding more than 8 percent will yield profits. However, a sound management decision is to allow several per-

Exhibit 3.5   Weighted Average Cost of Capital Method

Capital Structure	After-Tax Cost	Weight	Weighted Cost
Long-term debt	5.1%	35.7%	1.8%
Preferred stockholders' equity	8.2	14.3	1.2
Common stockholders' equity	10.0	50.0	5.0
Total		100.0%	8.0%

centage points over and above the average weighted cost of capital in case of errors in forecasting and unforeseen events. This decision will protect the investments' profitability in the long run. In this example, the minimum required cutoff rate would be 10 percent.

Earnings Per Share Goals

Both the financial community and shareholders give a great deal of attention to earnings per share (EPS). This is the amount earned during a period on the common shareholders investment as evidenced by the number of common stock outstanding. A more significant budget goal is the growth of EPS. The outside community (investment and shareholder) often considers that EPS growth is a positive barometer. However, this is greatly influenced by how much earnings is retained in the business for other uses; retirement of common share through the purchasing of treasury shares; acquisitions and/or divestitures; changes in the capital structure such as changes in the proportion of debt versus equity financing; and accounting adjustments. Caution should be used during the budgeting process to consider how budgeted changes affect EPS goals and what impact this may have on future stock prices as well as funding.

ESTABLISHING PERFORMANCE STANDARDS THROUGH RATIOS

Another way of establishing performance standards is to use historical ratios for either the company or a specific division. Ratios can be grouped into different categories to highlight trends at different levels of the company. Each category focuses on a different responsibility level within the company and relates to different parts of the business. Two different groupings can be used. One category of ratios is shown in Exhibit 3.6. Another grouping categorizes by performance ratios, managing ratios, and profitability ratios, which we detail in the following sections. In both groupings, data must be provided for the prior year's actual percentage results, the current budget period for which you are preparing data, the industry standard if available, and specific actions that are to be taken to reach your anticipated standard. This process provides a company with a ratio profile by which to develop both financial and nonfinancial performance standards.

Performance Ratios

These ratios follow the trend of the overall performance of the company. Because these ratios are viewed by the outside community as a way of measuring both current

Exhibit 3.6 Ratio Profile of a Company

Category Standard	Prior Year's Actual	Budget Period	Industry Standard	Actions To Be Taken
Measuring Liquidity				
Working capital				
Inventory turnover				
Days' sales in receivables				
Current ratio				
Days' sales in inventory				
Accounts receivable turnover				
Evaluating Debt				
Debt to equity				
Cash flow/debt				
Times interest earned				
Debt to assets				
Measuring profit				
Earnings per share				
Return on capital				
Return on equity				
Net profit margin				
Total asset turnover				

Ratio Profile of a Company

Company

Budget Period

and potential performance, they are important to the overall success of the company. They include such ratios as net earnings to shareholders' equity, net sales to shareholders' equity, and net earnings to total assets.

Managing Ratios

These ratios assist in evaluating the various components of the balance sheet and are used in managing such major areas of the company as cash, receivables, inventories, and debt relationships. They include such ratios as current ratio, acid test ratio, current liabilities to shareholders' equity, debt to equity, net sales to fixed assets (net), net sales to working capital, fixed assets (net) to shareholders' equity, days' sales outstanding, cost of sales to inventories and day's sales on hand.

Profitability Ratios

These ratios evaluate components of the earnings statement and effectively show how well a manager is performing, given his or her level of responsibility. They include such ratios as net earnings to net sales, gross margin percent, and selling expenses to net sales.

CHAPTER FOUR

Budgeting Shareholder Value*

The process of budgeting shareholder value assumes that shareholders will decide whether or not to invest in a company based on the company's increase/decrease in shareholder value. Therefore, it is incumbent upon management to budget, as well as to perform results that increase the value to the shareholders. This includes providing for tools necessary to the budgeting process such as utilizing resources to maximize return on investment, setting in place a productive employee compensation plan, and creating a measurement procedure to evaluate periodic performance.

SHAREHOLDER VALUE DEFINED

Common stockholders require adequate returns on their investment. This includes both dividends and appreciation of stock, or both. Since cash flow is generated through investments over the life of the business, assuming the impacts of risk, shareholder value can be expressed as the sum of after-tax cash flows in the future in today's dollars. The financial measure commonly used to measure future after-tax cash flows is discounted cash flow (DCF). Further discussions can be found in Chapter 25, Techniques of Evaluating Capital Investments.

---

*Contents of this chapter are partially based on *Handbook of Budgeting*, fourth edition, by Robert Rachlin (New York: John Wiley & Sons, Inc., 1998) Chapter 9, pp. 9.1–9.16.

A concentration on future after-tax cash flows is important since other measurement techniques, such as earnings per share and returns on equity and operating assets, do not add to value creation. This includes the element of risk, expectations of investors, and the time value of money. It is suggested that focusing on future cash flows is rewarded by higher share prices, whereas, focusing on accounting earnings can result in decisions that lessen company values.

METHODS OF EVALUATING SHAREHOLDER VALUE

The two methods used to calculate shareholder value are long-term valuation and economic value added (EVA), which measures short-term value creation.

Long-Term Valuation.   Based on the discounted cash flow (DCF) technique, long-term valuation is used to evaluate long-term projects such as capital investment proposals and potential acquisitions, to assess long-term plans and projects, and as an economic decision-making tool. This method links shareholder value to investment decisions.

The term *value* is used to define free cash flow, which is after-tax cash generated for a period after investments have been made from the operations of the business. It does not include financing transactions. Investments in the business, or reinvestments, refers to capital expenditures for plant and equipment, changes in receivables and inventory less accounts payables (operating capital), and investments in acquisitions, mergers, etc. An example of a Statement of Funds Flow, which results in the calculation of free cash flow, is shown in Exhibit 4.1.

Exhibit 4.1   Statement of Funds Flow, Calculation of Free Cash Flow ($ in millions)

Operating income (before interest and taxes)	$1,000
+ Other income	210
– Cash operating taxes paid	(360)
Income after cash taxes (before interest)	850
– Additions to plant (net of depreciation)	(120)
– Additions to operating capital	(60)
– Additions to investments	(80)
Reinvestment	(260)
Free cash flow	$590

If Exhibit 4.1 were spread out over the long term, 5–10 years for example, the free cash flows would be discounted using a rate equal to the cost of capital. Further discussion follows on how to calculate cost of capital.

Cost of Capital

Cost of capital is the average rate of earnings that investors require to induce them to provide all forms of long-term capital to the company when risk is considered. Two majors areas that generally involve the cost of capital and elements of capital are: internal decisions within a company as to how capital should be employed, that is, which projects should be selected for investments; and deciding what outside sources should be used to provide the services, facilities, and funds needed to operate the business.

A company has many sources and variations of capital to choose from, such as equity and debt financing. The cost of capital can be calculated using several techniques. One is opportunity cost, which measures the maximum yield from a specific investment that might have been earned if the investment had been applied to some alternative risk. Another approach is to use the internal rate of return, which measures the discount rate, equating current or future cash flows with the original investment. The incremental cost technique states that any rate earned above the cost of financing is a favorable investment. For example, a capital investment earning 25 percent after borrowing from outside sources at 12 percent is a favorable investment. Reviewing economic theory further supports this, as well as the following pronouncement made by Lord Keynes. "Businessmen would continue to invest as long as the return of one more dollar of investment (marginal efficiency of capital) exceeded the interest rate (marginal cost of capital)." From this statement, it appears that the incremental cost method makes sense and has substantial validity. Another technique is the weighted average cost approach, a discussion of which follows.

Weighted Average Cost Method.   Management has a responsibility for investing equity to ensure that the minimum rate of return on investment equals the return required to keep the value of the existing common equity unchanged. The cost of equity can be shown in two ways:

$$\text{Cost of Equity} = \frac{\text{Anticipated earnings}}{\text{Net price per share}}$$

or

$$\text{Cost of Equity} = \frac{\text{Dividends per share}}{\text{Net price per share}} + \frac{\text{Expected uniform annual rate of}}{\text{growth of dividends}}$$

Assuming the following facts, each method is calculated:

Anticipated earnings per share $2.00

Net price per share $20.00

Dividends per share $1.00

Growth rate   5%

$\dfrac{\$\ 2.00}{\$20.00} = 10\%$ and $\dfrac{\$\ 1.00}{\$20.00} + 5\% = 10\%$

Under both methods, management must invest retained earnings in a capital investment that will earn at least 10 percent or market value of the share.

When a company uses more than one type of debt financing, it is necessary to develop a composite rate, commonly referred to as the weighted average cost method. The calculated rate is the weighted average of the rates for long-term debt, preferred stockholders' equity, and common stockholders' equity. The following components of capital are presented:

Components of Capital

Source	Amount	Rate	Multiplication
Long-term debt	$250,000	A	$250,000 A
Preferred stockholders' equity	100,000	B	100,000 B
Common stockholders' equity:			
Capital stock	150,000		
Paid-in surplus	50,000		
Retained earnings	150,000		
Total	$350,000	C	$350,000 C
Total capital	$700,000		D

The weighted average cost of capital is computed as follows:

$$D/\$700,000$$

A particular type of capital should not be associated with a particular investment proposal. One component of capital affects the cost of another. Capital should be viewed as a pool, which results in an average cost from which funds are drawn for different capital investments.

Let's assume that the cost rate of long-term debt is 5.1 percent, which represents the yield rate on the net proceeds to the company on an after-tax basis. For example, a bond with a $100 face value is estimated to generate $98.00 net proceeds to a company after discounting and financing costs. In addition, the nominal interest is $10.00, or $5.00 after-tax, resulting in 5.1 percent after-tax cost rate ($5.00/$98.00).

Source	Amount	Rate	Multiplication
Long-term debt	$250,000	5.1%	$12,750

Assuming a similar example as above, the preferred stockholders' equity is as follows:

$$\$8.00/\$98.00 = 8.163\%$$

Source	Amount	Rate	Multiplication
Preferred stockholders' equity	$100,000	8.163%	$8,163

Of all the components, common stockholders' equity is the more difficult to handle in both concept and application. It must be determined whose cost is being measured; does in fact retained earnings have a cost; how is the cost measured; and what earnings per share should be used?

The cost to be measured is the stockholders' cost. From the stockholders' viewpoint, retained earnings has a cost. If retained earnings are retained in the business, the stockholders cannot use it elsewhere to earn money, and it also has an opportunity cost. In theory, retention is the same as if the amount had been paid in dividends which were used to buy the company's stock. It is part of the money which stockholders have invested in the ownership of the business. Therefore, it should be combined with the other common stock accounts in developing this cost measure.

The stockholders are investing because they expect to receive some benefits almost equivalent to what they would receive on the next best investment when risk is considered. In addition, the stockholders are looking forward to two benefits which induce them to pay a price for the common stock: dividends as they will be paid in the future and capital appreciation. Both benefits come from future earnings per share, the principal factor affecting the price of a stock in the long term. The cost of capital is then measured by the inverse of the price-earnings ratio or the earnings-price ratio.

In computing the cost of common stockholders' equity, the net amount a company would receive from the sale of stock is divided into the future earnings per share as estimated by the investors. For example, the market price of the stock is $100, with financing costs of $15, resulting in net proceeds to the company of $85. This is divided into the future earnings per share estimated by the investors of $12, and results in a cost rate of 14.1 percent.

Source	Amount	Rate	Multiplication
Common stockholders' equity	$350,000	14.1%	$49,412

A summary of all three components is as follows:

Source	Amount	Rate	Multiplication
Long-term debt	$250,000	5.1%	$12.750
Preferred stockholders' equity	100,000	8.2%	8,163
Common stockholders' equity	350,000	14.1%	49,350
Total capital	$700,000		$70,263

Weighted Average Cost of Capital = $70,263/$700,000 = 10.0%

The above weighted average cost of capital of 10.0 percent serves as the cut-off rate below which the company should not accept an investment proposal. If there were not capital investment proposals above the 10.0 percent rate, stockholders presumably would be better off if they invested their capital in other investments. This rate also serves as part of long-term profit goals and forms a minimum goal for management to exceed in maximizing earnings. These goals are only a part of the framework of a comprehensive and systematic program of management objectives.

FAILURE TO MEET COST OF CAPITAL GOALS

The impact of a company failing to meet its cost of capital can have many effects regarding the health and success of the company, both in the near term as well as the long term. The most obvious is the higher cost of capital which increases, since more external financing is required to provide the necessary capital requirements of the company. This assumes that outside financing is at a higher rate than internal financing. This higher financing cost can lead to slower reinvestments which has unfavorable implications for the shareholder, and ultimately, the marketability of the company's stock.

With slower reinvestment, a company's growth may be impaired by having to reduce dividends. This decreases the shareholder's expectations and both the risk and return become less competitive in the marketplace. This in turn can cause the market value and the stock price to decline, which completes the cycle. At this point, we are back to higher financing, and in some cases, unavailability of capital funds.

ECONOMIC VALUE ADDED (EVA) DEFINED

EVA measures period value added or depleted from shareholder value in the short term. It consists of net earnings, cash income taxes, and capital on the balance sheet and the cost of capital previously discussed.

Value is considered positive when the return rate exceeds the cost of capital rate, and measures operating returns over or below the cost of capital rate. For example, if you borrowed money at 6 percent and earn a 10 percent return through some investment, you are creating added value of four percentage points. Conversely, if you borrowed money at 6 percent and earned only 4 percent return, you have lost value by two percentage points.

EVA Formula.   To illustrate a positive EVA in terms of dollars, the following formula applies:

$$EVA = \frac{(\text{Return on Invested Capital Minus Cost of Capital})}{\text{X Average Invested Capital}}$$

Return on Invested Capital (ROIC) is calculated by dividing Net Operating Profit After-Taxes (NOPAT) by Average Invested Capital or:

$$ROIC = \frac{\text{Net Operating Profit After-Taxes}}{\text{Average Invested Capital}}$$

NOPAT consists of post-tax earnings before payment of interest and dividends. Average Invested Capital represents the cumulative cash invested in the company over time such as total assets less EVA liability (debt, deferred taxes, and shareholder equity).

Application to Budgeting

Budgeting shareholder value can be used in many ways, some of which are:

- Support for decisions involving resource utilization, such as for capital investments and R&D projects.
- Support for potential mergers, acquisitions, joint ventures, and divestitures.
- As part of the strategic planning process.
- Serves as an operating budget review process.
- Used as part of the monthly review process.

Utilizing shareholder value techniques can be a driving force in managing complex organizations, especially the impact of decisions affecting balance sheet data. It also provides another measurement toward reaching financial success when it becomes part of the budgeting process.

CHAPTER FIVE

Budgeting Return on Investment

For most companies, probably no other area of decisionmaking is as important to its success as resource utilization and evaluation. Management is constantly faced with a wide array of possible resource investment alternatives and is responsible for the funds entrusted to its care. The selection of the most profitable alternative, recognizing the availability of funds and resources required to finance the investment, can be considered a major function of management during the budgeting process.

The primary objective of the financial manager is to utilize company funds within the limits of the manager's authority, so that over the long term, the company receives at least as high a rate of return on its investment as might be obtained in alternative investments of similar risk. The second most important objective is the maximization of the present value of resource investments to obtain as high a return as possible without assuming undue risks. To maximize the earning power of the company, resources are allocated in such a way that the earning power will be converted into as high a rate of return as possible for the company. To accomplish these objectives, measures are needed to appraise company performance. One basic measure is budgeting return on investment (ROI), which describes the relationships between earnings and investment.

It is assumed that a business's prime objective is to generate an adequate return to its owner. As we will discuss, it is necessary to reduce as many of the intuitive factors of decisionmaking to a more systematic and mathematical approach. However, it is important to recognize that return on investment concepts will never replace sound business judgments, but rather, aid in supporting or raising questions as to the validity of these business judgment factors. It is intended to be a financial management tool which defines the problem, evaluates and weighs possible alternative investments, and brings into focus those qualitative factors affecting the decision which may not be expressed in quantitative terms.

WHY IS RETURN ON INVESTMENT IMPORTANT?

Return on investment is important because it aids in maintaining a company's growth by measuring historical results and assists in the evaluation of the company's short-term budgets and long-term plans. It is also important because the technique is acceptable to investors, the business and financial communities, economists, and most students of business concepts. Of course, it is highly recognized by most companies internally as a budget and evaluation technique. With this kind of recognition, and the fact that ROI can provide a technique for evaluating alternatives for changing a company's relative attractiveness to the concerned community, it is easy to see why ROI is important.

WHY USE RETURN ON INVESTMENT?

In today's complex business environment, technological, economic, and competitive pressures tend to complicate managerial decisionmaking. This management tool provides management with an easy method of evaluating and communicating both past and anticipated future performance more effectively, in an effort to increase growth as well as productivity. The following list highlights why ROI is recommended and what the concept may do to enhance the decisionmaking process:

- *It forces planning.* Corporate management must have a plan, whether it is short term or long term, in order to measure efficiency and to set goals. This is accomplished during the budgeting process and in longer term planning.
- *As a basis for decisionmaking.* It takes certain decisions out of the realm of intuition into the realm of supportive and quantitative basis.
- *To evaluate investment opportunities.* This can include not only initial capital investments, but also the cost of additional working capital, the economic life

of the investment, and the effect on company profitability. These investment opportunities will also include alternative investments or new product opportunities.

- *Aid in evaluating management performance.* This would include performance of responsibility or profit center heads, as well as total company performance or predetermined objectives. It aids in eliminating inequities which might arise between managers or operating units due to differences in size and make-up of operations, that is, highly intensified capital operations versus distributive operations which may have little capital investment. In addition, performance measurement can be used to evaluate management's use of assets, cash flow, capital, equipment or other facilities, and internal control.

- *Response to marketplace.* Measures management's response to changes in the marketplace on pricing and need, as well as profitability and cost reduction measures.

UNDERSTANDING THE DEFINITION

To understand ROI, it is necessary to review the term itself. A great deal of confusion sometimes arises regarding the term ROI. "Return on" refers to an additional sum of money expected from an investment over and above the original investment. This return may be before or after taxes. An investment may be defined as the employment of an economic resource such as money, machinery and equipment, manpower, etc., with the anticipation of producing a gain either in the form of income, appreciated value, greater efficiency, or cost savings. This gain is measured over a period of time. Therefore, return on investment measures gain on economic resources over a period of time, usually in the form of a ratio.

Management's Need for Involvement

Management's involvement is required during the budgeting process since justification of any investment opportunity is directly related to the participation of persons with both technical knowledge and the expertise to recognize the relationship of all input data. This also serves as an integral part of training and the development of manager skills. Management must recognize that the development of profitable investment opportunities frequently starts at the lower levels of management by both technical and nontechnical personnel. In addition, management aids in establishing the areas of responsibility as well as the level of authority.

MAJOR USES AND APPLICATIONS

While the list of uses and applications can be quite extensive, it is important to identify the major applications and to note that these applications and/or techniques must be used by a company that best serves their needs.

- *External measurement.* A technique used to compare ROI calculations to other companies and industries.

- *Internal measurement.* A technique of evaluating internal segments of a company resulting in increased earnings contribution through cost reduction and/or profit improvement.

- *Improving asset utilization.* Ways of improving the utilization of cash, inventories, receivables, and capital assets for greater profitability.

- *Capital expenditure evaluation.* Most recognized technique for providing the tools for effectively allocating capital resources.

- *Divestments.* Used to reflect the impact of divesting businesses or segments for improving ROI.

- *Profit goals.* Through internal and external measurements, a company's profit goals can be established.

- *Acquisitions.* Measures the impact of acquisitions on the short- and long-term growth of the company.

- *Management incentives.* Technique of rewarding incentives based on ROI performance measurements.

- *Elimination or addition to product lines.* Techniques that can strengthen the focus on profitable or unprofitable existing or new product lines.

- *Make or buy decisions.* Measurement of the ROI impact for making or buying a product.

- *Lease or purchase decision.* Similar to capital expenditures evaluation techniques used in comparing lease versus purchase decisions of acquiring capital assets.

- *Evaluating human resources.* This concept can determine the return on human resources.

- *Inventory control.* Measures the incremental changes of inventory and earnings generated from that additional inventory investment.

- *Pricing.* Guide in developing the price of a product using the desired rate of return.

CAUTIONS IN USING THE ROI CONCEPT

The use of return on investment techniques in evaluating external and internal performance as a tool for management decisionmaking should be used with caution. Like all methods of evaluation, improper interpretation can arise from measuring different sets of comparative data by relying too heavily upon a single measurement device. The tool of return on investment is a vital management tool, but certain cautions must be recognized in its use.

Too often, managers make decisions by comparing absolute relationships between sets of data, without giving consideration to the meaningful relationship of the components of the data. This misconception can lead to wrong decisions, unless further interpretations are given to the meaning of the results. Therefore, the first caution to consider in ROI is not to rely exclusively on the absolute numerical results in calculating ROI rates, whether it is between products, departments, divisions, companies, or industries. The nature of comparative products, quality of products, nature of selling, production costs, and corporate structure are only some of the areas of operations to be considered before reaching any sound conclusions. The rule of consistency is perhaps one of the most important cautions that can be mentioned. We will continuously refer to this rule, since it is the basis of the concept of ROI. Consistency must be adhered to if accurate decisions are to be reached. Since ROI measures comparative data over a period of time, it is important to be consistent in measuring like data. Once a method of comparison is chosen, the ground rules must remain consistent. For example, if comparisons are calculated using certain allocations, these allocations must continually be used in future comparisons if any valid conclusions are to be reached. If the ground rules change, both historical and future calculations must be changed accordingly to develop an accurate trend of operations. This rule would hold true for all comparisons of data and is most important in measuring ROI. ROI is only the tool to aid in reaching these decisions, and not the ultimate solution.

Failure to use other supporting measures of performance can put too much emphasis on ROI as a management tool. Other sound methods of evaluation should be used to support conclusions reached through ROI calculations, such as growth rates and other techniques and processes found in the budgeting and planning aspects of a company's short- and long-range planning. These processes along with ROI will provide a sound and intelligent basis for appraising performance in both the short and long run.

ALLOCATING COMPONENTS

It is important to properly assign the net sales, net earnings, and investment into segments for evaluating performance. These segments can be divisions, product lines, departments, accountability centers, marketing segment, etc. Should all data be allocated, or only data for which a manager has responsibility and authority? Let's address that problem.

If you accept the rule of consistency, it doesn't matter whether you allocate as long as you are consistent in measuring like data from period to period. The ultimate return on investment rate can be adjusted upward if lower investments are allocated, and adjusted downward if higher investments are assigned to the segment. Therefore, the more likely approach should be taken which measures only the data that a manager is responsible for and the authority a manager is given. It is recommended that only data, which can be identified as controllable by a manager, be used. Other data, which may be allocated and not under a manager's authority, could lead to erroneous decisions and force an operating segment into decisions detrimental to the operation, that is, increasing prices to meet ROI objectives. The other unassigned data can be used to complete the entire company's operation in the establishment of overall goals.

It is suggested that earnings before taxes be used on the controllable components, and net earnings on the overall company. Since taxes are difficult to compute on individual segments, only net earnings should be used for overall evaluation. In addition, it is recommended that for short evaluation periods (i.e., less than one year), period-end balances be used for the investment bases. For longer periods (i.e., one year or longer), year-end balances should be used for the investment base or a variation of the average of the beginning and closing yearly balances, moving averages, or any other variation. The conclusion will not alter as long as consistency is maintained. Remember that the absolute rates are not as important as the incremental changes that occur from period to period. This indicates the performance trend, and will act as an indicator of performance in the past, as well as the future.

Net sales and net earnings should be accumulated for each period, such as three months year-to-date for a quarter of a year, six months year-to-date for half of a year, etc. No averaging of balances is necessary for net sales and net earnings, since they are not balances at any given period in time like the balance sheet, but performance data after each period of operations and can be accumulated for any given period desired.

ELEMENTS OF RETURN ON INVESTMENT

Return on investment derives its source data from the two most commonly used financial statements, namely, the Earnings Statement and the Balance Sheet. ROI is nothing more than a series of ratios in a logical sequence, in an effort to develop management decisions based on past and anticipated earnings and asset utilization. With this in mind, ROI can be broken down into two basic components, using three different sets of data from the Earnings Statement and the Balance Sheet. These components are the Profitability Rate and the Turnover Rate.

Profitability Rate

The profitability rate is computed by dividing net sales into net earnings. This ratio highlights the relationship of how many earnings are generated from a sales dollar and measures the success in the controlling of costs. This is a familiar ratio in most businesses, and plays a major role in operating the business. This ratio has the greatest leverage in generating higher returns for a company because when sales decline, most companies will experience lower earnings. To offset these lower sales dollars, expenses are generally reduced in order to maintain certain anticipated earnings. Therefore, immediate actions can be taken to compensate for temporary malfunctioning of the business. In our illustration, the profitability rate is as follows:

$$\frac{\text{Net Earnings}}{\text{Net Sales}} = \frac{\$90,000}{\$1,500,000} = 6\%$$

This means those six cents of every dollar of revenue results in a profit after tax.

Turnover Rate

The turnover rate is computed by dividing the investment into the net sales and is expressed as a rate. This turnover rate reflects the rapidity with which capital committed to an operation is being worked. The biggest problem of this ratio is determining what investment base to use, since the results will vary depending on the type of investment used. For example, when using total assets the following turnover results:

$$\frac{\text{Net Sales}}{\text{Total Assets}} = \frac{\$1,500,000}{\$900,000} = 1.67 \text{ times}$$

or, using capital employed, the following results:

$$\frac{\text{Net Sales}}{\text{Total Assets}} = \frac{\$1,500,000}{\$700,000} = 2.14 \text{ times}$$
$$\text{Less}$$
$$\text{Current Liabilities}$$

The different types of investment bases can be many. However, whichever is determined, that base will assume the type of ROI used. For example, using total assets, ROI is referred to as Return on Total Assets. Using capital employed, ROI would be referred to as Return on Capital Employed. Therefore, the investment base will determine the technique used since ROI measures the return on some investment base.

RELATIONSHIP BETWEEN THE PROFITABILITY RATE AND TURNOVER RATE

Taking both the profitability rate and the turnover rate, the following results:

$$\frac{\text{Net Earnings}}{\text{Net Sales}} \times \frac{\text{Net Sales}}{\text{Investment}}$$

Looking at the above components, you can see that the net sales in both equations can be cancelled, resulting in the following:

$$\frac{\text{Net Earnings}}{\text{Investment}}$$

As previously mentioned, the ratio is broken down into two components to review the relationship of earnings to sales and the rapidity to which committed capital is being used effectively. In addition, you can see that to improve the ROI rate, a manager can increase the profitability rate by increasing sales, reducing expenses, or a combination of both. Also, the ROI rate can increase by working existing investments harder, thus increasing the turnover rate. It is assumed that all these factors are under the control of the manager being measured. For example, we will assume that two managers have the responsibility for individual operations. The following facts are presented to illustrate the point:

	Manager A	*Manager B*
Net sales	$1,500,000	$1,500,000
Net earnings	90,000	120,000
Investment—Capital employed	700,000	937,500
Profitability rate	6%	8%
Turnover rate	2.14	1.6
Return on investment	12.86%	12.8%

You can see that both managers have the same sales dollars and the same ROI rate. Which manager is more effective? Without a detailed analysis of each operation, Manager B could be considered the better manager due to the fact that Manager B generates greater flexibility in controlling the profitability rate based on the above facts. However, use caution in analyzing the details supporting Manager B's results in both financial and nonfinancial data.

Applying the profitability rate and the turnover rate for Manager A, the following return on capital exploded results:

Profitability Rate × *Turnover Rate*

$$\frac{\text{Net Earnings}}{\text{Net Sales}} \times \frac{\text{Net Sales}}{\text{Capital Employed}}$$

Equals

$$\frac{\$90,000}{\$1,500,000} \times \frac{\$1,500,000}{\$700,000}$$

or

$$6\% \quad \times \quad 2.14$$

results in

12.86%

or

$$\frac{\$\,90,000}{\$700,000} \times 12.86\%$$

ORGANIZATION CHART—RETURN ON CAPITAL EMPLOYED

The organization chart of ROI responsibility is presented in Exhibit 5.1 using Return on Capital Employed. Note that each function is assigned or contributes to the ultimate objective of return on investment. In this illustration, working capital (current assets less current liabilities) is used, plus fixed assets, resulting in the term capital employed. Other variations of the investment can be used, but the rule of consistency must be adhered to.

INDUSTRY COMPARISONS

External review and analysis is important to put a company's performance into perspective with that of its competitors and the industry in total. Composites of similar companies are meaningful to the extent that they show a company's relative position,

Exhibit 5.1   Organization Chart

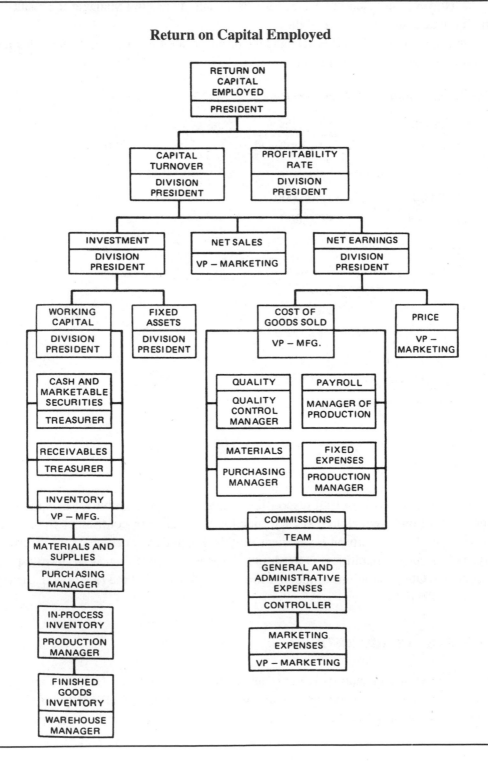

Return on Capital Employed

Exhibit 5.2 Competitive Relationship of the Profitability Rate and the Turnover Rate

		Competitor	
	Company A	B	C
Profitability Rate			
Net Earnings	$ 90,000	$ 60,000	$ 100,000
divided by			
Net Sales	1,500,000	2,000,000	1,000,000
Profitability Rate	6%	3%	10%
Turnover Rate			
Net Sales	$1,500,000	$2,000,000	$1,000,000
divided by			
Total Assets	900,000	1,500,000	1,250,000
Turnover Rate	1.67	1.33	.80
Return on Total Assets			
Profitability Rate	6%	3%	10%
multiplied by			
Turnover Rate	1.67	1.33	.80
Return on Assets	10.0%	4.0%	8.0%

and why a company may be favorable or unfavorable. Further analysis will be presented to show how this may be done in detail. However, utilizing the profitability rate and the turnover rate can lead to some clues and possible answers to a company's competitive position. Note that in Exhibit 5.2 competitor C has the highest profitability rate, but the lowest turnover rate. Company A has a profitability rate of 6 percent, which is four percentage points lower than competitor C, but is able to maintain a 1.67 turnover rate, which results in a 10 percent return on total assets. It is obvious that both components must be further analyzed and caution given to such internal variations as differences in accounting policies, nature of the business, and overall general structure. However, as a point of reference, this provides an excellent opportunity to put into perspective a company's position relative to its competitors.

It is possible to develop a table of the profitability rate and the turnover rate at different levels of return on investment rates. Exhibit 5.3 illustrates the relationship of the profitability rate and the turnover rate on investment rates of 5 percent and 10 percent.

Note that any combination of the profitability rate and the turnover rate will result in a specific return on investment. For example, at 10 percent return on investment, a profitability rate of 6 percent and a turnover rate of 1.67 equals 10 percent; 8.5 percent profitability rate and 1.18 turnover rate also equals 10 percent ROI, etc. Therefore, knowing one component will lead to decisions to generate the desired rate of the other component at a given rate of return.

Exhibit 5.3   Relationship of the Profitability Rate and the Turnover Rate at Different Levels of Return-on-Investment

5%			10%		
Profitability Rate	×	*Turnover Rate*	*Profitability Rate*	×	*Turnover Rate*
1.0%		5.00	1.0%		10.00
1.5		3.34	1.5		6.67
2.0		2.50	2.0		5.00
2.5		2.00	2.5		4.00
3.0		1.67	3.0		3.34
3.5		1.43	3.5		2.86
4.0		1.25	4.0		2.50
4.5		1.12	4.5		2.23
5.0		1.00	5.0		2.00
			5.5		1.82
			6.0		1.67
			6.5		1.54
			7.0		1.43
			7.5		1.34
			8.0		1.26
			8.5		1.18
			9.0		1.12
			9.5		1.06
			10.0		1.00

DETAILING ROI COMPONENTS

One of the interesting aspects of return on investment components is that it can be broken down in a chart detailing all of the data affecting each component's calculation. By this breakdown, it is possible to see the behavioral pattern of each component, and the reasons for the effect on the overall return on investment rate. The profitability rate using the financial data previously presented in the Earnings Statement is shown in Exhibit 5.4.

Note that each major income and expense items is charted, which results in a profitability rate of 6 percent.

Exhibit 5.4 Profitability Rate

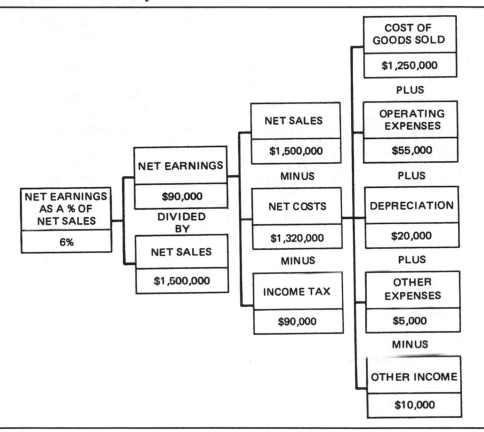

The turnover rate is also computed in a similar way and total assets will be used for the investment as shown in Exhibit 5.5.

Each asset item is included and totals $900,000 of total assets. This divided by the net sales equals a turnover rate of 1.67 times.

The combination of both components results in a Return on Asset rate of 10 percent as computed in Exhibit 5.6.

The profitability rate is multiplied by the turnover rate, resulting in a 10 percent Return on Total Asset rate. Assume a company's next year's budget is 16 percent. In order to attain this rate, either the profitability rate and/or the turnover rate must change. Many decisions can be made as follows:

- Increase sales volume
- Increase sales price
- Reduce production costs

Exhibit 5.5   Turnover Rate

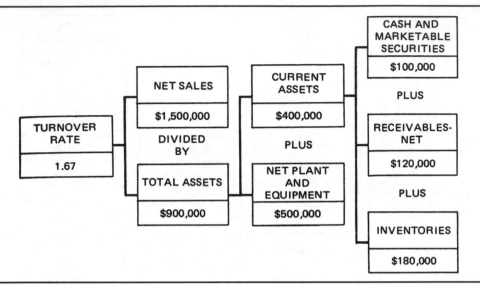

- Reduce operating expenses
- Reduce cash balances
- Reduce receivables
- Reduce inventory balances
- Dispose of unprofitable facilities

Exhibit 5.6   Return on Total Assets

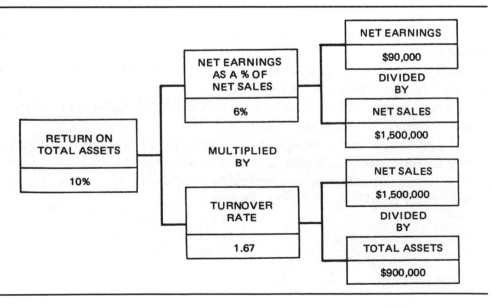

These are only some of the operating decisions that can be made to increase ROI rates. The type and magnitude of the changes will depend upon the achievable results that are desired. Some decisions may be easier than others. Remember that as pointed out earlier, decisions relating to the profitability rate may be easier to accomplish. This does not mean that areas relating to the turnover rate cannot be accomplished but greater earnings may be easier to accomplish due to greater control on expenses, particularly human resource costs.

In summary, this same technique can be used to measure two different sets of data whether actual versus budget, this year versus last year, competitive companies, etc. This presents an excellent tool for analytical decisions, since it provides the individual items making up the two components, the profitability rate and the turnover rate.

CHAPTER SIX

Developing Budget Segments

Most organizations are broken down into a series of budget segments, which can be considered well-defined subdivisions of an organization. They are designed in such a way that monies can be allocated, performance can be measured, and objectives can be established. This chapter covers the most common type of budget segmentation, as well as two that are not so common. It then examines the development of key goals and performance indicators. The most common form of budget segmentation is based on accountability/responsibility centers. Two less common forms of segmentation are the rule of three and Pareto's Law. It is advisable to use these methods for analytical purposes only and to use the more common form of segmentation for organizing the company into budget groups.

ACCOUNTABILITY/RESPONSIBILITY CENTERS

The terms *accountability center* and *responsibility center* are used interchangeably and represent segments of a business for which managers have responsibility, authority, and control. The head of this center generally has full control and responsibility for meeting budgeting performance within the entire company, a division, a department, or an operation. An example of this form of budget segmentation is provided in Exhibit 6.1.

Exhibit 6.1   Illustration of Budget Segments

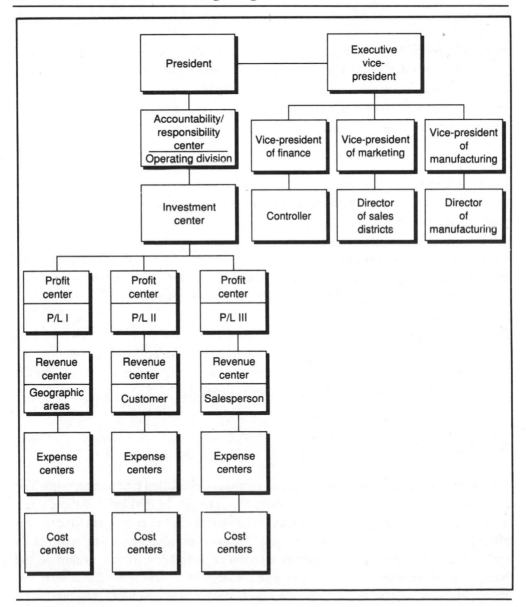

The different types of accountability/responsibility centers include the following:

Investment Center.   Segments of a company in which an accountability/responsibility head has assigned responsibilities for revenues and costs (or profits) and the capital invested in that operation, such as the property, plant, and equipment used to generate those revenues and incur those costs. The output of investment centers is usually measured by the relationship of profits to invested capital or return on investment.

Profit Center.   The profit center is a segment of the company in which assigned responsibilities encompass both revenues and costs without the impact of invested capital. Although we can consider the total company a profit center, it is generally more acceptable to have many different profit centers for control and manageability. An example would be a product line of a company or any subdivision of an operating unit of a division.

Revenue Center.   A revenue center is a budget segment in which performance is measured in terms of sales revenues such as a geographic sales area, product line, product, or salesperson.

Cost Center.   In a cost center, output is measured in terms of predetermined costs. In manufacturing, for example, standards would be developed for each manufacturing segment meeting certain predetermined levels of production.

Expense Center.   An expense center is a segment of a company in which functions are measured in terms of organizational structure. For example, the accounting and legal departments represent expense centers and their managers are responsible for the budgeting related to that specific department's expenses.

RULE OF THREE

In this method of segmentation, budget segments are classified into three groups. The operating divisions of an organization may, for example, be divided into those operations that are absolutely necessary to retain, those that are better to retain (due to benefits) than dispose of, and those that could be divested given poor performance or shifts in the direction of the company's business. Another variation would be the budgeting of human resources into three categories: key individuals who are absolutely necessary to retain, those who are better to retain than lose, and those who would be terminated given budgetary restraints. This part of the budgetary process can serve as a contingency plan should it be necessary to change human resource budgets. Obviously, these budgets must be kept in the strictest confidence.

PARETO'S LAW

It is an accepted rule of thumb that 80 percent of any output usually comes from 20 percent of the input. For example, a small portion of a product line's budget will generally account for the majority of sales. Using this as a guideline, a company can budget resources to obtain the highest maximum results. During the budget preparation the objective is to determine what 20 percent of the budget is expected to contribute 80 percent of your budget objectives. When this is known, final budget objectives can then reflect elimination and/or trimming down of product line activity.

DEVELOPING SPECIFIC KEY GOALS

Once the organization has been divided into workable budget segments, specific key goals can be established by each organizational segment. For example, a sound breakdown of the organization by budget segment usually follows the organizational chart. Within each box of the organizational chart, key budget goals can be established.

In Exhibit 6.1, the president's objective may be to increase return on investment by 5 percent and increase profits by 10 percent. The vice-president of manufacturing may be charged with reducing controllable operating costs by 10 percent. The vice-president of marketing may be asked to develop a marketing plan to increase sales by 25 percent. The vice-president of finance may be asked to increase efficiency by 10 percent, recommend new financing methods to reduce interest costs by 2 percent, and develop a computerized inventory control system.

The profit, expense, and cost center heads would also be required to meet certain budget objectives. Ultimately, these budget improvements would aim to accomplish the president's objective of increasing return on investment by 5 percent and increasing profits by 10 percent.

DEVELOPING PERFORMANCE INDICATORS

To accomplish the overall objectives, performance indicators are required for the various center segments of the organization. These performance indicators can be developed by assigning specific workload standards and measuring the actual output against them. This approach is accomplished by providing the following types of information broken down into five categories.

Category I   Resources needed by the segment under consideration (revenue center, expense center, profit center, and so on)

Category II   Effort required by that segment

Category III   Output of products and/or services

Category IV   Extent to which goals are achieved

Category V   Efficiency of performance indicators compared to actual results

Using these five categories, let us complete two organizational segments as an illustration, namely, a revenue center (Exhibit 6.2) and an expense center (Exhibit 6.3).

This method will ensure that each budget segment is assigned a performance or standard indicator that the organization is committed to achieving. It is suggested that budget segments be established before proceeding any further in the budgeting process.

Exhibit 6.2   Developing Performance Indicators for Northeast Region Revenue Center

Category I	Category II	Category III	Category IV	Category V
Amount of units available for sale	Number of calls on customers	Number of units sold	Number of units sold	Percent of marketing expense to sales
Marketing/ Sales Expenses:	Average shipments per day	Total revenues	Total revenues	Days' sales in receivables
		Number of new customers	Market share	
Salaries		Number of existing customers	Quality of customer service	Days' sales in inventories
Commissions			Return business	Average sales per salesperson, customer or customer calls
Overrides		Backlog of orders		
Advertising				
Promotion				
Freight				
Administrative				

Exhibit 6.3   Developing Performance Indicators for Production Department Expense Center

Category I	Category II	Category III	Category IV	Category V
Costs:	Number of units produced	Number of units completed	Backlog of orders	Cost variances
Direct materials			Delivery delays	Capacity utilization
Direct labor			Quality rejects	Day's amount of inventory on hand
Direct overhead			Customer complaints	
Carrying charges of raw and WIP inventories			Absenteeism	Changeover time
Resources:			Accidents per employee	
Number of labor hours				
Amount of machine time				
Amount of required inventories				

CHAPTER SEVEN

Organizing and Administering the Budgeting Process

Before the budgeting process can begin, many questions must be resolved and additional data provided. This chapter outlines the process of preparing a budget. It deals with the preliminaries needed to provide the many tools, techniques, policies, and procedures required for completing the budget—from the budgeting system checklist, to the role of the budget committee, to the development of the budgeting manual. The information presented here is for organizing and administering the budgeting process. The following list outlines some of these preliminary requirements.

- Establish responsibilities by segment of the company. This step is performed during the procedure discussed in Chapter 6.
- Where necessary, realign management responsibilities. This is part of the procedure outlined in Chapter 6.
- Determine and identify what financial and nonfinancial information is needed.
- Determine and identify what information is not presently available and how it can be developed.

- Establish a historical data base from the following sources:

  Departmental expense statements

  Operating statement and balance sheet

  Accounting records

  Vendor data files

  Customer data files

  Product data files

  Cost accounting records

  Long-range plans

  Prior year's budgets

  Wage and salary plans

  Market trends

  Raw material prices

  Payroll, sales, and other tax rates

  Insurance rates

  Capital investment projections from prior year

  Inflation rates and unemployment rates

- Establish performance targets as they relate to the long-range plans of the company.
- Develop regular performance reporting and analyze policies and procedures.
- Adjust commitments as needed.

BUDGETING SYSTEM CHECKLIST

Exhibit 7.1 is a step-by-step checklist of the sequence in preparing the budgeting process. It should be completed before starting the budgeting process. Each line item or sequence of preparation requires that an individual or individuals be assigned the responsibility for the completion of each preparation sequence. In order to maintain control of the completion of this process, required dates and the dates received should also be assigned. This checklist will help to alert the responsible parties to any scheduling changes needed and also assist in determining when completion can be expected. This checklist should serve as a guideline for the budget officer or person to whom responsibility for the completion of the overall budget is given. A further explanation of the role of the budget officer will be given later in this chapter.

Exhibit 7.1 Budgeting System Checklist

Budgeting System Checklist

Company _____

Sequence of Preparation	Responsibility	Date Required	Date Received
1. Establish overall goals and objectives			
2. Establish divisional, product, departmental goals and objectives			
3. Develop "grass roots" estimates of:			
a. Sales to new and existing customers			
b. Human resource requirements by department			
c. Additional new and replacement machinery and equipment			
d. Financial capabilities			
4. Prepare the required budgets:			
a. Sales and profit budget			
b. Production budget			
• materials budget			
• direct labor budget			
• manufacturing overhead budget			

Exhibit 7.1   (continued)

Sequence of Preparation	Responsibility	Date Required	Date Received
c. Marketing expense budget			
• sales personnel budget			
• sales administration budget			
• advertising and promotion budget			
• distribution budget			
• service and parts budget			
d. Research and development budget			
e. Administration budget			
f. Capital investment budget			
g. Cash budget			
h. Balance sheet budget			
• accounts receivable budget			
• inventory budgets			
• fixed asset budget			
5. Assemble the sub-budgets and prepare the master budget			
6. Review the master budget and negotiate changes			
7. Redo sub-budgets with changes			
8. Reproduce and distribute budgets			
9. Develop monthly performance reports			
10. Conduct monthly management reviews of performance compared to budget			
11. Keep track of necessary changes for future budgets			

BUDGET PLANNING MEETINGS

Budget planning meetings should be scheduled as often as necessary. These meetings are held by each budget segment before the budgeting process begins and should resolve the following key issues:

- How much staff should be involved in the budgeting decisions and input
- How objectives are going to be met, both in resources and time schedules
- Who the key personnel are in the development of budget objectives

This meeting should be short, but all these issues should be resolved before starting the budgeting process. At this time, responsibilities for preparation of various segments of the budget can be assigned.

BUDGET REVIEW MEETINGS

Budget review meetings play an important part in determining what people will get what they ask for, how much they will receive in resources, and, in some cases, how political power will be distributed within the organization. Here are some suggestions for organizing these important meetings.

- Determine beforehand who should attend and what data each person will bring to the meeting.
- Have an end objective and agenda in mind when entering the meeting.
- Do not belabor points so as to slow down the meeting and lose the attention of the group.
- Know when to stop talking and let others have a turn.

This meeting should be called and chaired by the segment head, who sets the tone for preparing his or her own segment budget. The segment head should also outline the key objectives of the organization's budget in an effort to focus on the overall guidelines established by the corporate office. These are spelled out in the memo issued by the chief executive (see Exhibit 7.2).

ROLE OF THE BUDGET COMMITTEE

Where feasible, a budget committee should be appointed that is composed of members of the organization, such as the president, the chief operating officer, certain staff and/or operational vice-presidents, the chief financial officer, and the budget director. Although not all these individuals need serve on the budget committee, as many as possible should participate. This committee should be rotated each year, with at least the budget director and one key executive remaining into the following year. A chairperson should be appointed whose responsibilities are to carry out the function of the budget committee.

The responsibilities and duties of this committee include the following:

- Reviewing budgeted estimates from each part of the organization and making recommendations to the respective responsibility heads
- Resolving budgetary conflicts between operating units of the organization and making these recommendations on behalf of the president and/or chief operating officer of the company
- Recommending and approving changes to the budgeting process
- Reviewing and making recommendations on periodic performance reports that compare budgetary standards and indicators to actual performance
- Approving or disapproving the contents of the budget manual

This committee represents the president of the company and recommends either approval or disapproval of the overall budget. A committee of this sort can sometimes deal more effectively with conflicts and recommendations than one or two individuals. It also acts as a training mechanism for all concerned to see how the budget is formulated as well as how a budgeting process works.

ROLE OF THE BUDGET OFFICER

The budget officer plays a major role in the preparation of the budgeting process. This person is responsible for coordinating all budget estimates developed by the line organization and for providing the necessary technical assistance in the preparation of certain budget reports.

The specific functions of the budget officer include:

- Advising the chief executive, budget committee, and others on budgeting matters
- Recommending procedures and other requirements for each component of the budgeting system
- Developing the organization of the budgeting program and timetables for the completion of each budgetary cycle

- Developing the forms, schedules, and other documentation necessary for completion of the budget
- Developing and maintaining an up-to-date budget manual
- Supplying some analytical data for operating units to use in their budget preparations
- Providing key executives with certain revenue and cost data as tabulated in the budgets
- Recommending certain courses of action to top management based on budget projections
- Analyzing and interpreting variations between actual and budgeted results
- Preparing and distributing the final budgets

The budget officer should always be part of the budget committee from year to year. This is extremely important to the continuity of the budgeting process.

EXECUTIVE MEMO

Each budgeting year, the chief executive of the company sends each segment head a memorandum outlining the schedule and guidelines for next year's budget. This memo establishes the overall guidelines on most key issues in preparing the year's budget. Exhibit 7.2 is an example of such a memo. However, keep in mind that every company should establish its own memo with key issues that apply to that particular organization.

Exhibit 7.2   Sample Executive Memo

Interoffice Memorandum

TO: Budget Segment Heads
FROM: Chief Executive Officer
RE: Annual Operating Budget Schedule and Guidelines

The enclosed budgeting package includes the various forms that have to be completed for our annual budget. In addition, you are expected to develop a narrative on your respective operations that addresses the following points:

- Summary and highlights (this year versus next year)
- Key problems and opportunities
- Marketing summary with product line profit and loss discussions

Exhibit 7.2 (*continued*)

- Strategies: Include description, why the strategy is necessary, who is responsible, how long it will take, how much it will cost, and what benefits are expected (include ROI expectations)
- Estimates on capital spending needs
- Human resource requirements (both cost and headcount)

We would also like to know all your budgeting assumptions, fully described and supported. Please discuss this requirement with the budget director if you have any questions. For budgeting purposes, use the following overall guidelines:

- Compensation:

Exempt	Cost of living	8% across the board
	Meritorious	10% average by department
Nonexempt	Cost of living	6% across the board
	Meritorious	8% average by department

- Inflation factors:

Materials and utilities	8%
All other expenses	6%

- Financial returns:

On capital investments	12%
Return on sales	8%

In addition, we expect to receive projections for your respective businesses as follows:

Sales by product	End of August
Standard cost by product	End of September
Expenses	End of October

Your complete budget is due in my office by the end of the first week in November. We plan to begin budgeting review meetings the second week in November, and you should be prepared for at least a three-hour meeting on your budget. The schedule of these review meetings will be sent in another memo. As in the past you should plan to make a presentation of this year's budget, highlighting the key performance indicators and your contingency plans for greater-than or less-than budget performance.

After your budget has been approved, you should also be prepared to discuss individual compensation plans to accomplish the goals and objectives set forth in the budget.

I am looking forward to your usual conscientious approach to the budgeting cycle. Please make a special effort to be objective and realistic in terms of your budgeting assumptions and not too optimistic in light of recent competitive and economic pressures. I also expect you to continue your close working relationship with the budget officer; you should use that person to help you accomplish an efficient budgeting exercise. If you have any questions about the corporate guidelines, contact the budget officer.

Of course, if there are any developments in your business that will materially affect the balance of this year's budget or create difficulties for you with the budget for next year, I expect to hear from you immediately. Let's use the monthly management meetings as the proper forum for this kind of discussion.

DEVELOPING THE BUDGET MANUAL

One of the tools that brings together all aspects of the budgeting process is the budget manual, which is a statement of the approved budget policies and procedures of the company. Like other operating manuals of a company, the budget manual contains all data needed for preparing a budget. The budget manual should include the following:

- The chief operating officer's statement of the objectives and potential of the budgeting program (see Exhibit 7.2 for example)
- Instructions and necessary forms
- Responsibility levels for developing inputs
- A budget calendar that specifies the dates when data must be completed, reviewed, and submitted (see Exhibit 7.1 for completion dates)
- Administrative details as to how the budget is to be prepared, how many copies are to be submitted, and to whom copies are to be sent
- Types and contents of performance reports to be prepared
- Responsibility levels for taking corrective actions
- Follow-up procedures

The budget manual is usually developed, maintained, and modified by the budget officer of the company. Any changes are usually presented to the budget committee for approval and then incorporated into next year's budget manual. It is important to keep track of copies of the budget manual in order to maintain control of who possesses a copy. Numbering each copy and having the recipient sign for each copy received is one way of maintaining control. In addition, old copies of the budget manual should be collected when replaced with a new edition. Although total control is almost impossible due to photocopying capabilities, it is nevertheless important to stress the need for maintaining some form of security of the budget manual so that copies do not end up in competitors' hands. An authorized list of those employees needing copies of the budget manual should be developed and approved by the chief operating officer. When an employee leaves the company, his or her copy should be turned in to the budget officer.

APPROACHES TO DEVELOPING A BUDGETING SYSTEM

A budgeting system can be developed in many ways. Each way has its own advantages and disadvantages. The method chosen should be based on its suitability to a specific organization. This suitability is determined by a company's needs, the nature of the organization, the reporting structure, the human resources involved, the complexities of the budgeting process, and the political nature of the organization. The three most commonly used methods are the top-down method, the bottom-up method, and the combination method. A brief description of each method will be presented. It is recommended that you use the method best suited to the nature of your organization.

Top-Down Method

In the top-down method a central staff determines the corporate goals, generates the budgets, and makes allocations to other parts of the organization for profit, expense, and investment objectives. This method has the advantages of simplifying the budgeting process and ensuring that all corporate goals are reflected.

However, it also has several disadvantages. It assumes that the central staff has extensive knowledge of all data needed to prepare the budget within every part of the organization. This assumption is generally not valid, since personnel at the operating level will usually be better prepared and more knowledgeable about what commitments can be made for that segment in future periods. If operating personnel do not have input into the budgeting commitments, there may be a lack of support for and commitment to the entire operating budget. The more effective systems try to develop firm budgeted commitments on which to base performance.

Bottom-Up Method

The bottom-up method starts from the bottom or operating level of the organization and is based on the goals and objectives for each segment of the company. However, the broad overall company objectives must be met by developing each of the commitments at the operating level. These overall goals and objectives include such guidelines as economic indexes, tax rates, pricing policies, expense allocations, minimum return on investment rates, growth rates, salary policies, and human resource requirements. The procedures and formats for budget preparation are also included.

The process of review and revision takes place at each higher level. Therefore, this method provides for participation and commitment at each operating level and affords each level with a greater understanding of the business in which it operates.

The principal disadvantage is the time it takes to prepare the many detailed schedules needed to support the budget. Quite often, operating units understate attainable performance to protect their performance records. They tend to be somewhat conservative in revenues and excessive in expense projections. Without proper reviews, some corporate goals may be neglected in an operating unit's projections.

Combination Method

In the combination method the operating units use a bottom-up approach to provide information to corporate managers, who then provide feedback and approval by the top-down method. In variation of this method certain objectives are established at the corporate level and submitted to operating managers (top-down) who use these objectives to prepare budgets on the operating level and submit them to corporate managers (bottom-up). The approval or disapproval would then be filtered back to operating managers (top-down), and the process would continue for any further actions.

DEVELOPING THE BUDGET MANUAL[1]

There are usually five steps involved in developing a budget manual. They include:

Step 1.   Determining the overall contents of the budget manual. While there are standards as outlined above, some companies may wish to customize the contents to their specific needs. Routing, distribution, preparation, and style vary from company to company.

Step 2.   How the manual is to be prepared and by whom. Usually the budget officer is responsible, but some companies may use a committee approach.

Step 3.   Distribution is usually made on a need-to-know basis. Copies must be tightly controlled by numbering each copy assigned to individuals, and making those individuals responsible for the security of the total manual and contents thereof.

Step 4.   Methods of revision such as who will be responsible for revisions, how often changes will be necessary (usually done for each budget period), and the mechanism for reproduction and distribution.

Step 5.   A vital part of the manual should deal with report formats for reporting budgeted data. Forms, as well as specific instructions, must be reviewed at least once a year for accuracy and usefulness.

The budget manual should take on the "flavor" or philosophy of the company, and fit into the style of management necessary to operate the company effectively.

---

[1]For further discussions on developing the budget manual, see the *Handbook of Budgeting,* third edition, by Robert Rachlin and H. W. Allen Sweeny (New York: John Wiley & Sons, 1991), pp. 7.1–7.10.

It is important to recognize some overall objectives regarding the budgeting process which must be considered and emphasized when developing the budget manual. They include:

Participation.   Should be developed at all levels of the organization.

Level of Attainment.   There must be a reasonable level of attainment on the overall objectives as set forth within the budgeting process.

Cost Control Mechanism.   Budgets should act as a cost control mechanism and not be used as a technique for cost reduction.

Personal Emotion.   Budgets tend to bring out personal emotions which are not always in line with corporate objectives. The manual should provide some mechanism to allow for managers to succeed and be measured fairly without fearing the loss of a job.

Reward System.   Reward systems should be attainable based on reasonable goals. Unrealistic goals at the outset can result in a meaningless budget.

CHAPTER EIGHT

Budgeted Costs

In order to prepare and analyze budgeted versus actual results, it is important to understand the behavior of various types of costs. These types of costs need to be defined and understood so that a business can categorize them properly and understand how they behave during the budgeting process. To budget properly, one must appreciate how costs relate to other variables such as volume, output, labor, overhead, and the like. Most of the cost definitions provided here apply to most organizations. The three principal cost definitions are variable costs, fixed costs, and semivariable costs. Therefore, more explanation will be provided for these terms.

TYPES OF COSTS

Variable Costs

Variable costs change in direct proportion to levels of activity. Examples include direct labor, direct materials, and utilities based on usage. Exhibit 8.1 illustrates the behavior pattern of variable costs. Note that as volume increases, the total variable costs increase, but the variable cost per unit remains constant. As you can see in Exhibit 8.1, the total variable cost for five units is $50 (point A). However, the variable unit cost remains the same $10 per unit produced at different levels of volume. For example, at point B, the total variable cost is $30; at point C, the total variable cost

Exhibit 8.1   Behavior Pattern of Total Variable Costs

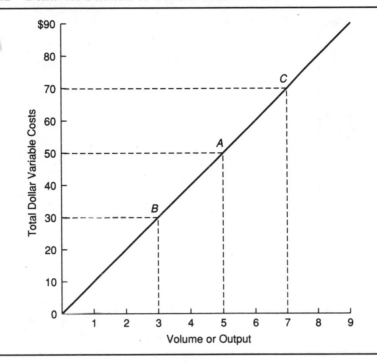

is $70. In all cases, the variable cost per unit is $10 (see Exhibit 8.2). This illustrates how variable costs change in direct proportion to activity.

An understanding of variable costs is extremely important in the application of breakeven, which is explained in Chapter 9.

Fixed Costs

Fixed costs do not fluctuate as levels of activity vary. Examples include such costs as fixed interest payments, insurance, and property taxes. For example, as shown in Exhibit 8.3, a cost at $600 remains the same as volume increases. Therefore, as volume increases, the unit cost decreases. This phenomenon supports the theory that higher output reduces the fixed portion of a unit's cost produced. In fact, it helps to reduce the total unit costs (variable and fixed) and is the reason for producing higher volume, since fixed costs are spread over more volume. In Exhibit 8.3, you can see that at the $600 level of fixed costs, the unit cost of fixed expenses is $200 per unit at point A, $100 per unit at point B, and $75 per unit at point C. As in the case of variable costs, fixed costs will be a main ingredient in calculating breakeven.

Exhibit 8.2   Behavior Pattern of Unit Variable Costs

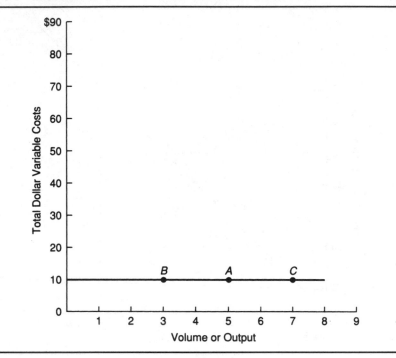

Semivariable Costs

Semivariable costs contain both fixed and variable costs. Sometimes they are referred to as mixed costs. An excellent example is telephone expenses, which usually have a monthly fixed charge and an additional charge for usage over and above a certain usage that is covered within the fixed charge. Other types of semivariable costs include mileage for auto and truck rentals and electricity usage.

Exhibit 8.4 illustrates the behavior of semivariable costs by focusing on an electricity charge with a flat charge of $400 per month for 10,000 kilowatts used plus a variable cost of $100 per 1,000 kilowatts used over 10,000 kilowatt hours of usage. In Exhibit 8.4 a usage of 15,000 kilowatts results in a fixed cost of $400 plus an additional $100 per 1,000 kilowatt used or $500. The unit per month of electricity is $900 ($400 plus $500).

Other Costs

Step Costs.   A step cost is a type of semivariable cost in which an abrupt change occurs at different activity levels. An example would be sales commissions that are

Exhibit 8.3 Behavior Pattern of Fixed Costs

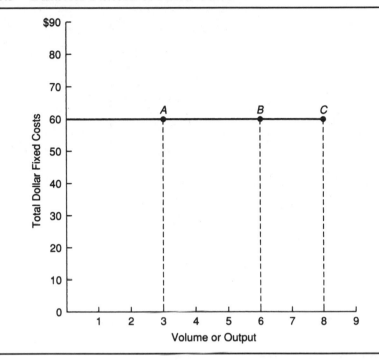

fixed over a specific range of volume and increase in steps as volume increases. The illustration of step costs in Exhibit 8.5 shows that the more units that are sold, the more commissions are generated. For example, Exhibit 8.5 shows that if 0–100 units are sold, $50 of commissions are earned; if 100–200 units are sold, $100 of commissions are earned; and so on.

Direct Costs.   Direct costs can be traced to a specific unit of activity, such as a product, geographic area, and the like. Two commonly known direct costs are direct materials and direct labor.

Indirect Costs.   Indirect costs cannot be traced to a specific unit of activity because they are common to many different activities. They are normally charged on some allocation basis such as indirect manufacturing costs.

Product Costs.   Product costs are tied to unit output and are charged to the cost of the product when it is sold. Examples include direct materials, direct labor, and overhead used in manufacturing.

Exhibit 8.4   Behavior Pattern of Semivariable Costs (Electricity)

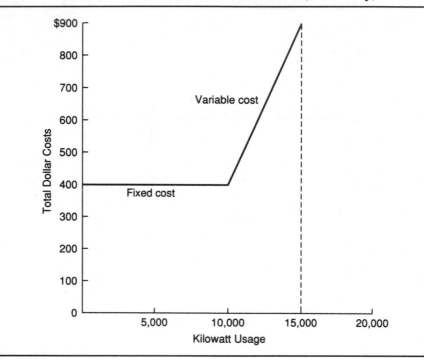

Period Costs.   Period costs are incurred as a function of time as opposed to level of activity and are neither directly nor indirectly tied to a unit of output. An example would be an executive's salary paid over a period of time.

Standard Costs.   Standard costs are anticipated or predetermined in the production of a unit of output under certain given conditions. Examples include standards that are established for material and labor costs.

Programmed Costs.   Programmed costs result from specific decisions without any consideration of volume activity or passage of time. Costs associated with research and development projects are a perfect example.

Assignable Costs.   Assignable costs can be charged to a specific project. An advertising campaign for a particular product would be an excellent example.

Exhibit 8.5   Behavior Pattern of Step Costs

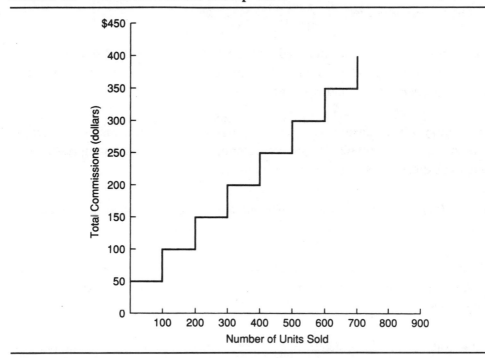

Unassignable Costs.   Unassignable costs cannot be directly traced to a specific product and/or segment of the business without arbitrarily allocating the cost. Corporate administrative expenses are an example of such a cost.

Controllable Costs.   Controllable costs can be directly influenced by an individual. An example would be the ability of the purchasing manager to choose at what price to buy materials.

Uncontrollable Costs.   Uncontrollable costs are not directly influenced by an individual. For example, the production manager does not control the cost of materials.

Opportunity Costs.   Opportunity costs represent benefits that are forgone as a result of not using another alternative. The return on investment on other capital project alternatives is an example.

Out-of-Pocket Costs.   Out-of-pocket costs require cash outlays either currently or in the future, such as wages.

Committed Fixed Costs.   Committed fixed costs cannot be easily disposed of without adversely affecting the operational structure of the company. Examples include a company's property, plant, and equipment.

Discretionary Fixed Costs.   Discretionary fixed costs can be easily changed to operate at capacities provided for under committed fixed costs. Examples include advertising expenditures and maintenance costs.

Relevant Costs.   Relevant costs represent anticipated future costs that can be changed or eliminated on the basis of economic conditions.

Irrelevant Costs.   Irrelevant costs are not affected by any decisions of management. An example would be the prior sunk costs of depreciation on a company's plant and machinery.

Incremental Costs.   Incremental costs are those that increase between alternatives. They are also referred to as differential costs. An example is cost of one supplier versus that of another.

Decremental Costs.   Decremental costs are those that decrease between alternatives. They are also referred to as differential costs. An example is cost of a domestic purchase versus an international purchase.

Shutdown Costs.   Shutdown costs represent fixed costs that continue to exist even if nothing is produced. For example, shutdown considerations associated with keeping a plant open or closing it include paying or not continuing to pay salaries, insurance, and other related costs.

Postponable Costs.   Postponable costs can be deferred to future periods without affecting the efficiency of an operation. Examples are maintenance and repair expenses.

Avoidable Costs.   Avoidable costs are those that can be saved by not entering into another alternative, such as the development of a new product.

Prime Costs.   Prime costs consist of direct material and direct labor costs directly related to production. It does not include factory overhead.

Conversion Costs.   Conversion costs consist of direct labor and manufacturing overhead costs, but do not include direct materials.

COSTING SYSTEMS

Many costing systems are used in both the accounting and budgeting of expenses. These costing systems will be mentioned and briefly defined in this section. For further explanations, the reader should refer to accounting texts, which will deal in more depth with each specific system.

Job Costing.   A job costing system accumulates costs of an identifiable product, known as a job, and follows that product through the production stages.

Process Costing.   A process costing system accumulates costs by a process or operation as it flows through production.

Direct Costing.   A direct costing approach allocates only variable costs such as direct materials, direct labor, and direct manufacturing overhead to the product. Fixed costs are treated as period expenses; that is, they are charged to the period in which they were incurred rather than to the product.

Absorption Costing.   Sometimes referred to as the full costing method, absorption costing charges both variable and fixed manufacturing costs to all units produced.

   The reader should become somewhat familiar with most of these definitions in order to determine the behavior patterns of costs within the budgeting process.

FLEXIBLE BUDGETING

In most cases, budgeted costs are difficult to forecast since levels of volume affect costs. To remedy this situation, flexible or variable budgets are used. This type of budgeting shows anticipated costs at varying levels of activity.

To illustrate this point, assume that there are three levels of production with the component of direct labor hours at each level of production and the impact on variable factory overhead costs.

Production Levels

Direct labor hours	2,400	2,750	3,075
Variable overhead costs:			
Indirect labor ($1.00 per direct hour)	$2,400	$2,750	$3,075
Indirect materials ($.70 per direct hour)	1,680	1,925	2,153
Maintenance ($.25 per direct hour)	600	688	769
Utilities ($.40 per direct hour)	960	1,100	1,230
Total variable overhead costs	$5,640	$6,463	$7,227

Fixed costs would not change. The budget preparer would need to determine the most realistic level of activity to use in preparing further budgets. Other similar analysis can be done for other types of variable expenses.

CHAPTER NINE

Using Breakeven Analysis to Make Budget Decisions*

The budgeting process involves many facets of decisionmaking, in particular, the "what if" scenario. Because many options are available in the budgeting of resources, the breakeven concept will provide insight into the volume of activity needed to cover all expenses over and above the cost directly associated with the product and/or company activity. To put it another way, it shows how many dollars of sales are needed to cover a company's budgeted fixed costs.

When revenues generated and costs incurred are equal, neither a profit nor a loss will materialize. This is called the breakeven point, that is, the point at which variable costs and fixed costs equal net sales dollars. This concept can be expressed numerically by formulas designed for this purpose or graphically by a breakeven chart. In any case, the shifts or changes in revenues and costs are ultimately reflected in the operations of the business. Thus breakeven analysis can be an important tool in budgeting the business by providing the necessary information for effective decisionmaking.

However, certain conditions have to be assumed when using this tool. Because various volume levels will be used to show the impact on the breakeven point, it is assumed that changing sales volume will not have any impact on the per-unit selling

---

*Robert Rachlin, *Successful Techniques for Higher Profits* (New York: MARR Publications, 1981), pp. 141–156.

price. It is also assumed that both types of expenses, variable and fixed, will react differently. For example, expenses categorized as variable will change in direct proportion to sales volume, whereas fixed expenses will remain constant regardless of the volume level.

DEFINING TYPES OF COSTS

In computing the breakeven point, it is necessary to divide budgeted costs into both variable and fixed costs. Variable costs vary in direct proportion to levels of activity and are directly related to the product. They typically include costs of materials (raw and packaging), labor (including fringe benefits), shipping materials, and commission. Fixed costs do not vary with the level of activity and remain constant within a given range of activity. They include such costs as rent, property taxes, depreciation, insurance premiums, salaries (not hourly), administrative costs, and general overhead.

What impact would production changes have on both these types of costs? Let us examine the following table:

	Total Costs	
	Variable Costs	*Fixed Costs*
Production Increase	Increase	No change
Production Decrease	Decrease	No change

Clearly production changes have no impact on fixed costs, but they affect variable costs in the same direction. However, if we look at the impact on per-unit costs, a different answer would result, as follows:

	Per-Unit Costs	
	Variable Costs	*Fixed Costs*
Production Increase	No change	Decrease
Production Decrease	No change	Increase

This is not to say that variable costs do not change on a per-unit basis. They vary with production levels. However, the more units produced, the lower the fixed costs per unit, because these costs are spread over more units. Conversely, the fewer units produced, the higher the fixed costs per unit, because fewer units must absorb more of the fixed costs.

In the hypothetical earnings statement shown in Exhibit 9.1, costs have been arranged to show classifications of variable and fixed costs. Costs directly related to the product are broken down into variable and fixed costs. The variable costs per unit were $4.70, and the fixed costs per unit were $1.30, or a total unit cost of $6.00. With a selling price of $7.00 per unit, the operating profit per unit was $1.00. In addition, 67.1 percent, or $0.671, of every dollar of revenue pays for variable costs for every unit produced. However, because fixed costs do not vary with volume activity, the total must be stated in terms of whole dollars. The difference of 32.9 percent, or $0.329 ($1.00—0.671), represents the amount needed for every sales dollar to cover fixed costs. This is referred to as the marginal income ratio. We will discuss this approach later.

BREAKEVEN CALCULATIONS

The basic calculation for determining the breakeven point is:

$$\text{Net sales} = \text{Variable costs} + \text{Fixed costs}$$

Exhibit 9.1   Hypothetical Earnings Statement

	Variable	Fixed	Total
Unit sales			100,000
Net sales			$700,000
Per unit			7.00
Operating expenses			
Cost of sales	$447,000	$ 78,000	525,000
Depreciation		5,000	5,000
Selling expenses	23,000	7,000	30,000
Administrative expenses		25,000	25,000
General expenses		15,000	15,000
Total	$470,000	$130,000	$600,000
Per unit	4.70	1.30	6.00
Operating profit			100,000
Other (income) expense			(2,000)
Income before income taxes			98,000
Income taxes			(48,000)
Net earnings			$ 50,000
Percentage of net sales	67.1%		7.1%

This point is reached when net sales equal variable costs plus fixed costs. At this point—that is, when both revenues and expenses are equal and neither a profit nor a loss results—the company is said to be at breakeven. The solution can be calculated either in units or in sales dollars.

Breakeven in Units

Let us review the breakeven point in units first, by using the following formula:

$$SP \times US = FC + VC$$

$$(SP \times US) - (VC \times US) = FC \times SP$$

$$US(SP - VC) = FC$$

$$US = \frac{FC}{SP-VC}$$

Applied to the data presented previously:

Sales price per unit (SP)	$7.00
Units sold (US)	100,000
Fixed costs (FC)	$130,000
Unit variable costs (VC)	$4.70

The formula yields this result:

$$US = \frac{\$130,000}{\$7.00 - \$4.70}$$

$$US = \quad 56,521.7 \text{ units}$$

The breakeven in units sold is 56,521.7 units. To prove that this many units are needed to break even, multiply the units by the selling price of $7.00 and by the variable unit cost of $4.70. Subtract the variable cost from the total sales dollars as well as the fixed costs of $130,000. The result should equal zero.

Net sales (56,521.7 × $7.00)	$395,652
Variable costs (56,521.7 × $4.70)	(265,652)
	130,000
Less fixed costs	(130,000)
Total	$ 0

If a specific profit were desired, the formula would be changed to include it.

Net sales = Variable costs + Fixed costs + Desired profit

Breakeven in Sales Dollars

Breakeven in sales dollars shows how many sales dollars are necessary to equal the fixed costs. The formula of breakeven is as follows:

$$BE = \frac{FC}{1 - (TVC/NS)}$$

Using the previous data:

Fixed costs (FC)	$130,000
Total variable costs (TVC)	470,000
Net sales (NS)	700,000

breakeven is calculated as

$$BE = \frac{\$130,000}{1 - (\$470,000/\$700,000)}$$

$$= \frac{\$130,000}{0.3286}$$

$$= \$395,617.77$$

The result shows that $395,617.77 is needed to equal the fixed costs without showing any profit or loss. This is proved as follows:

Net sales	$395,617.77
Variable costs at 67.14%	(265,617.77)
Variable margin	130,000.00
Less fixed costs	(130,000.00)
Total	$ 0

Contribution Margin

The contribution margin shows how many units are necessary both to recover fixed costs and to generate a desired profit. It is calculated as follows:

$$\text{Net sales} - \text{Variable costs} = \text{Fixed costs} + \text{Desired profit}$$

When this equation is applied to the previous data, the contribution margin is $230,000, assuming a desired profit of $100,000.

$$\$700,000 - \$470,000 = \$130,000 + \$100,000$$
$$\$230,000 \qquad = \$230,000$$

With a contribution margin of $230,000, or $2.30 per unit, the following number of units is needed to generate a profit of $100,000:

$$\frac{\text{Fixed expenses} + \text{Desired profit}}{\text{Unit contribution margin}}$$

or

$$\frac{\$130,000 + \$100,000}{\$2.30} = 100,000 \text{ units}$$

By comparing the data in the hypothetical earnings statement presented in Exhibit 9.1 to those presented in the following proof, you will recognize that the correct answer is 100,000 units.

Net sales (100,000 units at $7.00 each)	$700,000
Variable costs (100,000 units at $4.70 each)	(470,000)
Contribution margin	230,000
Less fixed costs	(130,000)
Desired profit	$100,000

In this case, the desired profit represents the operating profit.

Profit Contribution Ratio

The profit contribution ratio is computed by dividing the contribution margin by net sales:

$$\frac{\$230,000}{\$700,000} = 32.86\%$$

Note that this is the reciprocal of the relationship of variable costs to net sales (67.14 percent).

MARGIN OF SAFETY

The margin of safety reflects how much sales can decrease before losses can be expected. It is calculated by subtracting sales at the breakeven point ($395,618) from actual sales ($700,000) and by dividing this sum by the actual sales ($700,000). The following results:

$$\frac{\$700,000 - \$395,618}{\$700,000} = 43.48\%$$

Thus 43.48 percent of the actual sales can decrease before losses will occur. This is shown as follows:

Actual sales	$700,000
Less margin of safety at 43.48%	(304,360)
	395,640
Sales at breakeven	(395,618)
Total	$ 22

The total, or difference, of $22 represents rounding.

BREAKEVEN CHARTS

Breakeven can also be explained by the use of a chart. It is sometimes easier to visualize and demonstrate the relationships among volume, price, costs, and profits by such means. Knowing what these relationships are can be valuable in analyzing business performance as well as in preparing projections for budgeting and planning. Of particular interest are the effects of volume changes, cost changes, price changes, and tax changes on the breakeven point of the company and/or product. These effects will be explored later in the chapter. In addition, specific product data are necessary measures of performance in planning for changes in any of the elements that affect a product's financial performance.

The graphic approach charts data on both vertical and horizontal scales to measure volume and costs and profits or losses. The first step is to establish volume in units, sales dollars, capacity percent, or any other measurement relating to volume along the horizontal scale. In Exhibit 9.2, we use dollar sales volume. The vertical scale of the chart represents total costs and profits, as shown in Exhibit 9.3. A horizontal line, which represents total fixed expenses, is then drawn parallel to the horizontal axis, as shown in Exhibit 9.4. In this case, fixed expenses were $130,000.

Exhibit 9.2   Establishing Horizontal Scale

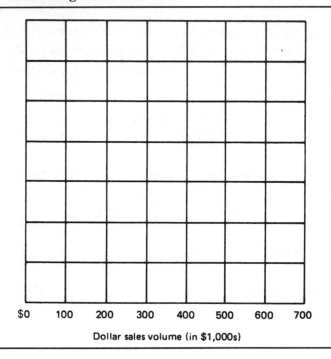

Dollar sales volume (in $1,000s)

In our previous illustration, each unit of sales had variable expenses of $4.70 per unit. Therefore, to graph each level of volume, a line is plotted upward, starting from the beginning of the fixed expense line, to a point that represents total expenses of $600,000 ($470,000 variable plus $130,000 fixed), as shown in Exhibit 9.5. A diagonal line is then drawn through the chart, representing total sales dollars. This is done from the left corner to the right corner, because the same scale is used on both axes (see Exhibit 9.6). The point at which both lines intersect in Exhibit 9.6 is the breakeven point. In this case it is $395,617.77.

HOW CHANGES AFFECT THE BREAKEVEN POINT

Changes in volume, cost, price, and desired profit—either singly or in any combination—affect the breakeven. One advantage of the breakeven concept is that it allows a business to simulate future business conditions and results and to show how many units are needed to break even. Once this has been established, decisionmakers can determine the most profitable course of action. Careful operating budgets will assist in reaching the desired goals.

Exhibit 9.3   Establishing Vertical Scale

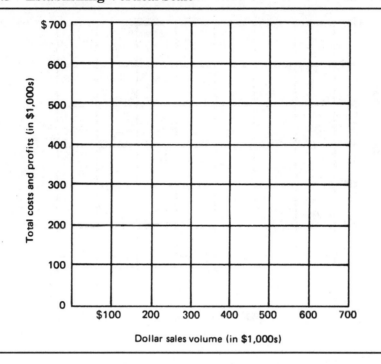

Let us use the data previously presented in this chapter to see how the various changes occur. These data are as follows:

	Total	Per-Unit Data
Unit volume	100,000	
Net sales	$700,000	$7.00
Variable costs	(470,000)	(4.70)
Variable contribution	230,000	2.30
Less fixed costs	(130,000)	(1.30)
Operating profit	$100,000	$1.00

Changes in Volume

What would be the impact on operating profit if unit volume increased to 150,000 units?

$$\$7.00 \times 150,000 = (\$4.70 \times 150,000) + \$130,000X$$
$$\$1,050,000 = \$705,000 + \$130,000X$$
$$\$1,050,000 = \$835,000X$$
$$X = \$215,000$$

Exhibit 9.4   Plotting Total Fixed Expenses

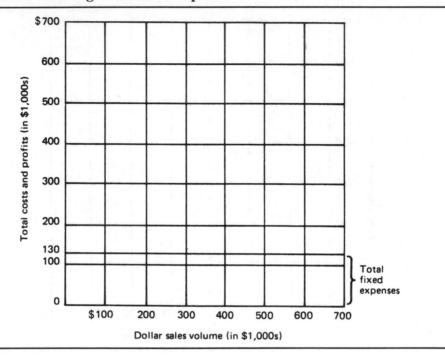

The operating profit would increase by $115,000, to $215,000. The revised data would be shown as follows:

Unit volume	150,000 units
Net sales	$1,050,000
Variable costs	(705,000)
Variable contribution	345,000
Less fixed costs	(130,000)
Operating profit	$ 215,000

The result shows that a 50 percent increase in unit volume increased operating profit by 115 percent.

Changes in Cost

Assuming that the same data are used, how many additional units would be needed to avoid a reduction in the original operating profit of $100,000 given an increase of $20,000 in fixed costs ($150,000)?

Exhibit 9.5   Plotting Total Variable Costs

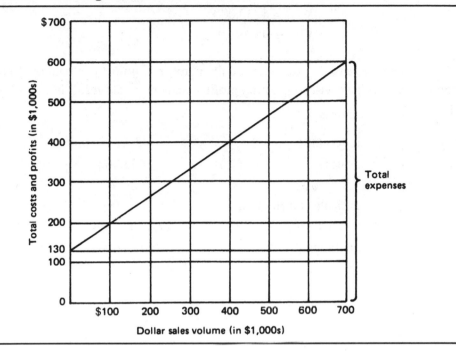

$$\$7.00X = \$4.70X + \$150,000 + \$100,000$$
$$\$2.30X = \$250,000$$
$$X = 108,695.7 \text{ units}$$

An additional 8,695.7 units are needed to absorb an additional $20,000 of fixed costs and maintain the same $100,000 of operating profit. The original data would now look like this:

Unit volume	108,695.7 units
Net sales	$760,870
Variable costs	(510,870)
Variable contribution	250,000
Less fixed costs	(150,000)
Operating profit	$100,000

Changes in Price

How many units would be needed to maintain the same operating profit of $100,000 if the price were increased from $7.00 to $10.00?

$$\begin{aligned}
\$10.00X &= \$4.70X + \$130,000 + \$100,000 \\
\$5.30X &= \$230,000 \\
X &= 43,396.2
\end{aligned}$$

A 42.9 percent increase in price reduced the number of units to be sold by 56,603.8, or 56.6 percent. The revised operating profit statement would result in the following data:

Unit volume	43,396.2 units
Net sales	$433,962
Variable costs	(203,962)
Variable contribution	230,000
Less fixed costs	(130,000)
Operating profit	$100,000

Exhibit 9.6   Breakeven Point Illustrated

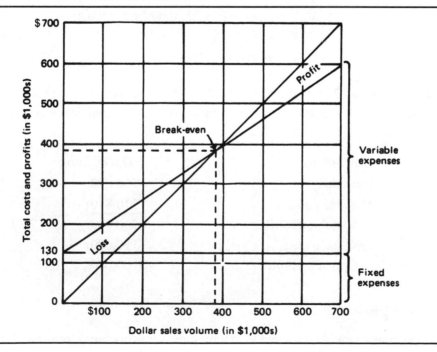

Changes in Profit

How many units would be needed to increase operating profit to $150,000?

$$\frac{\$130,000 + \$150,000}{\$2.30} = 121,739.1 \text{ units}$$

To increase operating profit by $50,000, an additional 21,739.1 units are needed. The following data now reflect the increase in operating profit:

Unit volume	121,739.1 units
Net sales	$852,174
Variable costs	(572,174)
Variable contribution	280,000
Less fixed costs	(130,000)
Operating profit	$150,000

USING BREAKEVEN DATA AS A DECISION-MAKING TOOL

The preceding analysis points out the flexibility that breakeven provides in projecting revenues and expenses under different assumed conditions. By reviewing these data, managers can see how certain actions can be integrated into the overall managerial decision-making process. However, caution should be taken in regard to certain problems in computing breakeven, such as the potential inaccuracy of revenue and expense projections and the extent to which competition will adjust their operating decisions to meet market conditions. Classifying expenses as variable and fixed can also be difficult, and some reasonable rationale is called for. Although breakeven analysis is a valuable tool, it can be oversimplified to the point where it does not conform to reality. The relationships among volume, cost, price, and profit must be studied carefully and in relation to the marketplace in which the business operates.

CHAPTER TEN

Budgeting Shared Resources or Common Costs

One of the more difficult parts of budgeting is the allocation of shared resources or common costs. Difficulties arise because there are often no fair and equitable methods of allocation. Whichever method is used, some inequities exist.

Common costs reduce overall costs through the efficiencies of scale by promoting internal cooperation among departments and other segments of the company. The allocation of these common costs affects budgets by developing complete cost data for specific operations of the company. In addition, it rations certain resources where resources are limited. This chapter describes methods of allocation for the most common types of shared resources.

ALLOCATING BY RATIO OF REVENUE OR SALES

The ratio of the revenue or sales of a segment is often used to allocate common costs in sales, marketing, advertising, billing, collecting, receivables and other departments. Exhibit 10.1 illustrates how this method works. Column 1 represents the total revenues or sales; column 2 represents each segment's percentage of the total. For example, Division III represents 27.5 percent of the total revenues of $1,000,000. Column 3 shows the actual allocation of a common cost of $50,000 by division. For Division III, the amount of the common costs allocated is $13,750, or 0.275 times $50,000.

Exhibit 10.1   Allocating by Ratio of Revenue or Sales of the Segment

Segment	*(col. 1)* *Total Revenues* *or Sales*	*(col. 2)* *Percentage* *of Total*	*(col. 3)* *Common Cost* *Allocated*
Division I	$ 100,000	10.0%	$ 5,000
Division II	200,000	20.0	10,000
Division III	275,000	27.5	13,750
Division IV	125,000	12.5	6,250
Division V	300,000	30.0	15,000
Total	$1,000,000	100.0%	$50,000

ALLOCATING BY ASSETS EMPLOYED

The assets employed method allocates such costs as depreciation, insurance, and general maintenance according to the amount of assets utilized for each segment of the company. Exhibit 10.2 illustrates the use of assets employed as an allocation method.

Note that column 3, the amount of common costs allocated, differs from the previous allocation method of segment or division. Although the total amount of the common costs of $50,000 remains the same, the allocations to individual divisions result in different cost figures. For example, Division III's allocation in Exhibit 10.1 was $13,750. In the assets employed method, $14,300 is allocated to Division III, as shown in Exhibit 10.2.

Exhibit 10.2   Allocating by Assets Employed in the Segments of a Company

Segment	*(col. 1)* *Assets* *Employed*	*(col. 2)* *Percentage of* *Total*	*(col. 3)* *Common Cost* *Allocated*
Division I	$ 125,000	11.4%	$ 5,700
Division II	200,000	18.2	9,100
Division III	315,000	28.6	14,300
Division IV	150,000	13.6	6,800
Division V	310,000	28.2	14,100
Total	$1,100,000	100.0%	$50,000

ALLOCATING BY SEGMENTS OF A COMPANY

Many different methods are available for allocating costs by segments of a company. The methods presented are representative of the types available. Keep in mind that different methods may result in different allocation amounts. Therefore, it is important to maintain consistency in methods from period to period.

Average Method.   The average method uses three key percentages to arrive at an arithmetic average that provides a single percentage for allocating. These three key percentages are: (1) the percentage of a company's total sales or revenues represented by the segment's sales or revenues, (2) the percentage of a company's gross payroll represented by the segment's gross payroll, and (3) the percentage of a company's total assets employed represented by the segment's assets employed. Exhibit 10.3 illustrates this method.

Gross Profit Method.   The gross profit method uses gross profits to allocate costs. Gross profits of each segment of the company are determined and a percentage is derived from the relationship of each segment's gross profit to the company's total gross profit. Exhibit 10.4 illustrates this method.

Working Capital Method.   The working capital method uses working capital, or current assets less current liabilities, as a basis for allocation. Exhibit 10.5 illustrates this method.

Exhibit 10.3   Average Method

Segment	(col. 1) Total Revenues or Sales	(col. 2) Gross Payroll	(col. 3) Assets Employed	(col. 4) Average Percentage— Col. (1 + 2 + 3)/3	(col. 5) Common Cost Allocated
Division I	10.0%	18.4%	11.4%	13.3%	$ 6,650
Division II	20.0	14.2	18.2	17.5	8,750
Division III	27.5	18.9	28.6	25.0	12,500
Division IV	12.5	28.4	13.6	18.2	9,100
Division V	30.0	20.1	28.2	26.0	13,000
Total	100.0%	100.0%	100.0%	100.0%	$50,000

Exhibit 10.4 Gross Profit Method

Segment	(col. 1) Gross Profits	(col. 2) Percentage of Total	(col. 3) Common Cost Allocated
Division I	$ 48,000	10.9%	$ 5,450
Division II	84,000	19.0	9,500
Division III	118,000	26.8	13,400
Division IV	50,000	11.3	5,650
Division V	141,000	32.0	16,000
Total	$441,000	100.0%	$50,000

METHODS OF ALLOCATING COSTS

Space and Related Support Systems.   Many costs related to square footage, such as office space, must be allocated on some basis of usage. Such costs can be allocated according to the number of square feet occupied or by the number of employees working within the allocated space.

Computer Services.   Costs relating to computer service can be allocated by units of output, units of input, or processing time.

Employee Fringe Benefits.   Costs relating to employee fringe benefits can be allocated by payroll dollars, employee headcount, or classification of types of employees.

Exhibit 10.5 Working Capital Method

Segment	(col. 1) Working Capital	(col. 2) Percentage of Total	(col. 3) Common Cost Allocated
Division I	$ 43,000	14.3%	$ 7,150
Division II	64,000	21.3	10,650
Division III	61,000	20.3	10,150
Division IV	43,000	14.3	7,150
Division V	89,000	29.8	14,900
Total	$300,000	100.0%	$50,000

Administrative Services.   These types of costs can be allocated by departmental expense dollars, employee headcount, or some calculation of a unit of service.

MANAGERIAL CONCERNS IN ALLOCATION

It is important that management resolve key issues relating to cost allocations before making any decisions on allocations. Such issues as the quality and demand for service during standby and peak periods, the type of method used as well as the means of allocation, and the cost effectiveness of the allocation. Remember, consistency in use of a single allocation method is important.

CHAPTER ELEVEN

Pricing*

An integral part of the budgeting process is how a product or service is priced. This major decision will impact most areas of the company since sales revenues will be generated, production levels established, and spending of costs associated with the marketing of products or services.

Both inside factors and outside influences will play a major role in the pricing strategy. These factors include manufacturing efficiency, earnings objectives, competitive conditions, and governmental regulations, economic circumstances, and changes in technology.

PRICING STRATEGIES

There are many pricing strategies available for use in budgeting. There is not any one acceptable technique, but rather several methods are used collectively to accomplish different objectives. The budget preparer may use different strategies for different products or services. A summary of these strategies follows:

---

*This chapter is based on the author's own works and some material is adapted from *Return on Investment Manual: Tools and Applications for Managing Financial Results*, by Robert Rachlin (New York: M. E. Sharpe Inc., 1997), pp. 140–157.

- *High price strategy.* Establishes higher prices for similar competitive products to imply greater value for the product or service. Most provide value in the long term for price to retain its high level.
- *Volume strategy.* Uses low margin, high volume philosophy.
- *Psychological pricing.* Refers to pricing just below the next dollar amount such as $14.99 instead of $15.00.
- *In-and-out pricing.* Utilizes the high price approach until the market is saturated and then the price is reduced. Works when there is not competition or substitute products/services.
- *Typical pricing.* Assumes a general pricing structure accepted by the marketplace as being a fair price.
- *Entry pricing.* Used when a company is trying to establish a position in the marketplace.
- *Elasticity pricing.* Occurs when a reduction in the price causes a decline in the demand for the product or services.
- *Cost-plus pricing.* A pricing strategy that is developed from the bottom up such as used in governmental units.
- *Phase-out pricing.* Usually occurs when a company is seeking to phase out a product or service.
- *Loss leader pricing.* A pricing strategy which uses lower prices on certain items to attract customers into an establishment, such as a retail store, in the hopes that they will buy other products once inside.

PRICING TECHNIQUES

There are five recognized techniques used in calculating the price of a product or service: mark-up technique, total cost method, contribution percentage method, margin approach, and the ROI approach. Each method is discussed below and illustrated with a calculation.

Mark-up Technique.   This technique is often used to establish a price but has several drawbacks, as you will see in the illustration. It does not allow for the treatment of fixed costs on profits since it treats fixed costs as a variable expense and does not allow the opportunity to cost a product based on volume. Assuming the following data, the calculation is made as follows:

Variable unit costs	*Per unit*
Manufacturing costs	$10.00
Selling and distribution costs	4.00
Fixed costs	8.00
Desired profit	5.00

Calculation

Variable costs	$14.00
Fixed costs	8.00
Total costs	22.00
Desired profit	5.00
Selling price	$27.00

Total Cost Method.   Another example of a pricing technique is sometimes referred to as the total cost method, or full costing. This method can be expressed as a formula using the following data:

SP = Selling price
MU = Mark-up percent—30%
DM = Direct material—$20.00
DL = Direct labor—$15.00
OH = Overhead—$5.00
TC = Total cost—$40.00

Calculation

SP = TC + MU(TC)
SP = $60.00 + 0.30 ($40.00)
SP = $60.00 + $12.00
SP = $52.00

Keep in mind that this pricing approach can be misleading due to the way overhead costs are allocated.

Contribution Percentage Method.   This method uses a contribution percentage and is an excellent method to be used in the short term. Be sure to review this percentage frequently in order to reflect changes in interest rates and other cost elements.
The following data is used to illustrate this method.

		Per Unit
Selling price		$75.00
Direct Costs		
Materials	$20.00	
Labor	18.00	
Overhead	12.00	50.00
Contribution		$25.00
Percentage of selling price		33.3%

If the selling price of $75.00 was not known, and the direct costs were $50.00 or 66.6 percent of the selling price, then the following calculation can be made to project the selling price.

Direct costs $50.00 = $75.00 selling price
Direct cost percentage   0.666

Remember that since data in this calculation changes frequently, it is not advisable to use this method in the long term.

Margin Approach.   This approach uses an agreed upon acceptable margin rate which is based on sales dollars as a basis for calculation. It allows the preparer the luxury of simulating different approaches to determine various selling prices at varying levels of margin. It also allows the preparer to use different cost data and reflect different price ranges.

Direct material	$20.00
Direct labor	15.00
Selling, general, and administrative expenses	5.00
Total per unit cost	$40.00

Using the above data, the following calculation results:

Total per unit cost	$40.00
Margin % desired	25%
Selling, general, and administrative expenses	10%
Remainder	65%

or

$$\frac{\$40.00}{.65} = \$61.54$$

The following is proof of the $61.54 selling price:

Selling price	$61.54
Less direct costs	40.00
Less selling, general, and administrative costs	6.15
	$15.39
Percentage of selling price	25%

Given the selling price of $61.54, management must determine whether this price is acceptable in the marketplace. If not, management can decide to lower the margin expectations, reduce costs, or both.

For example, lowering the margin return expectations from 25 percent to 20 percent, the selling price is calculated as $57.14 as follows:

$$\frac{\$40.00}{.70} = \$57.14$$

Return on Investment Approach. The last approach is used to determine the price based on an expected return on investment level. Be cautious about using the resulting selling price due to the sensitivity of sales volume estimates and the impact it may have on the estimated selling price.

Given the following data which assumes that an investment in a new product is required to earn a satisfactory return, the following selling price results:

Data Used

Investment	$500,000
Fixed costs	100,000
Variable costs	$50.00 per unit
Estimated units sold	20,000 units
Desired after-tax ROI	30%
Payback period desired	5 years

The formula that can be developed for computing the selling price under this approach is as follows:

$$P = \frac{(ROI)(I/PB) + FC + VC(US)}{US}$$

P = Price

ROI = Desired return on investment

I = Investment

PB = Desired payback period in years

FC = Fixed costs

VC = Variable costs per unit

US = Estimated units sold

or

$$P = \frac{(.30)(500,000/5) + \$100,000 + \$50.00(20,000)}{20,000}$$

$$P = \frac{(.30)100,000 + \$100,000 + \$1,000,000}{20,000}$$

$$P = \frac{\$30,000 + \$100,000 + \$1,000,000}{20,000}$$

$$P = \frac{\$1,130,00}{20,000} = \$56.50$$

The question that management must answer is whether the company can sell 20,000 units at a selling price of $56.50 per unit over the next 5 years. If not, management can choose to either lower the desired after-tax ROI estimate, reduce costs, or a combination of both.

CHAPTER TWELVE

Developing the Sales Budget

The development of the sales budget is pivotal to the success of the budgeting process. The sales budget allows a company to project such additional budgets as manufacturing, sales and marketing, cash, and major segments of the balance sheet. In essence it is the starting point of the budgeting process.

SALES AND MARKETING OBJECTIVES

Before sales and/or revenues can be projected, it is important to focus on the sales and marketing objectives of the company. These objectives will establish the philosophy and direction of the company during the budgeting year, as explained in the following discussion.[1]

Market Share Objectives

If the current market share is known, it is advisable to review it and estimate where the company would like to position itself within the marketplace during the following budget year. Increases in market share may require more unit sales, higher production

---

[1]Robert Rachlin, *Handbook of Budgeting*, fourth edition (New York: John Wiley & Sons, 1999), pp. 13.1–13.4.

levels, higher marketing and advertising expenditures, and other increases in marketing and sales support services. These increases must all be reflected in the budget projection.

Pricing Objectives

It is important for the projected budget to establish the pricing structure needed to accomplish market share objectives. For example, one way of achieving market share may be to lower the price of the product. An additional strategy may be to give higher discounts, offer special promotional deals, or support current price with more advertising. In any situation the support for your projected market share will depend heavily upon the established pricing structure.

Product Line Objectives

Management must reevaluate, and perhaps change, the mix of a product line when the company expands or contracts. Such changes may apply to the total product line or in some cases to specific product lines. Decisions to change product lines will greatly affect the company's ability to achieve its desired position within the marketplace.

Competitive Objectives

It is important to develop strategies for meeting competition, such as becoming a low-cost producer, a top-of-the-line company, a high-volume–low-price producer, or a low-volume–high-price producer. In addition, it is essential to consider how the product is going to be marketed, in what regions you want to achieve better results than your competition achieves, what products you want to emphasize to gain a competitive advantage, what position you want to achieve within the marketplace, and similar issues.

Profitability Objectives

It is vital to determine what level of profitability you desire within both the product line and the company. The level of projected volume will dictate the level of profitability you expect, since fixed costs will be spread over more units and production efficiencies will result when higher volume is anticipated. In addition, the company's profitability may be dictated by the expectations of the owners and/or stockholders.

Resource Objectives and Product Life Cycle

In Chapter 2, discussions centered on the impact of the product life cycle on the budgeting process. This consideration is also important in determining the amount of resources to allocate to a product that is on either the upward or the downward side of the life cycle. The effect of budgeting decisions on sales projections and marketing resources will depend upon the situation of a product within its life cycle.

Customer Buying Patterns

The buying patterns of your customers are important factors in forecasting sales. Such information as new account and customer retention rates, costs to acquire an account, sales call patterns, and customers' ordering history will provide critical support data in the development of sales forecasts. During the budgeting process a company may want to set an objective to increase or decrease certain factors in an effort to gain a competitive edge. For example, a program may be developed to increase the retention rates of existing customers by periodically visiting every customer during the budgeting year. Additional costs may then have to be factored into the marketing and sales budget to support this strategy. However, these costs would be more than offset by higher sales dollars due to a higher customer retention rate.

DISCRETIONARY EXPENDITURES

Certain budgeted expenses are considered discretionary. The marketing executive may budget these expenses as a means of developing sales revenues through other sales vehicles and use them at his or her discretion. However, the benefits of these expenditures to the sales effort would be expected to exceed the level at which they are expensed. In other words, revenues generated would exceed expenditures.

Discretionary expenditures include the following:

- Other methods of selling a company's product such as the use of brokers, special commission agents, or sales representatives.
- Expenses associated with sales promotion efforts such as trade shows, premium programs, or the modernization of retail stores
- Advertising of the product line or brand name
- Customer service efforts, including warranty support, training, and complaint handling
- Alternative methods of physically distributing the product

PROBLEMS AND SOLUTIONS IN MEASURING RESULTS

In sales and marketing budgeting many problems may arise in accurately measuring results of various expense budgets. These problems can be avoided by following some simple rules when dealing with such budgetary items as pricing adjustments, selling expenses, sales promotion expenses, advertising expenses, and customer service expenses. The following solutions are presented in an effort to avoid these problems.

Pricing Adjustments.   Prices can be adjusted in relation to cost or competitive environment. When new products compete with old products or enter existing markets, discounts may be necessary within the span of the budgeting period.

Selling Expenses.   Selling expenses should be budgeted in such a way that they can be analyzed when actual results are available. Comparative analysis by department, geographical area, product, customer calls, and the like must be available to assist in measuring actual expenditures against budgeted expenditures.

Sales Promotion Expenses.   Sales promotion expenses should be budgeted in such a way that they can be measured against actual results. Therefore, these expenses must be segmented and controllable on the expense and functional level.

Advertising Expenses.   Techniques must be developed for measuring the impact of advertising expenses on sales. These expenses must be controlled and measurable in relation to the level of sales activity.

Customer Service Expenses.   Expenses should be developed for warranties, based on such factors as percentage of sales, recall expenses, replacement expenses, and customer inquiries and complaints. In the preparation of a sales budget, it is important to review historical data regarding customer service. This experience will shed light on what might be expected in the following year's budget. The logical place to find these data is the internal accounting records. If records are properly maintained, you should be able to find the following information:

- To whom you sold the product
- Where the product was sold
- What salesperson sold the product
- To what industry the customer belongs
- How much was sold at what price
- The total value of the customer's order
- Discounts given and other special billing instructions

METHODS OF PROJECTING SALES

There are many different ways of projecting sales, and each company must choose one or more methods. Although one method may be advantageous for certain companies at certain times, all seven of the suggested methods are useful. Some of these methods merely provide an approach to or philosophy of sales forecasting in some cases. Others offer techniques that specifically assist the preparer in calculating the projected sales levels of a product and/or company. The seven methods or philosophies are briefly discussed in this section.

Causal Approach

The causal approach identifies the many variables that have a causal effect on future sales. Each of these variables is analyzed and used to project sales activity into some future period such as the next year's budget. There are causal variables over which a company has control and those over which it has no control. Variables over which a company has control include type of product line, pricing structure, sales territories, and amount of advertising. Variables over which a company has no control include such items as gross national product, overall and/or regional population, and general economic conditions.

Noncausal Approach

In the noncausal approach historical sales results are analyzed and projected into the future. No effort is made to identify and evaluate the underlying causal variables since it is assumed that future results will follow the same trend as historical results.

Direct Method

The direct method utilizes straightforward projections without any concern for the trend of the total industry in which a company competes.

Indirect Method

The indirect method takes into consideration the projections of the industry and uses these estimates to determine the percentage of the total industry a company wants to achieve. It is the complete opposite of the direct method.

Judgmental Methods

Judgmental methods are nonstatistical. Their time periods and the purposes for which they are used tend to overlap. It is advisable to use a combination of the following approaches in projecting the various segments of the sales budget.

Sales Force Composite. This method relies on the expertise of the sales force from the bottom up. Because projections are developed from the lowest level of the sales organization, it is important to analyze them carefully. Salespeople tend to be overly optimistic about what they can sell in the future. Here is an illustration of this method:

- The headquarters of the sales organization provides the sales personnel with data on historical results, changes in sales policies (as discussed previously in the chapter), and other valuable information that may provide a more accurate forecast, such as competitive and market data within the industry.

- The salespeople use these data to forecast unit sales within their territory, taking into consideration the customers they are servicing. They must also consider the general economic conditions within their sales territory.

- Once the salespeople have developed the estimates, they submit them to the local sales management for review and approval. Upon approval, these estimates are forwarded to the central sales organization.

- The estimates are then reviewed at the central sales organization by the sales executives, who develop dollar estimates on the basis of projected pricing policies. In addition, any adjustments for economic and other factors are made to the sales estimates, which are then finalized.

- The finalized sales estimates are presented to the budget committee for approval, taking into consideration the resources of the company such as manufacturing capacity, financial capability, storage capacity, distribution capabilities, and the like.

- Once approved, the sales estimates become part of the overall budget and are sent to the sales organization for implementation.

- In addition, budgets for such areas as manufacturing, marketing, and distribution are prepared on the basis of the sales estimates.

Sales Supervisors Composite. This method follows the same procedures as the sales force composite method with one exception: The sales forecasts are generated by the sales supervisors rather than the sales force.

Executive Opinion Method. This method is usually employed by smaller companies and represents the opinions of the key executives within the company. It is simpler, less sophisticated, and less time-consuming and expensive than other ways of preparing estimates.

Statistical Methods

Statistical methods require more technical knowledge and are more sophisticated than judgmental methods. Some knowledge of statistical applications would be helpful.

Trend Analysis. This method projects historical trends and uses indexes to forecast future trends. The wholesale price index, the industrial production index, the seasonal index, and similar indexes are commonly used.

To illustrate, let us assume that we are going to develop a sales forecast for the month of June. In trend analysis, we follow these steps:

1. Use the month's adjusted sales based on company records. $500,000
2. Develop a cyclical forecast index based on the industrial production index.   90%
3. Adjust sales according to the cyclical forecast index— line 1 × line 2. $450,000
4. Develop the seasonal index based on the experience of the company.   105%
5. Adjust sales according to both cyclical and seasonal indexes— line 3 × line 4. $472,500
6. Determine the wholesale price index.   110%
7. Calculate June's forecasted sales—line 5 × line 6. $519,750

Correlation Analysis. This method uses a correlation between a series of economic or business data and the company sales. Once the correlation is developed, the data are extrapolated in developing the forecast for the required monthly sales. An example of this method is shown in Exhibit 12.1.

This exhibit shows the historical sales dollars by month for the last three years. If you were projecting the sales dollars for the month of July, you would determine the total sales dollars for the past three years ($21.3 million + $20.5 million + $19.0 million), which amounted to $60.8 million. The total sales dollars for the past three years was $848.0 million ($286.0 million + $282.0 million + $280.0 million). Dividing the monthly totals of $60.8 million by the yearly totals of $848.0 million results in a per-

Exhibit 12.1   Correlation Analysis

| | Historical Data (in 000's) | | | Projection |
	Year 1	Year 2	Year 3	Year 4
January	$ 20.0	$ 21.5	$ 20.8	
February	19.0	18.6	19.8	
March	21.3	20.7	20.9	
April	24.6	23.9	24.1	
May	25.1	24.3	26.4	
June	28.5	27.2	27.9	
July	21.3	20.5	19.9	$ 20.8
August	19.2	20.3	18.1	
September	22.9	21.8	20.6	
October	23.1	24.2	23.4	
November	28.9	27.7	28.1	
December	32.1	31.3	30.9	
Total	$286.0	$282.0	$280.0	$290.0

centage of 7.17 percent. Assuming that the total year's sales projection for year 4 was $290.0 million, merely multiplying 7.17 percent by $290.0 million yields a projected July sales dollar estimate of $20.8 million. This same analysis can be applied to each of the other months. Such a correlation analysis can provide the basis for extrapolating historical averages into budget projections for future years.

Specific Purpose Methods

Specific purpose methods are used for analyses that have special data requirements, such as industry analysis, product analysis, and end-use analysis. A brief description will be presented for each of the specific methods.

Industry Analysis Method.   This method involves developing or using industry estimates and applying the share of market that you can reasonably expect to obtain during that budget year. However, this method assumes that industry data are available and that industry forecasts are somewhat accurate.

Product Line Analysis.   This method involves developing a forecast method from the product line estimate rather than by geographical area or by customer.

End-Use Analysis.   In this method, estimates are based on the end-user of the product. For instance, a tire manufacturer that sells all its tires to the automobile industry would have to develop and take into account new markets for its tires, such as the manufacturers of boat trailers, trucks, or lawn equipment.

LENGTH OF THE SALES BUDGETING PERIOD

Most budgets are based on either a calendar year—that is, January 1 through December 31—or a fiscal year, which is any period other than a calendar year. However, it may be advisable under some circumstances (discussed below) for the length of the sales budgeting period to differ from the typical 12-month time period; for example, an 18- or 24-month period could be chosen.

In most cases, the budget period should correspond to the period used in accounting. The data from these periods must be comparable to permit analysis of actual performance versus budget projection. Some factors may dictate changes in sales budgeting periods. Then both accounting records and budgets will be developed to meet these changes. The following situations influence the length of the budgeting period:

- When seasonal factors cause sales to be generated at a faster pace than inventory can be produced. In this situation the sales budget is developed on the basis of the selling season.
- When the length of the production period in manufacturing requires a change in the sales budget.
- When financing methods impose heavy financial requirements during periods of low volume when loans may be difficult to secure. In this situation longer budgeting periods may be needed to cover a period of time when financial institutions can be more confident that loans will be repaid.
- When fluctuating market trends require shorter budget periods.

ESTABLISHING SALES BUDGET STANDARDS

Sales budget standards can vary by company and industry. Because there are no universal standards, each company must develop standards that best suit its type of business and industry. However, there are some guidelines that will help the preparer develop reasonable standards.

These guidelines can be placed into three major categories, as we discussed in Chapter 3 in reference to establishing performance standards. Here they will be applied to the development of sales budget standards. The following list by no means represents the only standards that can be developed; it does, however, represent those standards that are commonly used today.

Standards of Effort

- Number of calls made per budget period
- Number of calls made on prospective customers
- Number of dealers and wholesalers established
- Number of units of sales promotional effort (demonstrations, pieces of direct mail, and the like) used

Standards of Result

- Percentage of prospective customers to whom sales are made
- Number of customers to whom new products are introduced or sold
- Number of new customers acquired
- Amount of sales dollars generated
- Number of sales units sold
- Amount of gross margins generated
- Amount of net earnings generated
- Number of units sold to the more established and larger customers
- Gross margin percentage returned

Standards of Relationship between Effort and Result

- The relationship of number of orders to number of sales calls
- The relationship of number of new customers to number of calls on new prospects
- The relationship of number of inquiries or orders to amount of sales promotional expenditures
- The relationship of individual direct selling expenses to volume or gross margin
- The relationship of administrative sales costs to volume or gross margin

TYPES OF SALES BUDGET CLASSIFICATIONS

There are many types of sales budget classifications. In many instances, an organization could use several types to supplement its overall sales budget. For example, one system of budget classification may be used to develop budgets that monitor the performance of salespeople. Another system of classification may be used to set objectives and monitor customer performance. Such a budget may require special promotional expenses in support of this effort, and other parts of the overall budget may therefore have to be reflected in terms of adding or subtracting expense dollars.

The following list provides a sampling of the types of budget classifications that can be developed. Within these major categories, there can also be subclassifications.

- Products or commodities (see Schedule A1, Exhibit 12.2)
- Territories (see Schedule A2, Exhibit 12.3)
- Customers (see Schedule A3, Exhibit 12.4)
- Salespeople (see Schedule A4, Exhibit 12.5)
- Channels of distribution
- Organization division (such as branches, stores, or departments)
- Terms of sale
- Method of sale
- Method of delivery
- Size of orders (such as full cases or small-unit sales)

Examples of the first four classifications are provided in the schedules cited. Instructions relating to Schedules A1 through A4 are presented later in the chapter.

SCHEDULE IDENTIFICATION SYSTEM

Throughout this book, schedules are presented to take the reader through the preparation of a company's budget. Each major schedule is labeled with an alpha letter such as A,B,C, and so forth. Within each alpha letter there is a numerical sequence that represents one or more schedules within that category. For example, Schedule A represents the Unit Sales/Revenue Budget. Within Schedule A, there are four schedules numbered A1, A2, A3, and A4. This is necessary to allow a company to generate unit sales and revenue figures by product (Schedule A1), by territory (Schedule A2), by customer (Schedule A3), or by salesperson (Schedule A4). In certain cases, more than one schedule would be prepared to allow for establishing performance standards by different categories, but only including one unit sales and revenue figure as part of the budget. Each line item (lines 1–25 or lines 26–50) indicates how the line item was calculated. For example, in Schedule A1, line 4, the sales revenue for product X is calculated by multiplying line 2 by line 3. Line 18 is a summary of unit sales and is calculated by adding lines 2, 6, and 10 together.

Exhibit 12.2 Unit Sales/Revenue Budget

Schedule _____ **A1**

Product _____

Company Name _____

Page _____ of _____

Period

☐ Six months ☐ Total year

LINE	($ in 000s)	Reference						Total
1	PRODUCT							
2	X – number of units							
3	– unit price							
4	– sales revenue (L2xL3)							
5								
6	Y – number of units							
7	– unit price							
8	– sales revenue (L6xL7)							
9								
10	Z – number of units							
11	– unit price							
12	– sales revenue (L10xL11)							
13								
14	Total gross revenues (L4+L8+L12)							
15	Less: discounts							
16	Net sales	To D1,L2						
17								
18	Total unit sales (L2+L6+L10)	To D1,L1						
19								
20								
21								
22								
23								
24								
25								

Exhibit 12.3 Unit Sales/Revenue Budget

Schedule _____ **A2** _____   Territory _____   Page _____ of _____

Period ☐ Six months ☐ Total year   Company Name

LINE	($ in 000s)	Reference							Total
1	TERRITORY								
2	NORTH								
3	X – number of units								
4	– unit price								
5	– sales revenue (L3xL4)								
6									
7	Y – number of units								
8	– unit price								
9	– sales revenue (L7xL8)								
10									
11	Z – number of units								
12	– unit price								
13	– sales revenue (L11xL12)								
14									
15	Total gross revenues (L5+L9+L13)								
16	Less: discounts								
17	Net sales	To D1,L2							
18									
19	Total units sales (L3+L7+L11)	To D1,L1							
20									
21									
22									
23									
24									
25									

Exhibit 12.4 Unit Sales/Revenue Budget

Schedule ____ **A3** Customers ____ Page ____ of ____

Period ☐ Six months ☐ Total year

Company Name

L I N E	($ in 000s)	Reference					Total
1	CUSTOMER NAME						
2	PRODUCT						
3	X – number of units						
4	– unit price						
5	– sales revenue (L3xL4)						
6							
7	Y – number of units						
8	– unit price						
9	– sales revenue (L7xL8)						
10							
11	Z – number of units						
12	– unit price						
13	– sales revenue (L11xL12)						
14							
15	Total gross revenues (L5+L9+L13)						
16	Less: discounts						
17	Net sales	To D1,L2					
18							
19	Total unit sales (L3+L7+L11)	To D1,L1					
20							
21							
22							
23							
24							
25							

Exhibit 12.5   Unit Sales/Revenue Budget

Schedule ___**A4**___   Salesperson _____   Page ____ of ____

Company Name

Period ☐ Six months ☐ Total year

LINE	($ in 000s)	Reference							Total
1	SALESPERSON								
2	E. JONES								
3	X – number of units								
4	– unit price								
5	– sales revenue (L3xL4)								
6									
7	J. SMITH								
8	X – number of units								
9	– unit price								
10	– sales revenue (L8xL9)								
11									
12	Z – number of units								
13	– unit price								
14	– sales revenue (L12xL13)								
15									
16	H.BROWN								
17	Y – number of units								
18	– unit price								
19	– sales revenue (L17xL18)								
20									
21	Total gross revenues (L5+								
22	L10+L14+L19)								
23	Less: discounts								
24	Net sales	To D1,L2							
25	Total unit sales (L3+L8+L12+L17)	To D1,L1							

118

The reference column indicates where a line number is posted to or where a line number is posted from. For example, Schedule A1, line 18 is posted to Schedule D1, line 1. Schedule B2, line 2, units to be produced, is posted from Schedule B1.

This identification system allows the preparer to follow the posting from schedule to schedule and line to line. It aids in the simplification of preparing a company's budget.

PREPARING UNIT SALES/REVENUE BUDGETS

As stated previously, a company may choose to develop different formats, or systems of classification, for projecting unit sales/revenue budgets. These formats assist the company in deciding how to budget units and revenues as well as how to measure results against performance standards. Before this process begins, however, the preparer must consider the following factors:

- The impact of competition on price, cost, and volume in the past and during the budgeting period.
- External economic factors that may affect the revenue capabilities of the product and/or industry, such as inflation; demographic changes; local, regional, or national political climate; and unemployment rates.
- Internal factors such as strategies for growth in specific markets, life cycle stage of the product(s), and management's pricing and distribution philosophies.
- Projected expenditures for advertising and sales promotion and the expected impact on revenues. This should be coordinated with the marketing department before projections are finalized.

The formats the preparer chooses should suit the company's needs and preferences. Organizational structure may also greatly influence the choice of budgeting format. Schedules A1–A4 illustrate some of the classification systems that are most commonly used. They include classification by product (Schedule A1), by territory (Schedule A2), by customer (Schedule A3), and by salesperson (Schedule A4).

Classification by Product (Schedule A1).   This budgeting classification system categorizes unit sales/revenues according to the various products within the company. Each product classification would include the estimated number of units to be sold, the unit price, and the total gross sales revenues (line 14). To this amount, discounts (line 15) must be deducted in accordance with credit and collection policies. Given no major changes in discount policies, it is advisable to use historical percentages. Net sales (line

16) are then posted to Schedule D1, line 2. Unit sales are posted to Schedule D1, line 1. In addition, the units are posted by product to Schedule B1 (Unit Production Budget), lines 2, 10, and 18, to determine levels of production.

Classification by Territory (Schedule A2).   This type of budgeting format deals with territorial segments such as regions, districts, cities, or towns and estimates unit sales and revenues to be sold within each territorial segment. Discounts, net sales, and unit sales calculations are similar to those in Schedule A1. Be sure that neither net sales nor unit sales are posted twice.

Classification by Customer (Schedule A3).   This type of budgeting classification system lists unit sales/revenues by major customer. Each major customer would be budgeted by products expected to be sold, and all other customers would be grouped into a one-line item. Discounts, net sales, and unit sales would be treated as they were in the previous formats and posted to Schedule D1, lines 1 and 2.

Classification by Salesperson (Schedule A4).   This classification system employs the same methodology as the formats just discussed, but it is categorized by salesperson.

ANALYZING SALES RESULTS

During the budget year it is important to analyze the budget projections in relation to the actual results. This process will highlight the variations that exist and help to identify the necessary corrective actions. In addition, such analysis provides a learning experience for developing future budgets. Below are key analytical questions to ask when analyzing product(s), customers, territories, and salespeople. They are designed to take the preparer through the many facets of analyzing actual results in relation to budget projections.

Analysis by Product

- Which product(s) are being neglected?
- Which product(s) are returning insufficient gross margin? Is this due to competitive conditions, unsatisfactory price policy, or excessive production costs?
- Which product(s) move too slowly, and what adjustments are necessary in production and inventory policies?
- Which product(s) require excessive distribution costs, and what items of cost are excessive?

- Which product(s) return insufficient net earnings? Why? What changes are necessary to make them profitable?
- Which product(s) offer no promise of profit and should thus be eliminated?

Analysis by Customer

- Which customers offer promise of more volume? In which product lines?
- Which customers return insufficient gross margins? Is this due to low prices, unfavorable restriction of terms, or purchases to low-profit lines?
- Which customers require excessive distribution costs, and what items are excessive?
- Which customers are unprofitable? Why? What adjustments are required to make them profitable?
- Which customers offer no promise of profit and should no longer be served?

Analysis by Territory

- Which territories offer promise of more volume? In what lines should it be secured?
- Which territories return insufficient gross margins? Is this due to competitive conditions, improper price policy, or neglect of high-profit lines?
- Which territories entail excessive distribution costs, and which cost item is excessive?
- Which territories are insufficiently profitable? Why? What changes in selling and service methods would be necessary to make them profitable?
- Which territories offer no promise of adequate profit? What indirect losses would be suffered by the abandonment of such territories? Which territory should be wholly or partially abandoned?

Analysis by Salesperson

- Which salesperson is generating inadequate volume? On which products? To which customers are sales unsatisfactory?
- Which salesperson is returning inadequate gross margins? Why?
- Which salesperson has excessive distribution costs including his or her own expenses? What cost items are excessive?
- Which salesperson is returning inadequate profit? What corrections are necessary to make his or her work profitable?

The preparer may also choose to analyze by channel of distribution, method of sales, organization, time of sales, customer retention rate, returns and adjustments, stock shortages, and the like.

CHAPTER THIRTEEN

Preparing Production Budgets

The next step in the budgeting process is the preparation of production budgets. Five major budgets are involved: the unit production budget, the direct labor budget, the direct materials budget, the manufacturing departmental expense budget, and the product budget. The following discussion illustrates how these budgets are prepared with appropriate instructions.

UNIT PRODUCTION BUDGET (SCHEDULE B1)

The unit production budget is developed on the basis of units produced. It supports the budgeted unit sales projections and must be coordinated with both the sales/marketing and finance departments. (See Exhibit 13.1.)

Steps in Preparing the Unit Production Budget

Preparation of this budget involves seven steps:

1. Determine what time period is to be used. This is usually based on the following data:
   - Length of sales budgeting period
   - Length of production cycle

Exhibit 13.1 Unit Production Budget

Schedule ____ **B1**

Period

☐ Six months ☐ Total year

Company Name _____

Page ____ of ____

L I N E	($ in 000s)	Reference					Total
1	PRODUCT X						
2	Unit sales	From A1,L2					
3	Beginning inventory						
4	Net production (L2-L3)						
5	Desired finished goods inventory						
6	Required production (L4+L5)						
7	Spoilage and waste allowance						
8	Units to be produced (L6+L7)						
9	PRODUCT Y						
10	Unit sales	From A1,L6					
11	Beginning inventory						
12	Net production (L10-L11)						
13	Desired finished goods inventory						
14	Required production (L12+L13)						
15	Spoilage and waste allowance						
16	Units to be produced (L14+L15)						
17	PRODUCT Z						
18	Unit sales	From A1,L10					
19	Beginning inventory						
20	Net production (L18-L19)						
21	Desired finished goods inventory						
22	Required production (L20+L21)						
23	Spoilage and waste allowance						
24	Units to be produced (L22+L23)						
25							

- Time needed for technical and style changes
- Time needed to acquire materials and supplies
- Possibility of hiring skilled laborers at the required times
- Stability of economic conditions in general

2. Determine the level of production, based on the following facts:
   - Level of customer service needed to avoid running out of inventory
   - Need for protection against raw material stockouts and anticipated labor problems
   - Cost of maintaining excessive inventory
   - Effects of obsolescence
   - Price trends of both raw materials and finished goods inventory
   - Financial capability of the company

3. Determine when and where inventory should be produced. This involves the following considerations:
   - The availability and cost of manufacturing and storage facilities
   - The ability of the current labor force to meet future peak periods
   - The feasibility of matching the economics of production levels with those of purchasing levels
   - The ability to finance buildups in inventory

4. Determine what manufacturing operations are needed.

5. Establish production standards for measuring production efficiency.

6. Develop the requirements for material, labor, overhead expenses, and types of equipment.

7. Revise estimates where necessary.

Instructions for Preparing the Unit Production Budget (Schedule B1)

The unit production budget determines how many units per product must be produced. This determination is made on the basis of sales estimates by product, as shown on the unit sales/revenue budget (Schedule A1). It takes into consideration the amount of inventory already on hand, the desired level of finished goods inventory, and the estimated allowance for spoilage and waste. The preparer uses this information to determine the number of units to be placed into production. It is assumed that these units will be manufactured in company-owned facilities. Finished components that are purchased as part of the manufacturing process must be included among the material requirements shown in Schedule B3.

DIRECT LABOR BUDGET (SCHEDULE B2)

The labor budget provides the company with a labor force that meets the requirements of the manufacturing environment. It performs many other functions as well:

- It determines the worker hours, skills, and timing needed to attain the required production levels.
- It determines the overall labor cost of production.
- It establishes the amount and timing of cash disbursements.
- It provides a basis for measuring labor performance and control in the following areas.

(See Exhibit 13.2.)

All these areas lead to higher production costs and can be prevented by including key ratios in performance reports, as listed below:

Various reasons for excessive labor time are:

- Worker inefficiency
- Wasted time
- Poor scheduling
- Inadequate supervision
- Defective tools, materials, and equipment
- Idle time
- Poor working conditions
- High percentage of trainees versus established skilled workers

Various reasons for excessive pay rates are:

- Wage increases
- High-priced workers doing low-priced work
- Excessive overtime
- Hourly rate guarantees

Data to be included in performance reports include:

- Percentage of actual performance to standard
- Output per labor hour and dollar and percentage of projected standard
- Ratio of indirect labor hours and costs to direct labor hours

Exhibit 13.2 Direct Labor Budget

Schedule __**B2**__   Product _____   Page _____ of _____

Period
☐ Six months ☐ Total year

Company Name _____

L-I-N-E	($ in 000s)	Reference						Total
1	DEPARTMENT A							
2	Units to be produced	From B1						
3	Standard hours per unit							
4	Total hours (L2xL3)							
5	Rate per hour							
6	Total direct labor (L4xL5)							
7								
8	DEPARTMENT B							
9	Units to be produced	From B1						
10	Standard hours per unit							
11	Total hours (L9xL10)							
12	Rate per hour							
13	Total direct labor (L11xL12)							
14								
15	DEPARTMENT C							
16	Units to be produced	From B1						
17	Standard hours per unit							
18	Total hours (L16xL17)							
19	Rate per hour							
20	Total direct labor (L18xL19)							
21								
22	Total direct labor (L6+L13+L20)	To B5,L8						
23								
24								
25								

127

- Average earnings per production worker
- Turnover rate and its causes

Instructions for Preparing the Direct Labor Budget (Schedule B2)

The direct labor budget represents the cost of wages paid to employees for performing work directly on a product during various stages of manufacturing, such as construction, fabrication, or assembly. Each product and all departments involved in the manufacturing process are budgeted to arrive at total direct labor costs. Historical cost data usually provide the basis for estimating standard hours and rates. The total direct costs are posted to the product budget (Schedule B5, line 8).

DIRECT MATERIALS BUDGET (SCHEDULE B3)

The direct materials budget establishes the raw material requirements for manufacturing a specific product. The number of units of raw materials needed by each product is calculated by multiplying the raw material usage requirements by the number of planned units of production. These raw material units are then multiplied by the unit cost to arrive at a material cost per unit of production by product. Each of the total raw material costs for each product is posted to Schedule B5, line 7. This amount also becomes the basis for the purchasing budget of raw materials, taking into consideration units required for production and inventory in stock. The total cost of raw materials to be purchased is calculated by multiplying the units to be purchased times the unit cost. (See Exhibit 13.3.)

MANUFACTURING DEPARTMENTAL EXPENSE BUDGET (SCHEDULE B4)

Manufacturing departmental expenses do not generally enter directly into the product nor are they usually directly chargeable to the product. The manufacturing departmental expense includes such costs as depreciation, plant utilities, property taxes and insurance, supplies, and indirect labor. (See Exhibit 13.4.)

Instructions for Preparing the Manufacturing Departmental Expense Budget (Schedule B4)

The manufacturing departmental expense budget establishes the manufacturing overhead for each department associated with the manufacturing of a product, such as producing and service departments. These overhead figures would be included in the

Exhibit 13.3. Direct Materials Budget

Schedule __B3__   Product _____   Company Name _____   Page __1__ of __2__

Period   □ Six months   □ Total year

LINE	($ in 000s)	Reference						Total
1	PRODUCT X							
2	Units of material A required							
3	Unit cost							
4	Material A cost (L2xL3)							
5								
6	Units of material B required							
7	Unit cost							
8	Material B cost (L6xL7)							
9								
10	Units of material C required							
11	Unit cost							
12	Material C cost (L10xL11)							
13	Total product X (L4+L8+L12)	To B5,L7						
14								
15	PRODUCT Y							
16	Units of material A required							
17	Unit cost							
18	Material A cost (L16xL17)							
19								
20	Units of material B required							
21	Unit cost							
22	Material B cost (L20xL21)							
23								
24	Units of material C required							
25	Unit cost							

Exhibit 13.3 *(continued)*

Schedule __B3 (continued)__   Product _____   Page __2__ of __2__

Period ☐ Six months ☐ Total year   Company Name _____

L I N E	($ in 000s)	Reference							Total
26	Material C cost (L24xL25)								
27	Total product Y (L18+L22+L26)	To B5, L7							
28									
29	PRODUCT Z								
30	Units of material A required								
31	Unit cost								
32	Material A cost (L30xL31)								
33									
34	Units of material B required								
35	Unit cost								
36	Material B cost (L34xL35)								
37									
38	Units of material C required								
39	Unit cost								
40	Material C cost (L38xL39)								
41	Total product Z (L32+L36+L40)	To B5, L7							
42									
43	Total direct materials (L13+L27+L41)	To D1, L5							
44									
45									
46									
47									
48									
49									
50									

Exhibit 13.4 Manufacturing Departmental Budget

Schedule ____ **B4**

Department ____

Page ____ of ____

Period ☐ Six months ☐ Total year

Company Name ____

	($ in 000s)	Reference						Total
1	LABOR							
2	Supervisory							
3	Indirect							
4	PAYROLL							
5	Vacations							
6	Holidays							
7	Overtime							
8	Insurance							
9	Pensions							
10	Taxes							
11	Other							
12	VARIABLE-OTHER							
13	Utilities							
14	Supplies							
15	Other							
16								
17	FIXED							
18	Training and development							
19	Depreciation							
20	Property taxes							
21	Insurance							
22	Other							
23								
24	OTHER							
25	Total	To B5,L9						

131

manufacturing departmental expense budget, and the totals of all departments would be posted to the product budget (Schedule B5, line 9).

PRODUCT BUDGET (SCHEDULE B5)

The product budget highlights the profit contribution by product. It represents the anticipated profitability of a product line and includes supplemental data relating to the product line such as key sales and cost statistics or standards. No postings are necessary to other schedules since this budget is merely for information purposes. (See Exhibit 13.5.)

The sum of Schedules B2, B3, and B4 equals the cost of sales.

STANDARDS

Standards for manufacturing allows a company the ability to measure results when they occur. It will also provide vital information for other parts of the budgeting process. The following manufacturing standards are recommended:

- Direct material and price standards
- Direct labor rate and quantity standards
- Manufacturing overhead standards

Exhibit 13.5 Product Budget

Schedule ____ **B5**

Product ____

Company Name

Period ☐ Six months ☐ Total year

Page ____ of ____

LINE	($ in 000s)	Reference						Total
1	Units	From A1						
2								
3	Price per unit	From A1						
4								
5	Sales revenues (L1xL3)							
6	COST OF SALES							
7	Direct materials	From B3						
8	Direct labor	From B2,L22						
9	Manufacturing overhead	From B4,L25						
10								
11								
12	Other							
13	Total cost of sales							
14								
15	Profit contribution							
16	Percent to revenues (L5)							
17	SUPPLEMENTAL DATA							
18								
19								
20								
21								
22								
23								
24								
25								

CHAPTER FOURTEEN

Preparing the Distribution Cost Budget

The distribution cost budget (Schedule C4, see Exhibit 14.1) represents the costs incurred from the time merchandise is produced until it is received by the customer. The following cost categories are used in preparing this budget:

- Direct selling expenses such as sales office expenses, incurred to solicit orders
- Transportation expenses associated with transporting and maintaining warehouses of inventory for customers
- Warehousing and storage expenses for storing and handling inventory
- Costs for other activities such as market research, distribution, accounting, and other distribution expenses not listed above

This budget serves many purposes. For example, it determines the most economical way of distributing the product and assists in coordinating the costs of distribution with such departments as sales, production, and finance. Ultimately, this budget will be a means to control distribution costs and effectively service the sales effort.

Exhibit 14.1 Distribution Cost Budget

Schedule ___ **C4** ___

Page ____ of ____

Period ☐ Six months ☐ Total year

Company Name

	Reference							Total
L I N E	($ in 000s)							
1	Direct selling							
2								
3	Transportation expenses							
4	Truck							
5	Rail							
6	Air							
7	Ship							
8	Total							
9								
10	Warehousing and storage							
11								
12	Market research							
13	Other (specify)							
14								
15								
16								
17	Total other							
18								
19	Total distribution costs	To D1,L14						
20								
21								
22								
23								
24								
25								

TYPES OF DISTRIBUTION COST BUDGETS

Three supplemental budgets can be used to support the preparation of the production budget. They deal with project-related costs, administrative costs, and volume-related costs.

Project-related Cost Budget. Not related to volume activity, but rather to the completion of specific tasks such as those found in research and development projects.

Administrative Cost Budget. Often required when dealing with administrative type costs such as staff departments found throughout the company. Costs usually focus around "people costs" such as salaries and employee benefits.

Volume-related Cost Budget. Tied into some form of volume activity and can be measured on a quantitative basis. Departments such as those found in some sales district warehouses and distribution centers would be prime examples of such budgets.

STEPS IN PREPARING THE DISTRIBUTION COST BUDGET (SCHEDULE C4)

The following steps should be used to prepare this budget:

1. Develop the necessary distribution information of the company and/or segment.
2. Determine the significant costs.
3. Segregate costs by responsibility head and subclassification where feasible.
4. Develop the most economical distribution channels.
5. Maintain effective control by establishing standards for items such as cost per call, auto mileage, and distribution cost as a percentage of sales.
6. Prepare distribution cost budget in consultation with sales executives as to the future.
7. Make appropriate revisions.

INSTRUCTIONS FOR PREPARING THE DISTRIBUTION COST BUDGET (SCHEDULE C4)

Complete each line item and post the total distribution costs to Schedule D1, line 14. Any expense items not listed on Schedule C4 should be included and budgeted accordingly.

CHAPTER FIFTEEN

Preparing the Administrative Budget

The administrative budget contains costs and headcounts for such areas of the company as the executive, legal, purchasing, human resources, finance, accounting, and treasury departments. This budget can be prepared either by responsibility or by expense classification.

TYPES OF FUNCTIONS

Many different departments throughout the organization generate administrative expenses. They are most commonly found at the so-called corporate level and other administrative departments in a decentralized organization. They include the following:

Executive Office.   Includes the president and staff.

Finance Office.   Includes the functions falling under the direction of the chief financial officer such as treasury, accounting, and planning departments.

Human Resources Office.   Includes the functions of personnel, pension, and medical departments.

Administrative Office.   Includes office management, computer administration, and other related functions.

FACTORS THAT INFLUENCE THE ADMINISTRATIVE BUDGET

Three major factors affect the content of the administrative budget. They include:

Nature of the Industry.   Includes the type of industry such as service versus manufacturing, the organizational structure, public versus governmental organization, and activity levels of the organization. Each of these may require higher or lower administrative costs as shown when comparing a service firm with a manufacturing firm. Service organizations tend to have more administrative expenses since they are people-oriented whereas manufacturing companies tend to be more automated and usually require fewer administrative expenses, especially in salaries, wages, and benefits.

Level of Maturity.   Companies usually have varying levels of administration, and therefore, varying levels of administrative costs depending on the level of maturity (e.g., a start-up company versus a mature company).

Organizational Structure.   Will determine the level of administrative costs. When companies are decentralized they require higher administrative costs, whereas in centralized organizations, administrative expenses are usually lower.

ESTABLISHING STANDARDS

For segments of the administrative budget, it is advisable to establish standards to measure performance. The following list indicates measurements to use in several areas:

- *Order handling.* Use the number of orders handled.
- *Mail handling.* Use the number of pieces handled.
- *Billing.* Use the number of invoice lines.
- *Filing.* Use the number of pieces filed.
- *Typing.* Use the number of lines typed.

INSTRUCTIONS FOR PREPARING THE ADMINISTRATIVE BUDGET (SCHEDULE C1)

Complete each line item on Schedule C1 (see Exhibit 15.1), and post the sum of lines 7–34, or line 36, to Schedule D1, line 10. Each department of the company should prepare a similar budget and post the totals to Schedule D1, line 10.

Exhibit 15.1 Administrative Departmental Budget

Schedule ____**C1**____   Department _____   Page __1__ of __2__

Period ☐ Six months ☐ Total year

Company Name _____

L I N E	($ in 000s)	Reference						Total
1	HEADCOUNT							
2	Professional							
3	Clerical support							
4	Other							
5	Total							
6								
7	PAYROLL							
8	Professional							
9	Clerical support							
10	Other							
11	Overtime							
12								
13	Total							
14								
15	EMPLOYEE BENEFITS							
16	Employee taxes							
17	Insurance							
18	Pensions							
19	Vacation							
20	Other							
21	Total							
22	Office supplies							
23	Rent							
24	Telephone							
25	Cable charges							

139

Exhibit 15.1 *(continued)*

Page __2__ of __2__

Schedule ___C1 (continued)___   Department _____   Company Name _____

Period ☐ Six months ☐ Total year

L I N E	($ in 000s)	Reference						Total
26	Travel and entertainment							
27	Depreciation-office equipment							
28	Utilities							
29	Insurance							
30	Office expense – other							
31	Advertising and promotion	From C2, L17						
32	Taxes							
33	Bad debt losses							
34	Outside fees (specify)							
35								
36	Total	To D1, L10						
37								
38								
39								
40								
41								
42								
43								
44								
45								
46								
47								
48								
49								
50								

140

Preparing the Advertising and Promotion Budget

The advertising and promotion budget constitutes a major financial commitment for the company, yet it is often hard to measure the effectiveness of these expenditures. Companies can use various methods of preparing these budgets. Such variance is due to the following factors:

- Some companies rely on outside advertising agencies, and costs may therefore vary.
- The advertising manager reports to the sales manager in some companies, whereas in others the advertising manager is independent.
- Some companies do only institutional advertising; others do only product advertising.
- Some companies do only local advertising, others only regional, and others only national.
- In some industries manufacturers do all the advertising; in others, manufacturers make advertising contributions to companies such as jobbers and dealers.

ADVERTISING OBJECTIVES

The advertising and promotion budget is designed to reach various objectives in the budgetary process. They include the following:

- To increase sales
- To maintain prices
- To provide an alternative to other selling efforts
- To educate consumers
- To maintain trademarks and brand names
- To establish new products and new markets
- To meet competition
- To create an image
- To change opinion and prevent hostile legislation

STEPS IN PREPARING THE ADVERTISING AND PROMOTION BUDGET

1. Determine purposes or objectives of the advertising program. For example, how much money will be needed, and how will it be spent?
2. Determine the cost of accomplishing the objectives listed in step 1, taking into consideration the amount of funds that can be released during the budget period, the amount necessary to make the program effective, and the nature of future expansion.
3. Develop detailed programs indicating when, where, how, and why advertising is necessary. Some methods of appropriating funds are:
   - By percentage of prior year's sales or budgeted sales
   - By fixed amount per unit of product
   - By arbitrary increase or decrease over last year
   - By competitor
   - By percentage of prior year's net earnings

4. Coordinate the advertising budget with other selling, production, and finance costs.

5. Where feasible, assign individual responsibility by product, territory, or project.

6. Develop advertising standards for control such as:

- Total cost per unit of space
- Cost per inquiry received
- Cost per sales transaction
- Cost per dollar of sales
- Cost per unit of time
- Total cost per account sold

INSTRUCTIONS FOR PREPARING THE ADVERTISING AND PROMOTION BUDGET (SCHEDULE C2)

The advertising and promotion budget includes all expenses for advertising and sales promotion with the exception of departmental operating expenses, which appear in specific departmental budgets. (See Exhibit 16.1.) Consideration should be given to the following factors:

- Last year's sales
- Mix of sales and products desired
- Relationship of last year's expenses to sales revenues
- Analysis of last year's media results to desired results

The total advertising and promotion expenses are posted to Schedule D1, line 10.

Exhibit 16.1   Advertising and Promotion Expenses

Schedule ____ **C2** ____

Page ____ of ____

Period

☐ Six months   ☐ Total year

Company Name

L I N E	($ in 000s)	Reference							Total
1	Newspaper ads								
2	Shopper ads								
3	Magazine and periodical ads								
4	Telephone directories								
5	Radio								
6	Telephone								
7	Direct mail campaigns								
8	House-to-house distribution								
9	Personal demonstrations								
10	Exhibits								
11	Catalogues								
12	Samples								
13									
14									
15									
16	Total advertising and	To D1,L10							
17	promotion expenses								
18									
19									
20									
21									
22									
23									
24									
25									

Preparing the Research and Development Budget

Research and development projects provide an organization with further growth and earnings. It is through this point of the budget process that new techniques, new products, and new ideas materialize in the company's future. All products/services have a life cycle. To maintain levels of growth during down life cycles, new products/services must be available to take the place of products/services that have reached the end of the life cycle.

Basic Research.   This type of research project represents original investigation for the advancement of scientific knowledge but does not involve any specific commercial objectives; however, it may be carried on in a field of current or potential interest to the company.

Applied Research.   This type of research project is directed to the discovery of new scientific knowledge with some specific commercial objectives for either products or processes.

Development.   This activity is technical by nature and is concerned with the non-routine problems encountered in translating research findings or other general scientific knowledge into products or processes.

ESTABLISHING GUIDELINES

Various guidelines can be used for estimating budgetary amounts for research and development activities. They include the following:

- Percentage of estimated sales for next year
- Percentage of operating profit before research and development expenses
- Percentage of net earnings
- Last year's expenditures adjusted
- Fixed amount per unit sold
- Percentage of cash flow
- Percentage of capital asset investments
- Estimated cost of selected projects

DEVELOPING STANDARDS OF PERFORMANCE

Some of the standards of performance used for measuring and controlling research and development expenses include:

- Cost per individual hour of supplies or total research expense
- Number of requisitions filled
- Number of tests per month
- Number of formulas developed per individual or week
- Number of pages of patent applications written per individual or day
- Estimated individual hours or hours by functional activity
- Cost per patent application
- Cost per operating hour

INSTRUCTIONS FOR PREPARING THE RESEARCH AND DEVELOPMENT BUDGET (SCHEDULE C5)

The expenses to be budgeted for research and development can be classified into three major categories. They include salaries and wages, materials and supplies, and other direct expenses. (See Exhibit 17.1.)

Exhibit 17.1 Research and Development Budget

Schedule ____ **C5**

Page ____ of ____

Company Name _____

Period ☐ Six months ☐ Total year

LINE	($ in 000s)	Reference					Total
1	SALARIES AND WAGES						
2	Administrative staff						
3	Nonadministrative staff						
4	Technical staff						
5	Other						
6	Total salaries and wages						
7							
8	MATERIALS AND SUPPLIES						
9	Expendable equipment						
10	Chemical and lab supplies						
11	Repairs						
12	Other						
13	Total materials and supplies						
14							
15	OTHER DIRECT EXPENSE						
16	Taxes and insurance						
17	Periodicals						
18	Dues and memberships						
19	Depreciation						
20	Utilities						
21	Travel and entertainment						
22	Other						
23	Total other direct expenses						
24							
25	Total R&D Expenses	To D1,L9					

Salaries and Wages (Lines 1–6).   This includes salaries and wages for the administrative staff (line 2); for nonadministrative staff (line 3); for technical staff such as lab technicians and draftspeople (line 4); and for others, including hourly and clerical workers.

Materials and Supplies (Lines 8–13).   This includes expendable equipment (line 9) that is not part of the basic equipment of the lab; chemicals, drugs, and laboratory supplies (line 10); outside repairs and supplies for existing equipment (line 11); and other materials and supplies (line 12) not included in lines 9–11.

Other Direct Expenses (Lines 15–23).   This includes payroll and property taxes and employee and property insurance (line 16); periodicals (line 17); dues and membership to professional organizations (line 18); depreciation on laboratory equipment (line 19); utilities such as phone, electricity, and gas (line 20); travel and entertainment incurred by professionals and administrative staff (line 21); and other expenses such as consulting fees and direct expenses not included in the other expense categories (line 23).

Post the total R&D expenses (line 25) to Schedule D1, line 9.

CHAPTER EIGHTEEN

Preparing the Other Income and Expense Budget

The other income and expense budget estimates income and expense projections for revenues received and expenses incurred from sources other than the basic business of the company. (See Exhibit 18.1.) Examples of such revenues and expenses include:

Other Revenue Items

- Gains from the sale of securities
- Dividends on shares of stock owned
- Gains from the sale of plant and equipment
- Interest earned
- Rent earned

Other Expense Items

- Interest on money borrowed from financial institutions
- Interest on notes given to creditors for inventory purchased
- Losses from the sale of plant and equipment

Exhibit 18.1   Other Income and Expense Budget

Schedule _____ **C3** _____

Company Name _____

Page _____ of _____

Period
☐ Six months   ☐ Total year

L I N E	($ in 000s)	Reference						Total
1	OTHER INCOME							
2	Gains from sale of securities							
3	Interest earned							
4	Dividends on company-owned shares							
5	Rent earned							
6	Gains from sale of plant and equipment							
7	Total other income							
8								
9	OTHER EXPENSE							
10	Interest on money borrowed							
11	Interest on notes given to creditors							
12								
13	Losses from sale of plant and equipment							
14								
15								
16	Total other expense							
17								
18	Other income (expense)	To D1,L13						
19								
20								
21								
22								
23								

INSTRUCTIONS FOR PREPARING THE OTHER INCOME AND EXPENSE BUDGET (SCHEDULE C3)

The totals from Schedule C3 are posted to Schedule D1, line 13, as either other income or other expense.

CHAPTER NINETEEN

Preparing the Estimated Statement of Earnings

The estimated statement of earnings (Schedule D1, Exhibit 19.1) brings together all the budget estimates from the previous income and expense budget schedules. It records estimated net earnings or net losses and becomes the input for other budgeting statements such as the statement of cash flows.

Both dividends and retained earnings calculations are based on this statement. Income tax calculations (line 17) must include anticipated federal, state, local, and other taxes such as franchise and excise. It is advisable to consult your tax professional in estimating this amount.

Exhibit 19.1 Estimated Statement of Earnings

Schedule ___ **D1** ___

Period
☐ Six months   ☐ Total year

Company Name _____

LINE	($ in 000s)	Reference						Total
1	Units	From A1–A4*						
2	Net sales	From A1–A4*						
3	COST OF SALES							
4	Direct labor	From B2,L22						
5	Direct materials	From B3,L43						
6	Overhead	From B4,L25						
7	Total cost of sales							
8	Gross profit (L2–L7)							
9	Research and development	From C5,L25						
10	Selling and administrative expenses	From C1,L36;C2,L17						
11	Earnings before other income (expense) and income taxes							
12								
13	Other income (expense)	From C3,L18						
14	Distribution costs	From C4,L19						
15	Earnings before income taxes							
16								
17	Income taxes							
18								
19	Net earnings							
20								
21	*Represents units and net sales from either A1,A2,A3,or A4 depending on how units							
22	and revenues are presented							
23								
24								
25								

CHAPTER TWENTY

Preparing the Cash Budget*

Every organization must provide the cash needed in both the short and the long term to ensure that the business operates smoothly and that sufficient funds are available to meet both current and future cash obligations. Generally, short-term cash forecasts are for one year, and long-term forecasts are for any period over one year. However, if a business requires shorter or longer budgeting periods, it is acceptable to change the amount of time covered by long- and short-term forecasts.

REASONS FOR CASH BUDGETING

Cash budgeting is needed for a variety of reasons. The reasons explored here are used to highlight the importance of cash budgeting. Some of these points may not immediately apply to a new company but will apply at some time during a company's life.

Expansion

For a company to expand, it requires large sums of cash. The demands for cash to provide for expansion will play an important part in your future plans. In order to predict

---

*Robert Rachlin, *Successful Techniques for Higher Profits* (New York: MARR Publications, 1981), pp. 31–40.

how much cash will be available at a given time, a cash forecast is necessary. Advance knowledge of monies needed will also assist you in making the best deal for additional funds from such sources as the equity and long-term capital markets.

Control

A cash budget will assist you in setting up centralized control mechanisms that identify the amounts of cash available in the system, indicate the amount and timing of additional cash requirements, and predict the timing of both receipts and disbursements of cash.

Payments

A cash budget highlights anticipated payments of loans, including interest payments, bonuses, accounts payable, and dividends. It indicates when these payments are to be made and whether sufficient funds are available. This knowledge can act as a valuable tool for avoiding temporary shortages of cash by shifting funds on a temporary basis to meet the demands of current payments.

Investments

A cash budget points out how much excess cash will be available for investment in short-term securities at a given time. Short-term securities generally yield high short-term interest, which is used to generate additional income as a part of your cash management program.

Borrowings

From time to time, shortages of cash will cause increases in working capital requirements. For instance, seasonality may create a temporary cash shortage. Money may therefore have to be borrowed to meet cash requirements caused by buildups of working capital such as for receivables and inventories. This irregularity of cash flows is in the nature of any business.

Requirements from Lending Institutions

Lending institutions require a company to prepare a cash budget in support of any loan application. This enables the lending institution to determine the applicant's needs as well as its ability to repay the loan. A cash budget is as vital to the operations of a business as are the company's financial statements.

DECISIONS THAT AFFECT CASH BALANCES

As will be seen in discussions of segments of the balance sheet budget in later chapters, many budgetary decisions have an impact on the balance sheet and are ultimately reflected in changes in cash balances. The following decisions, though not necessarily presented in priority sequence, can *increase* cash balances as shown on the balance sheet under both asset and liability accounts:

- Reduce accounts receivable.
- Sell old and obsolete inventory.
- Sell unproductive assets.
- Reduce deferred or prepaid expenses.
- Defer payments to creditors.
- Acquire both short- and long-term capital.
- Increase earnings retained in the business.
- Provide accounting entries for depreciation allowance and other noncash items.

    Other decisions *decrease* cash balances:

- Increase accounts receivable.
- Build up inventory.
- Acquire fixed assets and other investments.
- Increase deferred and prepaid expenses.
- Make tax and dividend payments.
- Make payments for other operational expenditures.
- Make payments for short- and long-term borrowings.
- Sustain losses in operations.

Many of these decisions must occur in the normal course of business, but prudent management can take steps to prevent certain decreases in cash balances, as discussed within each balance sheet budget in later chapters.

ESTIMATED CASH BALANCES[1]

There is a model, referred to as the Baumol Model, that can assist in estimating cash balances. It is used to assist the budget preparer in determining adequate levels of cash nec-

---

[1]Lawrence J. Gitman, *Principles of Managerial Finance*, sixth edition (New York: Harper Collins Publishers, 1991), pp. 720–722.

essary to maintain a healthy and prosperous business during the projected budget period and beyond. While this method is merely a tool, prudent judgment and common sense must be exercised to adequately estimate reasonable cash balances for the budget period.

Baumol Model

This approach treats cash as an inventory item and can be instrumental in predicting the demand for meeting transaction requirements with a fairly good degree of certainty. Cash is generated to replenish the need for cash in meeting transaction requirements from the portfolio of marketable securities, which can be converted into cash at a moment in time.

This cash inventory is based on the cost of converting marketable securities into cash, referred to as the conversion cost, and the cost of holding cash rather than in the form of marketable securities, known as the opportunity cost.

Since the objective of the Baumol Model is to determine what level of cash minimizes total cost, the formula for determining this is referred to as the economic conversion quantity (ECQ) and is expressed as follows:

$$ECQ = \sqrt{\frac{2 \times \text{conversion cost} \times \text{demand for cash}}{\text{Opportunity cost}}}$$

Conversion Costs.   Costs associated with placing and receiving an order for cash and its related paperwork.

Opportunity Costs.   The amount of interest earnings foregone as a result of holding on to funds in noninterest bearing accounts rather than funds being invested in an interest-bearing account.

Total Cost.   The sum of both conversion costs and opportunity costs.

An example of this model is as follows:

Demand for cash	$3,000,000
Cost of conversion	$50 per transaction
Percentage earnings	6%

or

$$ECQ = \sqrt{\frac{2 \times \$50 \times \$3,000,000}{.06}} = \$70,710$$

The $70,710 represents the amount of cash received each time cash is replenished. This translates into 42.4 conversion ($3,000,000/$70,710) during the budgeted year. The average cash balance is $35,355 ($70,710/2).

The total cost of managing cash is $4,241 as follows:

$$\text{Total cost} = (\$50 \times 42.4) + (.06 \times \$35,355) = \$4,241$$

A similar model can be used for inventory whereby the demand for cash is replaced by the demand for inventory; the conversion cost is replaced by the cost per order; and the opportunity cost is replaced by the holding cost per unit per budgeted period. The results are expressed in units as opposed to dollars.

CASH RECEIPTS AND DISBURSEMENTS BUDGET

The cash receipts and disbursements budget is used for short periods of time, such as days, weeks, months, and quarters. It allows a company to budget its cash inflows and outflows, or cash receipts and cash disbursements, in periods that are nearer to the current operating period. Data are usually obtained from historical patterns such as those that show how sales revenues are received and in what time period expenses are incurred.

A company that has no historical base must use the best educated guess available. However, some sources may provide data that would be of value in the estimation process. For example, market consultants, federal government statistics, trade organizations, local chambers of commerce, local colleges or universities, libraries, and local governmental agencies can provide data to help you estimate the potential market and ultimately the receipts you can expect during the period you are forecasting.

Determining the Collection Pattern of Sales (Schedule E2)

For companies with historical data, a simple analysis, as shown in Exhibit 20.1, will provide some basis for estimating cash to be received. The monthly sales forecasts can be obtained from Schedules A1–A4, keeping in mind that in most cases it will take several months before actual cash is collected from accounts receivable.

Once the cash received from collections has been estimated, the amount should be posted to Schedule E2 (Exhibit 20.3), in the appropriate line items (lines 5–9). The amount of money received from cash sales or from selling any assets and any other income received should also be estimated (line 10).

Determining the Disbursements of Cash (Schedule E1)

The next step in preparing the cash receipts and disbursements budget is to estimate the cash disbursements during the period. A realistic estimate should be made for each period. Many of these cash disbursements will always be the same, but caution should

Exhibit 20.1   Collection Pattern of Sales

| Month | Estimated Collections from Sales | | | |
	Current Month	1 Month Ago	2 Months Ago	Beyond 3 Months Ago
January	6.0%	67.0%	20.0%	7.0%
February	5.0	70.0	19.0	6.0
March	7.0	70.0	16.0	7.0
April	4.0	75.0	18.0	3.0
May	5.0	69.0	21.0	5.0
June	3.0	68.0	22.0	7.0
July	8.0	61.0	20.0	11.0
August	7.0	69.0	16.0	8.0
September	5.0	72.0	15.0	8.0
October	3.0	74.0	14.0	9.0
November	4.0	70.0	19.0	7.0
December	6.0	67.0	18.0	9.0
Monthly average	5.3%	69.3%	18.2%	7.2%

be taken to check the accuracy of each disbursement periodically and to reflect any changes that might occur in each forecast.

This budget provides estimates of cash disbursements for expenses such as raw materials, utilities, loans, capital additions, payroll, dividends, and other out-of-pocket expenses. Noncash items such as depreciation are not included. In addition, future cash payments must be considered in later months, as reflected in the accounts payable budget. (See Exhibit 20.2.) The total on line 24 is posted to Schedule E3, line 8.

PREPARING THE CASH BUDGET (SCHEDULE E3)

The cash budget is a summation of the cash receipts budget (Schedule E2) and the cash disbursements budget (Schedule E1). It provides an additional estimate of the desired minimum cash balance, based on historical patterns. It indicates whether to anticipate a need for financing as a result of greater cash outflows (cash disbursements + the desired minimum cash balance) or cash excess as a result of greater cash inflows (cash receipts + beginning cash balance) in each period. Schedule E3 (Exhibit 20.4) also predicts interest received from investment in cash excesses or interest expense resulting from temporary borrowings.

Exhibit 20.2 Cash Disbursements Budget

Schedule _____ **E1** _____

Period ☐ Six months ☐ Total year

Company Name _____

Page __1__ of __3__

($ in 000s)	Reference							Total
1	Cash purchases-raw material	From B3,L43						
2								
3	PAYMENTS OF ACCOUNTS PAYABLE							
4								
5	Payment within one month							
6	Payment within second month							
7	Payment beyond second month							
8								
9	Telephone	From C1,L24						
10	Rent payments	From C1,L23						
11	Utilities	From C1,L28						
12	Office supplies	From C1,L22						
13	EMPLOYEE PAYROLL AND BENEFITS							
14	Payroll	From C1,L13						
15	Benefits	From C1,L21						
16								
17								
18	Loan repayments							
19	Tax payments	From C1,L32						
20	Purchase(s)-fixed assets	From F4,L4						
21	Cash dividends							
22	Interest payments	From C3,L10-L11						
23	Other cash disbursements	From C1						
24	Total	To E3,L8						
25								

Exhibit 20.3 Cash Receipts Budget

Schedule __E2__

Company Name

Period ☐ Six months ☐ Total year

L I N E	($ ir 000s)	Reference								Total
1	Net sales	From A1,L16								
2										
3	COLLECTIONS OF ACCOUNTS									
4	RECEIVABLE*									
5	Collection within current month									
6	Collection within 1 month ago									
7	Collection beyond 2 months ago									
8	Collection beyond 3 months ago									
9	Total									
10	Other cash receipts	From C3,L7								
11	Total cash receipts	To E3,L3								
12										
13										
14										
15										
16										
17										
18	* Remaining balance from line 1									
19										
20										
21										
22										
23										
24										
25										

161

Exhibit 20.4 Cash Budget

Schedule _____ **E3** _____

Period _____

☐ Six months ☐ Total year

Company Name _____

L I N E	($ in 000s)	Reference							Total
1	Beginning cash budget								
2									
3	Plus: Cash receipts	From E2,L11							
4									
5									
6	Total cash available								
7									
8	Less: Cash disbursements	From E1,L24							
9									
10									
11	Ending cash balance	From F9,L4							
12									
13	Less: Desired minimum								
14	cash balance								
15									
16	Anticipated financing								
17									
18	Anticipated cash excess								
19									
20									
21									
22									
23									
24									
25									

CHAPTER TWENTY-ONE

Preparing the Accounts Receivable Budget

The accounts receivable budget provides an estimate of the monthly net accounts receivable less bad debts and collections. These monthly net amounts are part of the current assets on the balance sheet.

MANAGING ACCOUNTS RECEIVABLE

Part of budgeting accounts receivable is the ability to measure prior ratio relationships to current budgetary ratios. In addition, these ratios should be measured against industry standards, as well as budgeted objectives. The most commonly used ratios for measuring the relationship of accounts receivable to net sales and working capital are as follows:

Net Sales to Accounts Receivable – Net.   Used to measure the turnover of accounts receivable. The objective should be to generate higher turnover rates indicating that monies are being collected at a faster pace. This makes cash readily available more quickly. The ratio is calculated as follows:

$$\frac{\text{Net sales}}{\text{Accounts receivable} - \text{net}}$$

Average Collection Period.   Measures how long it takes a company to collect from its customers. Obviously, the quicker the collection period, the quicker cash is freed up to reinvest in working capital and other investments. The ratio is calculated as follows:

$$\frac{\text{Accounts receivable} - \text{net}}{\text{Net sales}} \times 365$$

Accounts Receivable – Net to Working Capital.   Measures how accounts receivable–net impacts on the liquidity of the company. Indeed this is an excellent barometer of a company's liquidity caused by changes in sales mix, and the extent of growth or shrinkage of past-due customer accounts.

INSTRUCTIONS FOR PREPARING THE ACCOUNTS RECEIVABLE BUDGET (SCHEDULE F1)

The beginning accounts receivable–net balance should be the last estimated balance from the month before the budget period begins. For example, if you are starting your budget with the month of January, the beginning balance would be the actual or latest estimate of the ending accounts receivable balance as of December 31.

To this balance add the monthly net sales revenues from Schedule D1, line 2. Deduct collections from Schedule E2, line 9, and anticipated uncollectible accounts, or bad debts, which can be calculated from historical ratios of each month's bad debt expenses to net sales revenue, expressed as percentages. Apply these historical percentages to each month's net sales revenues and post the totals to Schedule F1, line 7. (See Exhibit 21.1.)

After estimated collections and bad debts have been deducted, the results represent monthly estimates of accounts receivable–net (line 8) for each month of the budget. Post these totals to the balance sheet budget (Schedule F9, line 6).

Exhibit 21.1 Accounts Receivable Budget

Schedule ___**F1**___

Period ☐ Six months ☐ Total year

Company Name _____

Page ____ of ____

LINE	($ in 000s)	Reference						Total
1	Beginning accounts receivable							
2	balance	Y/E balance						
3	Plus:							
4	Monthly net sales	From D1,L2						
5	Less:							
6	Collections	From E2,L9						
7	Bad debts:	Company percentage						
8	Accounts receivable–net	To F9,L6						
9								
10								
11								
12								
13								
14								
15								
16								
17								
18								
19								
20								
21								
22								
23								
24								
25								

CHAPTER TWENTY-TWO

Preparing the Inventory Budget

The inventory budget summarizes the budgeted monthly ending inventory balance for the company. The amount of inventory that a company must maintain is dependent upon five factors. They include the following:[1]

LEVEL OF SALES

Budgeted sales level will be a main ingredient in projecting the monthly inventory level. Inventory levels relate to future sales, and it is therefore important to use projected levels of cost of sales to arrive at monthly inventory balances as calculated on Schedule D1, line 7.

Using the days' sales in inventory ratio, which results in the average days' sales in inventory,

$$\frac{\text{Inventory at end of period}}{\text{Cost of sales in future 3 quarters}} \times \text{Number of days in future quarter}$$

---

[1]Robert Rachlin, *Handbook of Budgeting*, fourth edition (New York: John Wiley & Sons, 1999), pp. 23.15–23.22.

or develop the budgeted inventory balance for the month of January assuming the following facts:

December 31	*inventory balance*	$1,500,000

Month		Cost of Sales
January	31 days	$ 690,000
February	28 days	630,000
March	31 days	480,000
Total	90 days	$1,800,000
April	30 days	$ 500,000

Given these facts, the average days' sales in inventory is calculated as:

$$\frac{\$1,500,000}{\$1,800,000} \times 90 = 75 \text{ days}$$

An average days' sales of 75 days means that the level of inventory at the end of each month should be equal to the next two months' cost of sales (59 days) plus 16/31 of the third month, or 51.6 percent of the month of April's cost of sales. Given these facts, the desired level of inventory for January 31 is calculated as:

Month	Cost of Sales
February	$ 630,000
March	480,000
April × 51.6%	258,000
	$1,368,000

Similar calculations would be made for the succeeding months in the budget.

LENGTH OF THE PRODUCTION PROCESS

Inventory levels will be dictated by the time it takes a product to be produced and become available for sale. If it takes one month to produce a product, the minimum inventory level should be at least one month. Shorter production periods require lower inventory levels.

AVAILABILITY OF RAW MATERIALS

The size of raw material inventories depends upon the time it takes to receive raw materials from suppliers—from order to delivery. Developing just-in-time inventory methods will reduce raw material levels, since these raw materials arrive at the production site and become available to enter the production cycle very near to the time they are needed.

DURABILITY OF FINISHED GOODS

The size of the finished goods inventory depends on the durability of the product in relation to perishability, style changes, technological change, and market demand. This amount should be coordinated with the amount of raw materials requested.

DISTRIBUTION METHODS

Inventory levels are also determined by the manner in which a product is distributed. A product that must be delivered within days of being manufactured will not have the same amount of inventory for the following reasons:

- Closer delivery patterns due to perishability. Products such as fresh baked goods, dairy products, and produce cannot be too heavily inventoried or spoilage will result.
- Under the above conditions, local distribution centers or manufacturing facilities are usually available.

In both cases, inventory is held at minimum levels. Products that are not subject to spoilage or market trends usually require higher levels of inventory since higher levels of production will generally result in greater efficiency and reduce unit costs.

METHODS OF EVALUATING INVENTORIES

Companies are faced with many methods of evaluating inventories. Some are impractical due to the nature of the business, while the Internal Revenue Service does not accept others. Following are commonly used methods of evaluating inventories with a brief description. One or more of these methods must be adopted for accounting purposes, which then becomes the basis for the preparation of budgeted data.

Last-In, First-Out (LIFO). Assumes that the last inventory unit purchased is the first to be used.

First-In, First-Out (FIFO). The opposite of LIFO in that inventory first received is used first.

Average Cost Methods. Calculated using simple average cost, weighted average cost, moving average, or monthly average.

Replacement Cost. Represents the cost it takes to replace the inventory at current rates.

Standard Cost. Establishes a predetermined cost and is reviewed periodically as conditions change.

Lower of Cost or Market. Assumes a costing structure as the title implies.

Ratios Used to Manage Inventory

The following ratios should be used to compare budgeted inventory to actual and industry standards. They include:

$$\text{Finished goods turnover} = \frac{\text{Cost of goods sold}}{\text{Average finished goods inventory}}$$

$$\text{Inventory} = \frac{\text{Net sales}}{\text{Inventory}}$$

$$\text{Supplies turnover} = \frac{\text{Cost of supplies used}}{\text{Average supply inventory}}$$

$$\text{Inventory to current assets} = \frac{\text{Inventory}}{\text{Current assets}}$$

$$\text{Inventory to total assets} = \frac{\text{Inventory}}{\text{Total assets}}$$

$$\text{Days outstanding} = \frac{365}{\text{Inventory turnover}}$$

$$\text{Inventory to working capital} = \frac{\text{Inventory}}{\text{Working capital}}$$

METHODS OF MANAGING INVENTORY

Several methods are available for the budget preparer to use in budgeting inventory. These are commonly used tools for managing inventory, but should be used in the budgeting process.

ABC Method[2]

This method prioritizes levels of inventory into three groups. The logic behind it is that a small proportion of physical units account for the major share of investments in inventory. Those types of units are categorized as A items.

On the opposite extreme are C items, which represent a large percentage of items but with little investment in inventory. All other items fall into the B item classification.

A items must be monitored carefully since they represent the greater investment in inventory. An illustration of this method is shown in Exhibits 22.1 and 22.2.

Exhibit 22.1 classifies the various levels or classes of inventory and estimated percentage of dollar usage and percentage of total inventory items.

Using Exhibit 22.1 as a guideline, an ABC calculation can be made as shown in Exhibit 22.2.

Exhibit 22.2 illustrates the decisionmaking process needed to control and budget inventories. You will see that Class A inventory accounts for 77.9 percent of the annual dollar volume, but only 14.0 percent of the number of items stocked. Purchasing should spend more time developing suppliers and more time in budgeting these items given the significance of this class of inventory. This is not the case in Class C inventory, where only 1.5 percent of annual dollar volume and 26.2 percent of the number of items stocked is shown.

Exhibit 22.1   ABC Classification of Inventory

Class of Inventory	Level of Volume	% of Dollar Usage	% of Total Inventory Items
A	High	72–80%	12–14%
B	Moderate	18–19%	33–36%
C	Low	2–4%	53–63%

---

[2]Jay Heizer and Barry Render, *Production and Operation Management* (Needham Heights, MA: Allyn and Bacon, 1988), pp. 531–532.

Exhibit 22.2   Calculation of ABC Analysis

Inventory Number	% of Number of Items Stocked	% of Annual Dollar Volume	Class
#1	9.1%	40.5%	A
#2	4.9	37.4	A
#3	17.0	8.2	B
#4	19.8	7.2	B
#5	23.0	5.2	B
#6	9.1	.6	C
#7	8.5	.5	C
#8	8.6	.4	C
	100.0%	100.0%	

Just-in-Time (JIT)

This method gets inventory back into the hands of the supplier. When inventory is needed, suppliers provide inventory directly to the production line. Therefore, quality and reliability are sometimes more important than price in order to prevent production shutdowns due to defective parts. Remember that there is usually no back-up inventory if parts are defective.

Materials Requirement Planning (MRP)

This method uses the economic order quantity (EOQ) model to compare adequate production needs and determine the timing of ordering inventory. Its advantage allows companies to plan for what is needed within the production cycle, instead of stockpiling investments in inventory.

INSTRUCTIONS FOR PREPARING THE INVENTORY BUDGET (SCHEDULE F2)

Beginning Balance. Use the ending inventory balance from the prior month. Depending on when the budget is prepared, it will be necessary to estimate the ending inventory balance for the first month of the budget. For example, if the budget starts on January 1 and you are preparing the budget in October of the prior year, you will need to use the total actual ending inventory balance (preferably for October) and estimate the remaining months of November and December. The estimated balance for December 31 will become the beginning balance for January 1 (line 2).

Goods Manufactured.   Use the data from the manufacturing budget.

Cost of Sales.   Deduct these balances from Schedule D1, line 7.

Work-in-Process Inventory.   Add the estimated work-in-process for each month of the budget. This inventory represents raw materials that are in process but not totally completed and therefore not available to be sold.

Raw Material Inventory.   Use the data from the direct materials budget (Schedule B3, line 44).

Total Ending Inventory.   This represents the value of ending inventory for each budget period and becomes the beginning balance for the following month. See Exhibit 22.3.

Exhibit 22.3 Inventory Budget

Schedule ____ **F2** ____

Company Name _____

Page ____ of ____

Period ☐ Six months ☐ Total year

LINE	($ in 000s)	Reference					Total
1	FINISHED GOODS INVENTORY						
2	Beginning balance	Prior month					
3	Plus:						
4	Goods manufactured						
5	Less:						
6	Cost of sales	From D1,L7					
7	Total						
8	Work-in-process inventory						
9							
10	Raw material inventory	From B3,L44					
11							
12	Total ending inventory (L7,L8,L10)	To F9,L7					
13							
14							
15							
16							
17							
18							
19							
20							
21							
22							
23							
24							
25							

CHAPTER TWENTY-THREE

Preparing the Other Current Assets Budget

This budget provides an estimate of the other current assets on the balance sheet. The most common asset accounts are prepaid expenses, current assets that are paid for before they are actually used or acquired. Expenses such as rent, insurance, supplies, and interest are normally prepaid for several periods at a time. Therefore, the unused remaining balances are considered current assets at that specific time.

INSTRUCTIONS FOR PREPARING THE OTHER CURRENT ASSETS BUDGET (SCHEDULE F3)

Determine the amount of each prepaid expense. In the absence of accurate forecasted data, it is advisable to budget these accounts at a constant amount or at a percentage similar to the percent change in net sales. The totals (line 10) should be posted to the balance sheet (Schedule F9, line 8). See Exhibit 23.1.

Exhibit 23.1 Other Current Assets Budget

Schedule _____ **F3** _____

Period _____

☐ Six months ☐ Total year

Company Name _____

Page _____ of _____

LINE	($ in 000s)	Reference						Total
1	PREPAID EXPENSES							
2	Rent							
3	Interest							
4	Insurance							
5	Supplies							
6	Other							
7	Total							
8								
9	Other							
10	Total (L7+L9)	To F9, L8						
11								
12								
13								
14								
15								
16								
17								
18								
19								
20								
21								
22								
23								
24								
25								

CHAPTER TWENTY-FOUR

Preparing the Capital Investments Budget

The preparation of the capital investments budget is a complex exercise because there are no universal standards to follow. The contents, approach, and format vary by company and industry. However, certain basic guidelines are followed by most companies. These guidelines will be discussed here in a general way, but you are encouraged to make any additions and/or deletions that fit your company's specific needs.

UNDERSTANDING CAPITAL INVESTMENTS

Capital investments provide funds for the following major categories:

- Additions or improvements to plant and equipment and other depreciable assets (buildings, machinery, and equipment) and nondepreciable assets (land).
- Related work in the installation or creation of plant or equipment (where capitalized).
- The amount of time spent and money currently invested in tangible assets in order to obtain positive benefit over a period of time. This includes working capital, marketing research and development, production research and development, and financial research and economic analysis.

Before the budgetary process begins, it is important to understand the importance of capital investments; profit expectations and their relationship to interest rates; priorities to be established; problem areas; complex variables; and replacement options.

Importance of Capital Investments

Capital investments deserve serious attention for the following reasons:

- They involve substantial amounts of money.
- They are made over long periods of time.
- Once capital investment commitments are made, they are hard to reverse without substantial losses in funds.
- In many instances, capital investments depend upon the survival of the business: If a major capital investment fails, the company's existence is in jeopardy.
- Investments made today will result in both cash flows and profits in some future period.

Profit Expectations and Interest Rates

Capital investment decisions involve risk. As a reward for this risk, a company expects some benefits, usually profits, to materialize. These profits are closely related to interest rates.

For example, when interest rates rise, higher returns from capital investments are expected. To be profitable, an investment must return more than alternative investments—even interest on securities such as bonds. Therefore, assuming that no other factors are present, capital investments with higher return rates become harder to find when interest rates increase, and the number of acceptable projects available therefore tend to decline.

Establishing Company Priorities for Capital Spending

Capital investments are expected to accomplish various objectives. For example, they may be expected to make a company a low-cost producer, to add more volume, to upgrade technology, and so on. These categories establish the level of priority that a company wants to give a capital investment. Why?

Investments with different levels of priority generate different levels of profitability and cash flow. For example, the purchase of equipment to meet governmental regulations for safety, pollution control, or employee morale will rarely provide profits or positive cash flows but is necessary to maintain the business. The company should determine what percentage of the total capital investments budget is going to be spent on high- and low-priority projects. This provides a guideline for the preparer to follow in allocating funds for capital investment expenditures. Exhibit 24.1 will help your company provide this input.

Problem Areas Companies Face in Capital Expenditure Decisions

It is important to recognize that preparing the capital investments budget can create problems in decisionmaking. These problems are generally unique to the preparation of capital investments and are therefore briefly explored in the following list:

- Alternatives are not disclosed. This leads to:

  The possibility of overlooking superior alternatives in risk, return, and adaptability. The inability to collect estimates of costs and benefits for incremental analysis.

- Difficulties in forecasting are used as an excuse for inefficient methods of handling capital expenditure analysis.

Exhibit 24.1   Establishing Company Priorities for Capital Spending

	Company Budget Year Percentage of Total Budget	
	High Priority	Low Priority
Making your company a low-cost producer		
Replacing and modernizing normal plant and equipment		
Meeting required environmental standards		
Bringing in major new high technology		
Consolidating existing product lines		
Starting up new product lines		
Adding to present productive capacity		
Other: (List)		

- Accuracy in estimating costs.
- Failure to express benefits in quantitative terms causes difficulty in estimating benefits.
- Some benefits are difficult to measure in quantitative terms.
- Operating personnel are unable to understand the logic behind the evaluation of capital projects because they do not know why projects are accepted or rejected.
- Analysts and reviewers are not well qualified because they don't know the business, understand the evaluation theory and its application, or raise the right questions.
- Background and interests prevent top management from lending its support to the methods and techniques used.
- Lack of standardization in methods and assumptions creates confusion and lack of direction.
- Accounting practices create confusion and inaccuracies because:
  Cash flow projections are not consistent with accrual accounting techniques.
  The time value of money is different from typical recording of accounting records.
  Opportunity cost is ignored in financial accounting.
  The capital investment process lacks unified and consistent treatment.

Complex Variables in the Capital Investment Decision

The decision to accept or reject a capital project involves many complex variables. Some may be more important in the decisionmaking process than others. This depends upon the nature of the project. For example, a capital proposal may be forecasted to generate an acceptable return on investment rate as well as payback but may be rejected because of legal implications. As a way to understand the complexities involved, let us review the following variables:

Economic Desirability. Does the proposal meet minimum return on investment objectives such as discounted cash flow (DCF) rates and maximum payback criteria?

Relative Importance. How important is the investment in relation to the overall objectives of the company? For example, how important is this proposed capital investment to the survival of the company?

Alternative Opportunities. What alternatives are available in addition to the proposed capital investment? It is this author's opinion that every capital investment proposal should have one or more alternatives for the company to select. One alternative is not to approve the proposal, but sufficient reason must be given.

Perception of Risk and Consequences of Potential Failure. How risky is the proposed capital investment? For example, it is important to understand both the extent of the risk and the potential consequences of failure. Would the continuance of the company's operation be in jeopardy?

Compatibility with the Long-Range Character and Image of the Company. Most companies have an image that they want to project to the buying and investing public. This is usually found in the company's mission statement. Is the capital investment proposal acceptable in terms of the mission statement of the company?

Acceptability to All Concerned. Are all reviewers and approvers in full agreement with the contents of the proposal?

Potential Competitive Reactions. How will the competition react to your company's competitive edge? It is not reasonable to think that a capital investment will confer a permanent advantage. Therefore, the projections for profits and cash flows should be reviewed and adjusted at given times throughout the life of the project.

Reliability of Information. Relating other capital projects of a similar nature to a current project under review.

Political Considerations. How might the political environment affect the capital project? Will local, regional, or national laws or proposed legislation have an impact?

Potential Future Investment. Will future investments be needed to support the capital investment during the life of the project? For example, most capital investments require further funds for maintenance, parts replacement, updating technology, and the like, at some time. This must be considered as part of the total dollar investment in the capital project.

Intuition. What does the intuition of experienced managers tell you? This variable is difficult to evaluate, and caution should be taken not to rely on it exclusively. However, this factor should not be ignored.

Effect on Both Short- and Long-Range Financial Performance. How will larger capital investments affect both the short- and long-term financial performance of the company? Management must understand how financial performance will be affected in the next few years and beyond. The investment must be evaluated in terms of the overall financial objectives of the company.

Required Changes in the Company's Financial Structure. Will the capital investment alter the financial structure of the company by requiring further financing through equity, debt, or both? This sort of change is reflected in the balance sheet relationships between debt and equity and may further affect the type of financing that the company may desire in the future.

Timing of the Investment.   Is it the right time to invest in such a project? Although this may seem a minor point, it is important to fully explore whether a proposed capital investment is right in relation to the marketplace, economy, technology, cost, and other time-sensitive factors.

Legal Implications.   Is the capital project in keeping with current and proposed legislation? A capital project may have all the positive ingredients—that is, profitability and cash flow—but may violate laws, such as certain requirements to meet pollution or safety standards. Therefore, most projects must be reviewed by the legal department before being accepted.

Replacement Options

Too frequently, companies replace plant and equipment without considering options such as the following:

- Do nothing. This option is acceptable if the preparer can satisfactorily answer these questions:

  How long can I do nothing?

  What are the consequences?

  What is the cost?

  If these questions can be satisfactorily answered, then doing nothing is an acceptable option.
- Go out of business (disinvestment).
- Replace with the same type and capacity of equipment.
- Replace with a larger or smaller piece of equipment.
- Replace with a new and more productive process.

USING THE CAPITAL EXPENDITURES BUDGET

The capital expenditures budget is one of the largest expenditures budgets within the budgeting process. It serves the company in the following ways:

It Forecasts Next Year's Cash Requirements.   The capital expenditures budget provides a summary of cash requirements needed for capital expenditure proposals.

Estimates of both the timing and amounts of money needed help the company antic-ipate any additional financing. In addition, such estimates assist in determining what capital projects can be deferred or abandoned if funds cannot be made available.

It Provides Operational Targets. The process of preparing the capital budget alerts management to plans and targets being requested for types of projects such as product expansion, cost reduction, productivity improvement, or new product devel-opment. In addition, it encourages division and plant personnel to develop realistic appraisals of the overall targets and objectives of their operations.

It Eliminates Duplication. Developing overall company capital expenditure bud-gets highlights the existence of equipment duplication throughout the company. Fre-quently, various operational units request the same equipment for different operations.

It Establishes Project Priorities. When capital projects are summarized, spending priorities can be established depending upon the need for and the availability of funds.

It Meets Company's Objectives. The capital expenditures budget assists in detect-ing proposed capital projects that do not meet the overall objectives or goals of the company. For example, capital expenditure requests for monies to be spent on a prod-uct line that the company is considering abandoning would be rejected. Also when uncertainty exists, projects may be deferred pending further analysis.

CONTENTS OF THE CAPITAL EXPENDITURES BUDGET

A company needs to define how the capital expenditures budget is to be organized and administered. This definition is usually contained in a capital expenditures manual that is reviewed and updated each budgeting period. It contains all the necessary poli-cies and forms as well as instructions for completing the capital expenditures budget. The following discussion highlights the major segments contained in this manual. These are by no means the only data contained; the material provided will merely serve as an operating guideline.

Policy Statement

The policy statement should describe the following:

- Major changes and directions in product lines
- Changes in location of certain facilities

- Economic outlook as it affects product demand
- Money availability and costs
- Minimum return on investment rates and maximum payback period
- Specific funds available for each operating unit

Definitions

Concepts and terms should be clearly defined. Of particular interest are the issues stated below:

- What is considered a capital project? What types of capital outlays are involved?
- What constitutes major versus minor projects? What is expense versus capital? What are the classifications of expenditures?
- How should rentals and leases be handled?
- What is involved in underruns and overruns, depreciation methods used, interdivision pricing, tax rates, taxes used, asset transfers, disposals, and other important data?

Responsibility and Authorization Levels

The level of authorization and responsibility for the company's overall administration of the capital budget should be clearly spelled out. The list should specify:

- The duties of appropriate budget officer or other designated individual
- Levels of authority for dollar approvals
- Appropriate routing and sign-off responsibilities
- Individuals and parts of the organization responsible for submitting capital budgets
- Where capital budgets are to be submitted
- Who will assemble, organize, and analyze the capital budgets

Procedural Details

Equally important are the procedural details in the preparation of the capital budgets. These issues must be made clear to the preparer so that consistency in preparation can be achieved. The details to be established include:

- Standard forms with clear instructions
- The required supplemental and backup materials
- Where and how to submit completed capital budgets
- When data should be presented
- How data are to be rounded (to thousands, to millions)
- The length of the budget period
- The types of project classifications, such as cost reduction, facility replacement or improvement, expansion or addition, product improvement, and others
- Level of priority—for instance, absolutely urgent, necessary, economically desirable
- The financial requirements, including working capital and expenses
- Carryovers from prior years
- Carryforwards to future years

Review and Timing Details

To establish an efficient review schedule, it is vital to determine:

- The necessary timetables for reviews and approvals
- The person responsible for reviews and approvals
- Feedback procedures for revisions and/or approvals
- The basis for approval

INSTRUCTIONS FOR PREPARING THE CAPITAL EXPENDITURES BUDGET

As indicated previously, most companies and/or industries prepare capital expenditure proposals differently. That is, they use different forms, but usually record similar information. The following forms are typically used and provide a solid foundation for preparing the capital expenditures budget.

Preliminary Budget Request Form (Exhibit 24.2)

This form is used by operating units as a preliminary request for funds for a capital asset. It contains all the information management needs to accept or reject the proposal. The information contained in this form includes:

Exhibit 24.2 Preliminary Budget Request Form

XYZ CORPORATION
Capital Expenditure
Preliminary Budget Request

Department _____   Number _____

Division _____   Date _____

Project Classification: Request (check one):
_____ Replacement/Cost Reduction   ☐   Original
_____ Expansion   ☐   Supplementary
_____ New
_____ Other _____
              (please specify)

Description of Proposed Investment

Amount Needed: $ _____ (as shown below)

$_____ Fixed Assets + $_____ Working − $_____ Net Cash Flow = $_____ Net
                                 Capital   from Replaced   Investment
                                                   Items

Expected Cash Flow (Benefits):

Expected Time Schedule and Priority:

Expected Benefits and Returns on Investment:

Approvals and Acknowledgements:

	Signature	Date
Project Originator	_____	_____
Department Head	_____	_____
Division Controller	_____	_____
Division Head	_____	_____
Corporate Controller	_____	_____
Director of Budgets	_____	_____
Corporate President	_____	_____

Department, Division, and Date.   Here the preparer lists the names of the department and division requesting the proposals and the date requested.

Number.   The capital budgeting system should have a numbering system to identify the division from which the project request originated and the budgeting period to which it applies. For example, division X may use the following number to request funds for budget year 20X1: X-01-X1. This means that division X is requesting project number 01 (numbered in sequence order) for the budgeting period 20X1. More sophisticated numbering systems can be developed to identify the types of projects and their priority status.

Project Classification.   In this section the preparer indicates the project classification as defined in the capital expenditures budget manual. Additional classifications may be added if they suit the requirements of the industry or meet the specific needs of the company.

Request.   This section indicates whether the request is original or a supplement to an existing proposal.

Description of Proposed Investment.   In this section, the preparer describes the proposed investment as briefly as possible. Because detailed supporting data will accompany this form, only a summary is needed.

Amount Needed and Cash Flow (Benefits) Expected.   This element is self-explanatory, but keep in mind the additional investment in working capital.

Expected Time Schedule and Priority.   Here the preparer indicates the expected schedule, considering the starting and ending dates. For example, the preparer should mention if the ending completion date will carry over beyond the current budgeting period. Remember, funds for projects that are budgeted in a given budget year are lost if they are not used in the approved year. Therefore, a proposal must be resubmitted the following budget year.

   In addition, it is necessary to indicate the priority level of the project as defined in the capital budget manual. Acceptance of the project may depend on the priority level established. However, the preparer should be realistic and set high priority levels only when actually demanded.

Expected Benefits and Returns on Investment.   This section indicates the estimated payback period and return on investment rate for the project over the life of the project.

Approvals and Acknowledgments.   The capital budget manual should establish an approved limits schedule for various types of fixed asset acquisitions at different organizational levels. For example, the following is an illustration of what an approval schedule might look like:

	Capital	*Expense*	*Office Equipment*
Board of Directors	N O	L I M I T S	
Chairman and President	$2,000,000	$2,000,000	$200,000
Senior Vice-President	500,000	500,000	50,000
Vice-Presidents	250,000	250,000	25,000
Plant Manager	50,000	50,000	10,000
Directors	20,000	20,000	2,000
Production Managers	10,000	10,000	1,000

Variations on the above should be developed to meet the needs of the company. The responsible person assigned to coordinate the capital expenditures program, such as the budget director, should be sure that all the proper signatures are contained in the request and that they are dated by each individual.

Capital Budget (Exhibit 24.3)

The capital budget form summarizes all the proposed capital projects for the budget year by operating unit. The column headed "Expenditure this budget" becomes the amount of addition to the fixed assets budget (Schedule F4), and the totals of all operating divisions should be posted to Schedule F4, line 4.

Capital Expenditures in Process Report (Exhibit 24.4)

The capital expenditures in process report keeps track of the progress of each project and is used to determine underruns and overruns.

Plant Appropriation Request (Exhibit 24.5)

The plant appropriation request (PAR) form is used by the operating unit to detail all the supporting data for the capital proposal. This analysis is used to evaluate the viability of the proposed capital project. In most companies, it does not automatically give authority to expend funds. When the project is scheduled to start, the operating division must request an authorization for funds form that authorizes the company to issue funds to specific vendors against the approved plant authorization request (PAR). This is done merely to control the outflow of funds by management.

Exhibit 24.3 Capital Budget Form

Page Number _____

XYZ CORPORATION
Capital Budget
For Year 20XX

Department/Division _____

Department	Item number	Description	Status		Total expenditure	Expenditure this budget	Estimated R.O.I.	Priority 1, 2, or 3	Classification			
			New	Cont.					Replacement cost reduction	Expansion	New	Other
Total												

Exhibit 24.4   Capital Expenditures in Process Report

XYZ CORPORATION
Capital Expenditures in Process Report

Item number	Description	Approval amount	Original project completion date	Spent to date	Needed for completion	Total	Expected variation	Favorable (F) Unfavorable (UF)	Expected completion date	Comments
Example X1-A-601	Replacement of casting machines	3.000.000	12/31/X1	2.000.000	1.100.000	2.100.000	100.000	UF	March 31. 20X1	Approval was obtained for 100.000 overrun

189

Exhibit 24.5   Plant Appropriation Request (PAR) Form

1. Plant appropriation request (PAR)   No. _____

.... Group   Approval required
.... Division
.... Department   ....
.... Product line
.... Project location   (Dollar amounts in thousands)

2. Summary description of proposed project

3. Project expenditures

	This request	Previously approved	Future requests	Total project
Basis for approval				
Related expense	_____	_____	_____	_____
Total	_____	_____	_____	_____

4. Key financial measurements

Chart of cumulative funds flow

	Reported	Inflation-adjusted
DCRR	____%	____%
Payback period (years)	____	____

Amount

_____ Reported
...... Inflation-adjusted

0

20 20 20 20 20 20 20 20 20 20

Exhibit 24.5 *(continued)*

5. Business history and forecast of .... Department/operation

Reported						Inflation-adjusted (c)			
Market position (a)	Sales		Net income				Net income		
	Amt.	Price index (b)	Amt.	ROS	ROI	Sales	Amt.	ROS	ROI
Year									

a. Last five years:
   20
   20
   20
   20
   20

b. Forecast with proposed project:
   Current year
   20
   Next five years
   20
   20
   20
   20
   20

6. Business history and forecast of ....
   ...., product line

a. Last five years:
   20
   20
   20
   20
   20

b. Forecast with proposed project:
   Current year
   20
   Next five years
   20
   20
   20
   20
   20

c. Increment resulting from project:
   Current year
   20
   Next five years
   20
   20
   20
   20
   20

a- Basis -   Federal income tax rate used -
b- 20 = 100; Basis -
c- Base year -

Exhibit 24.5   (*continued*)

7. Summary of project expenditures

	This request	Previously approved	Future requests	Total project
Investment expenditures..............................				
Associated deferred charges..........................				
Lease-commitments not capitalized plus lease related expenses.............................				
Subtotal – Basis for approval.........................				
Patterns and tooling.................................				
All other related expense				
Grand total				
As a memo:				
All other starting costs................................				
Trade-in value of surplus equipment				

8. Category(s):

	Total	Investment	Expense
Category (prime)			
Category (other)			
Category VII (if applicable)			
Total, this request			

Two calendar years following project completion	10. Facility to be replaced
9. Estimated gain (loss) 20____ 20____ in net income to other G.E. Components:	First cost.................................... Year purchased............................. Book value .... Description of facility and proposed disposition
11. Starting date . . . . month/year Completion date . . . . month/year	

12. Utilization anticipated in first year after project completion – 20 . . . . % Basis	13. Number of employees Location

	Before	After	Before	After
Manufacturing				
All other				
Total				

Exhibit 24.5 (*continued*)

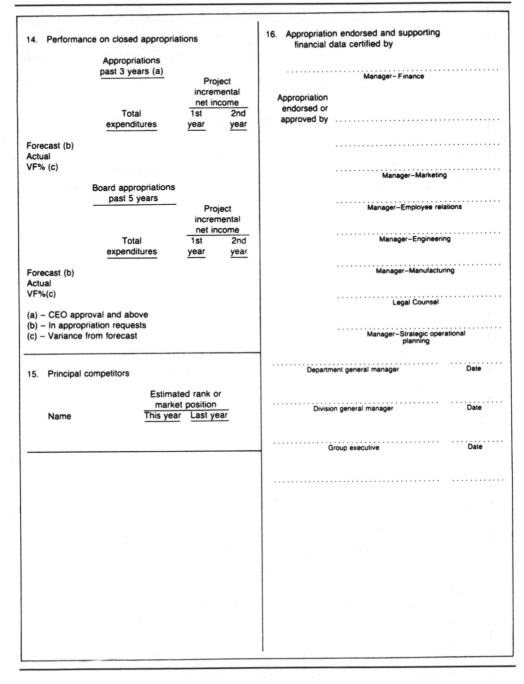

14. Performance on closed appropriations

Appropriations past 3 years (a)

	Total expenditures	Project incremental net income	
		1st year	2nd year
Forecast (b)			
Actual			
VF% (c)			

Board appropriations past 5 years

	Total expenditures	Project incremental net income	
		1st year	2nd year
Forecast (b)			
Actual			
VF%(c)			

(a) – CEO approval and above
(b) – In appropriation requests
(c) – Variance from forecast

15. Principal competitors

	Estimated rank or market position	
Name	This year	Last year

16. Appropriation endorsed and supporting financial data certified by

....
Manager–Finance

Appropriation endorsed or approved by ....

....

....
Manager–Marketing

....
Manager–Employee relations

....
Manager–Engineering

....
Manager–Manufacturing

....
Legal Counsel

....
Manager–Strategic operational planning

....
Department general manager   Date

....
Division general manager   Date

....
Group executive   Date

....

Capital Investment Proposal (Exhibit 24.6)

The capital investment proposal includes the information needed to provide a commentary on the nature of a capital project proposal. It accompanies the previously mentioned forms (see Exhibits 24.2 through 24.5) and provides management with a verbal commentary to support the financial projections.

Capital Expenditure Proposal—Project Schedule (Exhibit 24.7)

The capital expenditure proposal—project schedule form projects the cash flows for the estimated life of the project. To reflect the time value of money and inflation, discounted cash flow calculations are made (see Chapter 25 for further explanations). In addition, the payback period is also calculated (see Chapter 25).

Exhibit 24.6   Capital Investment Proposal

Division or company: _____

1. *General description and justification.* This is, for example, the underlying situation and the solution; assets to be acquired; market profitability.

2. *Classification.* Projects are slotted for ongoing business or as new ventures. They are further classified according to objective, for example:

   a. Reduce costs.

   b. Improve quality.

   c. Increase output.

   d. Improve market position.

   e. Comply with legislation.

3. *Profitability.* The future effect on the firm or unit of the firm.

4. *Inflation.* Indexes used and their sources.

5. *Assumptions.* The main variables affecting the project, plus:

   a. Project yield sensitivity to changes in these variables.

   b. Estimated probabilities of such changes.

6. *Project risk.* Based on the analysis for (5) above, estimate the probability of a significant variance from estimated project profitability.

7. *Alternatives considered.* Include plausible options and the reasons for their rejection.

8. *Staff comments.* Include advisory and service groups and other management groups consulted, and their opinions. Explain where these opinions were not accepted.

Exhibit 24.7   Capital Expenditure Proposal—Project Schedule

Company/Group _____   Proposal no. _____
Title of project _____

	Years	0	1			10	11
Year-on-year general inflation rate (%)							
Fixed capital (including residual values)							
Land							
Buildings							
Plant and machinery							
Vehicles							
Other fixed assets							
Subtotal							
Proceeds of disposals							
Subtotal							
Working capital (including residual values)							
Subtotal							
Repairs							
Initial expenses							
Profit before tax and depreciation							
Tax payable (see below)							
Net cash flow in current terms							
Net cash flow in constant terms							
Tax calculation in current terms							
Profit before tax and depreciation							
Depreciation							
Other allowances/adjustments—detail:							
Taxable amount							
Tax incurred, at _____ (%)							

Indicators
DCF yield in constant terms   _____ (%).
DCF yield in current terms   _____ (%).
Payback period in current terms_____ years

Fixed Assets Budget (Schedule F4, Exhibit 24.8)

The fixed assets budget reflects both additions and deletions to the fixed assets—net balance. It calculates the amounts projected in the capital expenditures budget, as well as amounts that are to be charged during the budget year for construction in progress, amounts for disposals projected for the budget period, and depreciation adjustments. The ending fixed assets–net balance is posted to the balance sheet (Schedule F9, line 15).

Exhibit 24.8   Fixed Assets Budget

Schedule _____ **F4**

Page _____ of _____

Period _____

☐ Six months   ☐ Total year

Company Name _____

LINE	($ in 000s)	Reference						Total
1	Fixed assets–net beginning balance	Y/E balance						
2								
3	Plus:							
4	Additions							
5	Less:							
6	Disposals							
7	Depreciation allowance							
8								
9	Fixed assets–net ending balance	To F9,L15						
10								
11								
12								
13								
14								
15								
16								
17								
18								
19								
20								
21								
22								
23								
24								
25								

Capital Expenditure Checklist[1]

Some companies complete an extensive checklist of items to consider when preparing a capital expenditure request. Some of these items do not pertain to all projects; in many cases, they relate to projects in which new products are involved. Nevertheless, it is important to have such a checklist so that all areas of the project are at least considered. The checklist is broken down into the following segments:

- Financial
- Investment
- Distribution/warehousing
- Pricing
- Market
- Technical
- Production
- Labor
- Inventory

Questions to Consider

Some significant questions must be answered or explored for each capital expenditure request. The following checklist covers questions vital to each of the preceding segments. It is by no means comprehensive and should be supplemented by other questions that are unique to a particular company.

Financial

- What is the financial risk?
- Can product investment generate sufficient cash flow?
- What is the cash risk or payout?
- What is the expected rate of return?
- Is there any internal or external transfer of profits? If so, how much?
- What is the breakeven point?
- What financing will be required?
- What are the tax implications?
- How will overhead be allocated?

---

[1]Robert Rachlin, *Successful Techniques for Higher Profits* (New York: MARR Publications, 1981), pp. 85–88.

Investment

- If this project is a replacement of existing machinery and equipment, what disposition will be made of the old machinery and equipment?

Distribution/Warehousing

- If capacity is increased, what will be the impact on storage and distribution facilities?
- Are any new distribution channels required?
- Can the product be distributed by the current sales force?
- By what method will the product be distributed?

Pricing

- Is the selling price dependent upon the production costs?
- What is the elasticity of the price in relation to supply and demand?
- What pricing strategy has been planned?
- At what price will the breakeven point occur?
- What is the expected price trend?

Market

- What is the ease of entry by competitors if the product is new to the marketplace?
- What is the nature of the market, that is, size, industry, and so forth?
- At what state is the current market? That is, is it expanding, contracting, or maintaining position?
- How do customers react to changes in the economy, in needs, and in trends?
- Who are the major competitors?
- How strong a position do the competitors have in the marketplace?
- Are our proposed products competitive?
- Are any restrictions set forth by the marketplace or by governmental regulations that limit both production and sales?
- Is this product for domestic consumption only?
- What is the demand for potential business?
- If the investment is product related, has the product been tested?
- Are any additional costs involved in promoting the product?

Technical

- What are the risks in technically completing the project?
- How likely are changes in technology that may lead to obsolescence?
- If this is a new product, what are the potential problems?
- Are there any additional requirements for maintenance?
- What technical know-how is needed for the proposed project?
- Will new machinery and equipment require new design?
- Does the project require new plant layout?
- Will the start-up situation require additional resources?
- Can technical service be provided to new customers for new products?
- Are any patent problems involved?
- Is specialized know-how needed to produce this product?
- Are there any salable by-product as a result of this project?

Production

- How will this project affect production rates?
- Does the projected volume of production seem reasonable given the current rate?
- How flexible are the planned facilities for future expansion?
- Why are changes to current production facilities necessary?
- What is the history of repair and maintenance costs if equipment and machinery are being replaced?
- Can new facilities produce other related products?
- Is the product seasonal, and if so, what is the impact on production levels?

Labor

- Will the project require any additional labor?
- Will the project reduce labor costs and by how much?

Inventory

- Are new sources of raw materials needed?
- What are the required inventory levels?
- How accessible are producers of raw materials to production facilities?
- Is there more than one supplier of raw materials?

CHAPTER TWENTY-FIVE

Techniques of Evaluating Capital Investments*

The success of most companies depends upon the maximum use of capital investments. Capital investments generate profits by providing additional earnings from each specific investment. Growth companies continue to plow earnings back into profitable investments and in some cases borrow funds to finance profitable opportunities.

This chapter explains the many concepts that can be used to evaluate capital investments. Each of these concepts has its advantages and disadvantages. Ultimately, the method that fits a company's needs is the one that should be used. The key is to establish consistency both in technique and in computation so that each investment can be evaluated against each other. The next step is to select investments that are necessary to the growth of the company.

PREREQUISITES OF AN ACCEPTABLE METHOD OF CALCULATION

Certain prerequisites are important for the effective evaluation of capital investments. Each criterion is central to the overall process, and its importance cannot be overemphasized. The prerequisites are as follows:

---

[1]Robert Rachlin, *Successful Techniques for Higher Profits* (New York: MARR Publications, 1981), pp. 89–109.

Universal Application.   The method must be applicable throughout the entire organization. Its universal application must be understandable and workable for all parts of the organization.

The Time Value of Money.   Because money has a cost and is related to time, it is important that a method of calculation include the time value of money. This is found when computing discounted cash flow, which will be discussed later in this chapter.

The Life of the Project.   The method must consider the life of the project—whether the economic, technological, or physical life—to evaluate fully the effectiveness of the project.

The Payback Period.   This consideration requires the use of the payback method of evaluation. As will be discussed later in this chapter, the payback method measures recoverability and not rate of return. Therefore, it is one of the calculations used in conjunction with other methods to evaluate capital investments.

Ease of Calculation.   Because the preparers will be from different disciplines throughout the company, and because the expertise of these individuals may not be uniformly sophisticated, the calculation should be reasonably easy to carry out.

Risk.   The method must be capable of highlighting certain elements of risk—whether cash risk, financial risk, or risk of obsolescence—by a good method of calculation.

CALCULATION OF CASH FLOW

The financial justification of capital investments can be evaluated by calculating the cash flow generated from a specific project. The cash flow projections are found in the capital expenditures request form and include the following information:

Financial

- Land
- Buildings
- Machinery and equipment
- Working capital
- Capitalized costs
- Other

Earnings

- Net sales
- Cost of sales
- Advertising
- Research and development
- Depreciation
- Selling
- General and administrative
- Taxes
- Other

Cash flow projects are made for each time period over the life of the investment, as are earnings projections. With this information, cash flows are calculated by applying the following formula to the yearly projections over the life of the investment:

Accounting net earnings + Depreciation charges = Cash flows

The cash flow statement in Exhibit 25.1 is based on the following data about a project:

Machinery and equipment	$80,000
Working capital	40,000
Depreciation method	Straight line
Life of asset	4 years

The data in Exhibit 25.1 are used in calculations to determine the payback period and the return on investment. To further explain why depreciation is added back to net earnings and used to calculate cash flow, let us look at the preceding data for all four years of cash flow, as shown in Exhibit 25.2. Assume also that Example A in Exhibit 25.2 has no charge for depreciation and that Example B is as given.

The increase of $40,000 in cash flow represents the after-tax savings of depreciation. Although depreciation is not a source of cash, it provides higher cash flows by reducing income taxes paid.

PAYBACK METHOD

The payback method has long been used in capital expenditure evaluations. As will be seen, it is used in conjunction with other methods to determine the acceptability of an

Exhibit 25.1   Illustration of Cash Flow for a Project (in $1,000s)

	Year				
	0	1	2	3	4
Machinery and equipment	$ 80				
Working capital	40				
Total investment	$120				
Net sales		$120	$120	$120	$120
Costs (excluding depreciation)		60	60	60	60
Depreciation		20	20	20	20
Earnings before taxes		40	40	40	40
Taxes		20	20	20	20
Net earnings		$ 20	$ 20	$ 20	$ 20
Cash flow		$ 40	$ 40	$ 40	$ 40

investment, primarily because payback is not a true rate of return and does not measure profitability or return on investment.

To understand payback, it is important to recognize its advantages and disadvantages. The advantages are as follows:

It Is Easy to Calculate and Understand.   Of all the evaluation methods, payback is the easiest to calculate and understand. It merely requires identifying the total investment dollars of the project and dividing this by the annual cash flows.

Exhibit 25.2   Impact of Depreciation on Cash Flow (in $1,000s)

	A	B	Difference
Net sales	$480	$480	—
Costs (excluding depreciation)	240	240	—
Depreciation	—	80	$80
Earnings before tax	240	160	(80)
Taxes	120	80	(40)
Accounting net earnings	120	80	(40)
Plus depreciation	—	80	80
Cash flow	$120	$160	$40

It Indicates Cash Risk. As compared to other methods of calculation, payback is an excellent indicator of the riskiness of a project. The longer the payback period, the higher the risk; the shorter the payback period, the lower the risk. In times of a tight cash position, payback will play a major role in a decision to invest. Remember that in a rapidly changing economy the longer you wait to recover your investment, the more risk you face in recovering that investment.

It Measures Recoverability. Payback measures the recovery period when annual cash flow equals the total investment. At this point, the project is said to be at payback, meaning that the investment has been fully recovered. The importance of this calculation applies only until the payback period is reached.

It Gives Greater Weight to Earlier Cash Flows. Because payback is measured only up to the recovery period, annual cash flows have greater weight in the earlier years. Beyond the payback period calculation, they are not significant for this calculation. Therefore, it is important that a project be structured so that cash flows are generated more heavily in the earlier periods. Also, as will be discussed later in this chapter, the payback period will have a favorable impact on other methods of calculating return on investment.

Two of the disadvantages of payback are as follows:

It Does Not Represent a True Rate of Return. As discussed previously, payback indicates at what period the investment will be recovered from cash flows generated from the project. Therefore, it does not measure return on investment, because any method of return on investment would consider the total cash flows for the life of the project.

It Is Not a Good Way to Compare Projects. Because the result of the payback calculation is expressed as a time period—that is, years and months—it does not provide a comparable basis on which to measure projects. For example, different types of projects can have the same payback as well as different amounts of project investment. Therefore, the projects assume an equal status, but in reality they are quite different. The only similarity is that they have the same payback period.

Calculation of Payback

The calculation of payback is based on the cash flow projections previously discussed. Based on the previous calculations, the annual cash flow data (in $1,000s) are as follows:

| | Year | | | | |
Investment	0	1	2	3	4
Machinery and equipment	$80				
Working capital	$40				
Annual cash flows		$40	$40	$40	$40

The formula for determining the payback period is:

$$\frac{\text{Investment}}{\text{Annual cash flows}}$$

The following number of years are therefore required to recoup the initial investment detailed above:

$$\frac{\$120,000}{\$\ 40,000} = 3 \text{ years}$$

The preceding calculation assumes that the annual cash flows are even each year. In reality this will not be the case, because sales volume and costs vary from year to year. Assuming this variance, the following annual cash flow data (in $1,000s) result:

| | Year | | | | |
Investment	0	1	2	3	4
Machinery and equipment	$80				
Working capital	$40				
Annual cash flows		$45	$50	$40	$35

The payback period has now changed from 3 years to 2.625 years, calculated as follows:

Total investment to be recovered	$120,000
Two years' cash flows	(95,000)
Remainder to be recovered	$ 25,000

A partial year's calculation is therefore:

$$\frac{\$25,000}{\$40,000} = 0.625$$

and the payback calculation is:

Total full years to recover investment	2.0 years
Partial year to recover investment	0.625 year
Total payback period	2.625 years

Note how much shorter the payback period is when heavier cash flows are received in the earlier periods. As will be seen later in this chapter, the return on investment rates for projects with heavier cash flows in earlier periods tends to be favorable.

Discounted Payback

When the discounted cash flow concept has been applied (approximately 16 percent over four years, to be discussed later in the chapter), payback can reflect the time value of money. Assuming the previous data, let us apply a 16 percent discount rate, which was calculated using discounted cash flow. The results are shown in Exhibit 25.3.

Payback Reciprocal

One way of relating the payback period to the rate of return is to use the payback reciprocal. This represents a rough estimate of the rate of return at which the project's life is at least twice the length of the payback period. The reciprocal is calculated as follows, using the data previously presented:

$$\frac{\text{Average annual cash flows}}{\text{Investment}} = \frac{\$\,40,000}{\$120,000} = 33.3\%$$

Exhibit 25.3   Calculation of Discounted Payback

Year	Investment	Annual Cash Flows	Present Value Factors—16%	Net Present Values
0	($120,000)		1.000	($120,000)
1		$45,000	0.862	38,790
2		50,000	0.743	37,150
3		40,000	0.641	25,640
4		35,000	0.552	19,320
Total				$ 900

In this case, a three-year payback period is equivalent to a 33.3 percent rate of return. Note that, when the payback period is multiplied by the rate of return, the answer will always equal one.

ACCOUNTING METHODS

Accounting methods of evaluation involve various methods of calculation. These calculations can be based on the original investment or an average investment. Other methods of calculation also exist. The basic difference between these methods and others that have been discussed is that the calculations are derived only from reported accounting data and not from cash flow. These methods of calculation will be explained later in the chapter.

Two advantages of accounting methods are as follows:

They Are Easy to Calculate. These methods are easy to calculate, because the data are the same as those used to prepare accounting statements. No consideration is given to adding back depreciation to arrive at cash flow.

They Tie in with Accounting Records. When financial data are forecast into the future for capital investments, they are prepared as if they were future accounting statements. Therefore, in future periods, these forecasted data can be measured against actual performance.

Some of the disadvantages of these methods tend to outweigh the advantages, and therefore they are not as widely used as some other methods. The disadvantages include the following:

They Rely on Accounting Data. The reliance on accounting data can create problems, because some accounting principles change periodically, as do certain adjusting entries. These changes sometimes distort projections based on historical data. In addition, a knowledge of accounting is needed, and not all contributors to the input of a capital project may have this technical knowledge.

They Give Equal Weight to All Cash Flows. Because all cash flows are treated as equal entities, they are given equal weight. No distinction is made for earlier monies, which have more value because they can be reinvested at an earlier period. This problem is compensated for by the use of discounted cash flow (discussed below).

They Assume That the Project Will Last Its Estimated Life. Because all cash flows must be calculated for the entire life of the project, it is assumed that the project will last the entire estimated life.

They Ignore the Time Value of Money. No consideration is given in each of the yearly cash flow projections for the time value of money. Money is assumed to be more valuable in the earlier years because it can be reinvested that much quicker.

Calculation

Based on the previous data, return on original investment is calculated as:

$$\frac{\text{Yearly cash flows}}{\text{Original investment}} = \frac{\$40,000}{\$120,000} = 33.3\%$$

and return on average investment is calculated as:

$$\frac{\text{Yearly cash flows}}{\text{Average investment}} = \frac{\$40,000}{\$60,000} = 66.7\%$$

DISCOUNTED CASH FLOW

The theory of discounted cash flow (DCF) is a rather difficult concept to understand. By following a logical sequence of events, we will see that discounting is the reciprocal of compounding and that both methods relate to the interest rate. The basic theory of DCF says that a dollar today is worth more than a dollar in the future. It is that rate of difference, or percentage return, that indicates what an investor may expect to receive on funds left to the company to invest over the life of the project. The common denominator for DCF calculations is the interest rate.

Discounted cash flow has many advantages. It provides a basic common ground for all types of projects, therefore providing an ideal method of ranking projects. To measure the DCF rate, one must include all cash flows throughout the life of the project. Most important is the fact that DCF assumes the time value of money.

Some of the disadvantages include a lack of relationship to accounting records and the uncertainty of forecasted cash flows. The latter problem is extremely important because each year's cash flow will carry a different present value factor. In addition, the calculated cash flows are assumed to be reinvested at the assigned discount rate.

Compounding

To understand the concept of discounting, it is important to understand compounding. Both methods have a common factor—the interest rate. Therefore, compounding uses a compound interest rate that computes a sum of money (principal) at the present to

Exhibit 25.4   Illustration of Compounding

Year	Principal	Interest—10%	Total
0	$10,000	—	$10,000
1	10,000	$1,000	11,000
2	11,000	1,100	12,100
3	12,100	1,210	13,310
4	13,310	1,331	14,641
5	$14,641	$1,464	$16,105

another sum of money at the end of X years. To illustrate, let us assume that you deposit $10,000 in a savings account at 10 percent interest. How much will you have after five years? The results are shown in Exhibit 25.4.

Clearly, after five years a $10,000 deposit is worth $16,105 at a 10 percent interest rate. A more simple method is to refer to a compound interest table (Exhibit 25.5) for the compound factor (1.1611) that equals five years at 10 percent and apply it to the initial deposit of $10,000, arriving at the same answer, as follows:

$$\$10,000 \times 1.611 = \$16,110$$

The difference of $5 between this result and the one obtained from the calculations is due to rounding.

Exhibit 25.5   Compound Interest Table

Year	10%	12%	14%	15%	16%	18%	20%
1	1.100	1.120	1.140	1.150	1.160	1.180	1.200
2	1.210	1.254	1.300	1.322	1.346	1.392	1.440
3	1.331	1.405	1.482	1.521	1.561	1.643	1.728
4	1.464	1.574	1.689	1.749	1.811	1.939	2.074
5	1.611	1.762	1.925	2.011	2.100	2.288	2.488
6	1.772	1.974	2.195	2.313	2.436	2.700	2.986
7	1.949	2.211	2.502	2.660	2.826	3.185	3.583
8	2.144	2.476	2.853	3.059	3.278	3.759	4.300
9	2.358	2.773	3.252	3.518	3.803	4.435	5.160
10	2.594	3.106	3.707	4.046	4.411	5.234	6.192

Discounting

As explained previously, discounting is the reverse of compounding. Whereas compounding shifts the value of money from the present to the future, discounting shifts the value of money to be received in the future back to the present. To illustrate, let us take the same data used in compounding and apply them to discounting. If you need $10,000 in five years, how much must you deposit today at 10 percent annual interest? Or at what discount factor will X principal equal $10,000? The results are shown in Exhibit 25.6.

By applying each of the interest factors, or present values, one arrives at $10,004. Therefore, given a principal amount of $16,110 for five years at 10 percent, the value of that money today is $10,000. The interest factors in this case are referred to as the discounted cash flow factors (see Exhibit 25.7). A simple technique is to apply the discount factor of 0.621 to the principal of $16,110 to arrive at the same answer.

Compounding and Discounting as Reciprocals

To further illustrate that compound interest rates and present value factors are reciprocals, let us take both factors for the same period at the interest rate of 10 percent and multiply them by each other:

Number of Periods	Compound Factors	$\times$	Present Value Factors	$=$	Reciprocal
1	1.100		0.909		1.000
2	1.210		0.826		1.000
3	1.331		0.751		1.000
4	1.464		0.683		1.000
5	1.611		0.621		1.000

Clearly, when both factors are multiplied by each other, the result will always equal one, proving that compounding and discounting are reciprocals.

Selection of a Discount Rate

It is important to select a DCF rate that ties in with the company's objective. Because capital investments provide future profits with today's cost of money, it is important to choose a DCF rate that complements the way the company establishes its corporate objective. This approach includes such techniques as cost of capital, corporate rate of return, risk potential, industry averages, and so forth. This DCF rate then becomes the minimum rate that is acceptable for capital investment proposals.

Exhibit 25.6   Illustration of Discounting

Year	Principal	Interest Factor	Total
0	$16,110	1.000	$16,110
1	16,110	0.909	14,644
2	16,110	0.826	13,307
3	16,110	0.751	12,099
4	16,110	0.683	11,003
5	16,110	0.621	$10,004[a]

[a]The $4 is added because the interest factors are not carried out to more decimal points.

Interest Rates and DCF Rate: An Illustration

As previously indicated, the DCF rate is equated to the interest rate. To illustrate this point, let us look at what happens when someone borrows $10,000 at 10 percent annual interest (see Exhibit 25.8). The repayment schedule is $2,638 at the end of each year for a total of five years. The payment of $2,638 represents both principal and interest. You will note that the borrower pays an interest rate of 10 percent and the lender earns 10 percent.

Applying this concept to discounted cash flow, we obtain the results shown in Exhibit 25.9. The discounted cash flow rate is 10 percent, because when the cash flows are discounted at 10 percent, the outflows and inflows of cash equal zero.

Exhibit 25.7   Present Value Table

Year	10%	12%	14%	15%	16%	18%	20%
1	0.909	0.893	0.877	0.870	0.862	0.847	0.833
2	0.826	0.797	0.769	0.756	0.743	0.718	0.694
3	0.751	0.712	0.675	0.658	0.641	0.609	0.579
4	0.683	0.636	0.592	0.572	0.552	0.516	0.482
5	0.621	0.567	0.519	0.497	0.476	0.437	0.402
6	0.564	0.507	0.456	0.432	0.410	0.370	0.335
7	0.513	0.452	0.400	0.376	0.354	0.314	0.279
8	0.467	0.404	0.351	0.327	0.305	0.266	0.233
9	0.424	0.361	0.308	0.284	0.263	0.225	0.194
10	0.386	0.322	0.270	0.247	0.227	0.191	0.162

Exhibit 25.8   Illustration of a Loan Repayment

Year	Outstanding Balance at Beginning of Year	Interest at End of Year	Annual Payments	Reduction of Principal
1	$10,000	$1,000	$ 2,638	$ 1,638
2	8,362	836	2,638	1,802
3	6,560	656	2,638	1,982
4	4,578	458	2,638	2,180
5	2,398	240	2,638	2,398
Total		$3,190	$13,190	$10,000

Calculation of Discounted Cash Flow

The calculation of DCF is relatively simple. There are basically two methods of computation, both of which will be illustrated. There are other variations, but these two methods are the most commonly used.

Net Present Value Method.   The net present value (NPV) method calculates the net present values of cash flows by means of a given discount rate—the rate used as the minimum requirement for all capital investments. If the net present values are positive, that is, higher than the investment, then the project is acceptable at that specific rate. If the net present values are negative, then the project is unacceptable at that rate, since cash flows, when discounted, are insufficient to cover the investment dollars. In addition, this method will indicate which projects should be selected when several projects are calculated. The ones with the higher net present values would have a higher priority. The example shown in Exhibit 25.10 illustrates this point.

Exhibit 25.9   Illustration of Discounted Cash Flow to a Loan Repayment

Year	Transaction	Cash Flows	Present Value Factors at 10%	Net Present Values
0	Borrow	$10,000	1.000	$10,000
1	Repayment	(2,638)	0.909	(2,398)
2	Repayment	(2,638)	0.826	(2,179)
3	Repayment	(2,638)	0.751	(1,982)
4	Repayment	(2,638)	0.683	(1,802)
5	Repayment	(2,638)	0.621	(1,639)
Total		($3,190)		—

Exhibit 25.10   Illustration of Discounted Cash Flow Using a 15% Discount Factor

Year	Cash Flows	Discount Factors at 15%	Net Present Values
0	($120,000)	1.000	($120,000)
1	40,000	0.870	34,800
2	40,000	0.756	30,240
3	40,000	0.658	26,320
4	40,000	0.572	22,880
5	40,000	0.497	19,880
Total	$ 80,000		$ 14,120

Based on the $14,120 net present value, the project illustrated would be an acceptable project.

Internal Rate of Return Method.   The internal rate of return (IRR) method solves for the discount rate (interest rate) that discounts the cash flows to equal the investment. This method solves for a discount rate, whereas the net present value method assigns a rate. The projects giving the highest internal rate of return are the ones accepted. Also, the calculated rate can be compared to the overall company objective to determine the acceptability of the investment. The example shown in Exhibit 25.11 illustrates this method.

The residual at the 15 percent rate is $14,120 and at the 20 percent rate ($400). This means that the internal rate of return is between 15 percent and 20 percent.

Exhibit 25.11   Illustration of Net Present Values

Year	Cash Flows	Discount Factors at 15%	Net Present Values	Discount Factors at 20%	Net Present Values
0	($120,000)	1.000	($120,000)	1.000	($120,000)
1	40,000	0.870	34,800	0.833	33,320
2	40,000	0.756	30,240	0.694	27,760
3	40,000	0.658	26,320	0.579	23,160
4	40,000	0.572	22,880	0.482	19,280
5	40,000	0.497	19,880	0.402	16,080
Total	$ 80,000		$ 14,120		($ 400)

Therefore, an interpolation is required in order to arrive at the exact rate. It is calculated as follows:

$$15\% + \left(5\% \times \frac{\$14,120}{\$14,520} \right) = 19.86\%$$

APPROACHES TO ADJUSTING FOR RISK

There are many approaches to adjusting for risk. However, the three most commonly used methods are as follows:

Judgmental.   Assessing the relative risk of an investment depends upon the common knowledge of management. Caution should be taken in being too subjective in the assessment.

Adjustment of Objective Rates.   Each investment carries a different objective rate, depending upon the riskiness of the investment. Although this is easy to understand, too much is left to the arbitrary assignment of different rates.

Adjustment of Cash Flows.   Cash flows are adjusted on the basis of the probabilities of each of the cash flows.

Two major drawbacks to the third method are (1) that the actual assignment of probability levels is difficult and (2) that high and low ranges are not revealed. Assume for example, a project of $10,000, with a five-year projection of cash flows of $3,500, $3,500, $3,000, $2,500, and $2,000. Given a current interest rate of 14 percent, will the investment be acceptable if interest rates rise? When the net present value method is applied, the discount factors for each of the interest rates are calculated for each of the cash flows. Results are shown in Exhibit 25.12. The conclusion is that, if interest rates approach 16 percent, the project should not be undertaken.

Exhibit 25.12   Cash Flows at Different Discount Rates

Year	Cash Flow	14%	16%	18%
0	($10,000)	($10,000)	($10,000)	($10,000)
1	3,500	3,070	3,017	2,965
2	3,500	2,692	2,601	2,513
3	3,000	2,025	1,923	1,827
4	2,500	1,480	1,380	1,290
5	2,000	1,038	952	874
NPV	$ 4,500	$ 305	($ 127)	($ 531)

Adding another dimension that brings probability estimates into the calculation will validate management's judgment as to the correctness of rising interest rates. Given the preceding data, what should be done if the probability levels shown in Exhibit 25.13 were established for each year at different interest rates?

When probability levels are applied to expected interest rates, each year's cash flow is adjusted and summarized under the adjusted NPV column. Because the NPV is positive, the project should proceed, assuming that the probability estimates are fairly reasonable.

Exhibit 25.13   Adjusting for Probable Interest Rates

Year	14%	16%	18%	Adjusted NPV
1	90%	10%		$ 3,065
2	90	10		2,683
3	80	10	10%	1,995
4	70	20	10	1,441
5	60	20	20	988
Cash Inflows				$10,172
Cash Outflows				(10,000)
NPV				$ 172

CHAPTER TWENTY-SIX

Developing the Loan Budget

The loan budget deals with both short- and long-term loans and is used to anticipate future financing as well as to project these items on the balance sheet.

INSTRUCTIONS FOR PREPARING THE LOAN BUDGET (SCHEDULE F5)

The beginning balance (line 2) for short-term debt represents the prior month's balance. This balance is usually estimated from the month before the new budget period. To this balance, all new projected loans (lines 3–5) from the referenced schedules are added and repayments (line 6) are deducted. Line 8 represents the ending balance for short-term loans and is posted to Schedule F9, line 30. It also becomes the beginning balance for the second month of the budget period. Similar calculations are made in succeeding budget periods.

Long-term debt projections start with the beginning estimated balance for both the current and long-term portions of the long-term debt. To this balance, new loans (line 15) are added and repayments (line 16) deducted.

The ending balance should be estimated for both the current portion (line 19) and the long-term portion (line 20). Both balances are posted to Schedule F9, lines 32 and 38 respectively. These balances are used as the starting or beginning balance for future budget periods.

See Exhibit 26.1.

Exhibit 26.1 Loan Budget

Schedule ____ **F5** ____

Period ____ ☐ Six months ☐ Total year

Company Name ____

LINE	($ in 000s)	Reference						Total
1	SHORT-TERM DEBT							
2	Beginning balance	Y/E balance						
3	New loans-disbursements	From E3,L16						
4	New loans-fixed assets additions	From E1,L20						
5	New loans-other	From E3						
6	Less: repayments	From E1,L18						
7								
8	Ending balance	To F9,L30						
9								
10								
11	LONG-TERM DEBT							
12	Beginning balance							
13	Current	Y/E balance						
14	Long-term	Y/E balance						
15	Plus new loans-L3,4,5							
16	Less repayments-L6							
17								
18	Ending balance							
19	Current	To F9,L32						
20	Long-term	To F9,L38						
21								
22								
23								
24								
25								

CHAPTER TWENTY-SEVEN

Developing the Accounts Payable Budget

The accounts payable budget represents a short-term obligation, or current liability to remit payment arising from the purchase of raw materials, material and supplies, and other items for which payment is due at a later date. The accounts payable balances are posted to the balance sheet and are based on input from other schedules such as Schedules B5, C1, and E3.

INSTRUCTIONS FOR PREPARING THE ACCOUNTS PAYABLE BUDGET (SCHEDULE F6)

The beginning balance (line 1) represents the ending balance (line 11) from the prior month. The first month of the budget usually represents an estimate of the ending balance prior to the start of the budgeting period. To this balance are added estimates of accounts payable from prior schedules as indicated on Schedule F6. Deductions are made for estimated disbursements from Schedule E3, line 8. The result is the accounts payable ending balance, which is posted to Schedule F9, line 33.

　　See Exhibit 27.1.

Exhibit 27.1 Accounts Payable Budget

Schedule _____ **F6** _____

Company Name _____

Page _____ of _____

Period ☐ Six months ☐ Total year

L-I-N-E	($ in 000s)	Reference						Total
1	Accounts payable—beginning balance	Y/E balance						
2	Add:							
3	Materials—manufacturing	From B5,L7						
4	Other—manufacturing	From B5,L9,L12						
5	G&A	From C1,L36						
6	Other							
7								
8	Deduct:							
9	Disbursements	From E3,L8						
10								
11	Accounts payable—ending balance	To F9,L33						
12								
13								
14								
15								
16								
17								
18								
19								
20								
21								
22								
23								
24								
25								

CHAPTER TWENTY-EIGHT

Developing the Other Liabilities Budget

The other liabilities budget establishes monthly balances for other noncurrent liabilities not budgeted in prior schedules, such as accrued expenses, income taxes, deferred income tax, and others. Brief explanations of some of these items follow:

- *Accrued expenses.* These are expenses that have been incurred in a given period but have not been paid. For example, interest and wage expenses are incurred in a given period but have not necessarily been paid and therefore constitute a liability.
- *Deferred income taxes.* This item represents the difference between income taxes that are actually paid in a period and the amount of tax computed on the basis of accounting income for that same period.
- *Other noncurrent liabilities.* These liabilities include such items as rent received in advance, and the like.

INSTRUCTIONS FOR PREPARING THE OTHER LIABILITIES BUDGET (SCHEDULE F7)

In the absence of any concrete estimates, it is advisable to use the following guidelines in budgeting these amounts:

- Use last year's balance when no major changes are anticipated.
- Use a percentage of sales or total operating expenses.
- Use a percentage of employees or total payroll expenses.
- Use current or proposed tax rates.

All the budget estimates are posted to Schedule F9 in the appropriate line items. Sec Exhibit 28.1.

Exhibit 28.1 Other Liabilities Budget

Schedule ____ **F7** ____ Company Name ____ Page ____ of ____

Period ☐ Six months ☐ Total year

L I N E	($ in 000s)	Reference							Total
1	Accrued expenses	To F9,L34							
2	Income taxes	To F9,L35							
3	Deferred income taxes	To F9,L39							
4	Other noncurrent liabilities	To F9,L40							
5									
6									
7									
8									
9									
10									
11									
12									
13									
14									
15									
16									
17									
18									
19									
20									
21									
22									
23									
24									
25									

CHAPTER TWENTY-NINE

Developing the Equity Budget

The equity budget summarizes the components of the stockholders' equity of the company and represents the owners' interest in the company. The owners' equity may be obtained through retained earnings in the business and investments made by the owners.

EQUITY BUDGET ACCOUNTS

The equity budget consists of the following accounts: retained earnings, dividends, capital stock, and paid-in capital in excess of par.

Retained Earnings

Retained earnings represent the increase in stockholders' equity that results from profits generated in operating the business, less any dividends declared and paid during the period. Therefore, the retained earnings account changes with budgeted earnings and anticipated dividends.

Dividends

Dividends represent distribution of profits by a company to its stockholders. The two most commonly used dividends are cash and stock dividends.

Cash Dividends.   Cash dividends are dividend payments made to stockholders in the form of cash. They reduce the retained earnings account as well as the cash account.

Stock Dividends.   Stock dividends are dividend payments made to stockholders in the form of stock. They represent distributions of a company's stock, such as common stock to its common stockholders.

Capital Stock

The capital stock account should reflect anticipated changes in stock issuances and purchases of treasury stock. This amount is posted to the balance sheet (Schedule F9, line 44).

The capital stock of a corporation consists of common stock, preferred stock, and treasury stock.

Common Stock.   A business corporation usually has some common stock outstanding. The common stockholders usually have legal rights to share earnings in the form of dividends, to purchase an amount of common stock in proportion to that which they currently own, to share in the asset value should liquidation occur, and to share in management decisions by electing members to the board of directors, and so forth.

The common stock value on the balance sheet depends upon the legal value or par value of the stock as stated in the corporation's charter and printed on the stock certificate. When the stock is initially sold, it is usually sold at par value and is recorded as such. However, if the stock is sold below or (usually) above par value, the differences will be recorded in an account titled Paid-in Capital in Excess of Par Value. See discussions of this subject later in this chapter.

Preferred Stock.   Preferred stock is different from common stock in that its stockholders take precedence over common stockholders in dividends, liquidation, cumulative rights to dividends, and convertible provisions. Other examples of preference may also exist. Concepts relating to par value are similar to those explained in the discussion of common stock.

Treasury Stock.   Treasury stock can be either preferred or common stock that was previously issued by the corporation and later reacquired on the open market for many reasons. A company may reacquire shares to acquire another company; to use for employee stock option plans, stock purchase plans, or bonuses; and to increase earnings per share since the purchase of such shares reduces the number of shares outstanding. These shares do not confer the privilege of voting, nor can dividends be paid on them.

Paid-in Capital in Excess of Par

This account represents the amount above or below the price received at the initial sale of the stock and is based on the par value of the stock. When stock is issued above the legal par value, the excess is recorded in the paid-in capital in excess of par account.

For example, if a company is authorized to issue 500,000 shares of common stock at a per share par value of $5.00 and sells 200,000 shares at $7.00 a share, the amount recorded in this account is as follows:

Stockholders' Equity

Common stock—$5.00 per value; authorized 500,000 shares; issued and outstanding, 200,000 shares	$1,000,000
Sold 200,000 shares at $7.00 per share	1,400,000
Paid-in capital in excess of par value	$ 400,000

The amount of $400,000 appears on the balance sheet and continues to change when more stock is sold and the selling price changes from the par value of the stock.

The paid-in capital in excess of par account reflects anticipated market price conditions for future sales of stock and is also posted to the balance sheet (Schedule F9, line 45).

EQUITY BUDGET AS SUMMARY

As you can see, the equity budget is determined by the sum of the other budgeted activity as well as by market conditions. For example, the retained earnings account changes with budgeted earnings and anticipated dividends, and capital stock is reflected by market price and par values. Therefore, those accounts must be reflected by budgeted growth, anticipated dividends, anticipated stock sales, and the amount of debt versus equity (leverage) a company anticipates.

INSTRUCTIONS FOR COMPLETING THE EQUITY BUDGET (SCHEDULE F8)

The ending prior month's balance (or estimate) is posted on line 1. To this amount are added the net earnings from Schedule D1, line 19. The anticipated dividends (line 3) are deducted by month, as calculated per the company policy. The remaining balance represents each month's ending balance for retained earnings (line 4). This amount is posted to the balance sheet (Schedule F9, line 46). (See Exhibit 29.1.)

Exhibit 29.1 Equity Budget

Schedule _____ **F8**

Page _____ of _____

Company Name _____

Period _____ ☐ Six months ☐ Total year

LINE	($ in 000s)	Reference						Total
1	Retained earnings—beginning balance	Y/E balance						
2	Plus: net earnings	From D1,L19						
3	Less: dividends	Company policy						
4	Retained earnings—ending balance	To F9,L46						
5								
6	Capital stock	To F9,L44						
7	Paid-in capital in excess							
8	of par	To F9,L45						
9								
10								
11								
12								
13								
14								
15								
16								
17								
18								
19								
20								
21								
22								
23								
24								
25								

CHAPTER THIRTY

Developing the Balance Sheet Budget

The balance sheet budget summarizes the estimates from Schedules F1 through F8. It reflects the anticipated financial position for each of the budget periods and accomplishes three main objectives:

1. It provides a direction for operating the business with the least amount of investment.
2. It provides a cushion of financial strength to overcome economic downturns.
3. It provides the ability to exploit unforeseen opportunities.

Schedule F9 is used to post these data as indicated by the references of schedules and represents the company's balance sheet. (See Exhibit 30.1.)

Exhibit 30.1 Balance Sheet Budget

Schedule ____F9____

Page __1__ of __2__

Period

☐ Six months ☐ Total year

Company Name

LINE	($ in 000s)	Reference						Total
1	Assets							
2								
3	Current assets							
4	Cash	From E3,L11						
5	Short-term securities	From E3,L18						
6	Accounts receivable-net	From F1,L8						
7	Inventories	From F2,L12						
8	Other current assets	From F3,L10						
9	Total current assets	L4-L8						
10								
11	Property, plant and							
12	equipment-gross							
13	Less:accumulated depreciation							
14	Property, plant, and							
15	equipment-net	From F4,L9						
16								
17	Other noncurrent assets							
18								
19	Total assets	L9+L15+L17						
20								
21								
22								
23								
24								
25								

Exhibit 30.1 (continued)

Schedule __F9 (continued)__

Period ☐ Six months ☐ Total year

Company Name

LINE	($ in 000s)	Reference						Total
26	LIABILITIES AND STOCKHOLDERS'							
27	EQUITY							
28								
29	Current liabilities							
30	Short-term debt	From F5,L8						
31	Current installments of							
32	long-term debt	From F5,L19						
33	Accounts payable	From F6,L11						
34	Accrued expenses	From F7,L1						
35	Income taxes	From F7,L2						
36	Total current liabilities	L30-L35						
37								
38	Long-term debt	From F5,L20						
39	Deferred income taxes	From F7,L3						
40	Other noncurrent liabilities	From F7,L4						
41	Total noncurrent liabilities	L38-L40						
42								
43	STOCKHOLDERS' EQUITY							
44	Stock (specify)	From F8,L6						
45	Capital surplus	From F8,L8						
46	Retained earnings	From F8,L4						
47	Total stockholders' equity	From F8,L4						
48								
49	Total liabilities and	L36+						
50	stockholders' equity	L41+L47						

CHAPTER THIRTY-ONE

Preparing the Statement of Cash Flows

The statement of cash flows was formerly known as the funds statement, statement of source and application of funds, and, most recently, the statement of changes in financial position. The new statement of cash flows reflects where, why, and how much cash was generated or spent and reflects the changes in cash balances from one period to another. It provides standards and information about the flows of cash from operating, investing, and financing activities of the company.

STATEMENT OF CASH FLOWS—FASB NO. 95

This Statement of Cash Flows is based on the Financial Accounting Standards Board (FASB) pronouncement titled "Statement of Financial Accounting Standards No. 95. The purpose is to provide relevant information about both cash receipts and payments of a company during a specific period of time. In addition, it provides information for creditors, investors, and others to assess a company's ability to generate positive cash flows; ability to meet its obligations to creditors and/or stockholders; and as an analytic tool for assessing variances in cash receipts and disbursements, as well as the financial position of both its cash and noncash investing and financing transactions during a specific period.

There are two methods of developing Statement of Cash Flows: the direct and indirect methods, with the direct method favored by the FASB.

Direct Method. This method deals with cash and its cash flow from components of operating cash receipts and payments as compared to converting or adjusting net income by items that do not affect the funds of the company.

Indirect Method. This method deals with cash and its cash flow from components of operating activities by adjusting revenues and expenses not resulting from cash transactions on the net income of the company.

For further details refer to FASB No. 95.

ACTIVITIES THAT AFFECT CASH FLOWS

Operating Activities

Operating activities include all transactions and events that are not classified as either investing or financing activities. They involve the generation of cash flows that result from net income activities. These activities are broken down into the following cash inflows and outflows:

Cash Inflows. These result from the following transactions and events:

- Cash receipts from the sale of goods or services
- Collection or sale of accounts and short- and long-term notes receivable arising from these sales
- Cash receipts from return on loans (interest), other debt instruments, and dividends on equity securities
- Others not classified as investing or financing activities and events

Cash Outflows. These result from the following transactions and events:

- Cash payments to suppliers for purchased inventory
- Cash payments to employees and other suppliers for goods or services
- Cash payments to governmental agencies for taxes due
- Cash payments of interest to lenders and other creditors
- All other expenses classified as operating activities

Investing Activities

Investing activities include lending and collecting on loans and buying and selling debt or equity investments and long-term productive assets. These activities are also broken down into cash inflows and cash outflows.

Cash Inflows.   These result from the following transactions and events:

- Cash receipts from the sales of productive assets such as property, plant, and equipment
- Cash receipts from the sales of debt or equity instruments of other companies
- Cash receipts from the collections or sales of other entities' debt instruments that were purchased by the company

Cash Outflows.   These result from the following transactions and events:

- Cash disbursements to purchase productive assets such as property, plant, and equipment
- Cash payments for the purchase of debt or equity instruments of other companies
- Disbursements of loans to other entities

Financing Activities

Financing activities include liability and owners' equity capital and result in a return on the owners' investments. It also involves acquiring cash from creditors and repaying amounts borrowed.

Cash Inflows.   These result from the following transactions or events:

- Cash receipts from the sale of equity instruments
- The receipt of proceeds from the issuance of such debt instruments as bonds, notes, mortgages, and other short- or long-term borrowings

Cash Outflows.   These result from the following transactions or events:

- Dividend payments or other distributions to stockholders
- The acquisition of capital stock
- The repayment of long-term debt

PREPARING THE STATEMENT OF CASH FLOWS

The data provided on each of the activities in the statement of cash flows are derived from the following sources:

- *Balance sheet (Schedule F9).* This source provides data on changes from the beginning of a period to the end of the period in assets, liabilities, and equities.
- *Estimated statement of earnings (Schedule D1).* This source reveals how much cash was provided or used by the company during a specific period.
- *Other selected sources.* These sources provide additional data on how cash was generated or applied during a specific period.

Operating activity data are obtained from items within the estimated statement of earnings, investing activity data are obtained from changes in long-term assets found on the balance sheet, and financing activity data are generally obtained from changes in long-term liability and stockholders' equity activities also found on the balance sheet.

In the statement of cash flows, cash inflows and outflows of operating activities are listed first. Those of investing activities are listed second, and those of financing activities are listed last. Schedule F10 provides a sample format of the statement of cash flows (see Exhibit 31.1).

There are three major steps in preparing this statement:

Step 1

In step 1 the preparer determines the change in the cash balance (Schedule F9, line 4) from one period to another.

Step 2

In step 2 the preparer determines the net cash flows from operating activities as found on the balance sheet (Schedule F9) and the estimated statement of earnings (Schedule D1). It is important to note that the estimated statement of earnings generally follows the accrual basis of accounting; that is, revenues are recorded before they are collected, and expenses are recorded before they are actually paid. Net earnings (Schedule D1, line 19) must be converted to record revenues that were actually received in cash and expenses that were actually paid in cash.

For example, consider the illustrations of simple financial statement presentations in Exhibits 31.2 and 31.3.

Exhibit 31.1 Statement of Cash Flows

Schedule ____F10____   Company Name _____

Period _____

☐ Six months   ☐ Total year

LINE	($ in 000s)	Reference						Total
1	CASH FLOWS FROM OPERATING							
2	ACTIVITIES							
3	CASH INFLOWS							
4	Cash receipts from sales							
5	Collections of receivables							
6	Interest/dividends-loans							
7	Other							
8	CASH OUTFLOWS							
9	Payments to suppliers							
10	Payments to employees							
11	Payments for taxes							
12	Payments of interest							
13	Other							
14	Net cash flow from operating							
15	activities							
16								
17	CASH FLOWS FROM INVESTING							
18	ACTIVITIES							
19	CASH INFLOWS							
20	Sale of productive assets							
21	Receipts of sales of debt or							
22	equity							
23	Other							
24	CASH OUTFLOWS							
25								

Exhibit 31.1   *(continued)*

Schedule _____ **F10 (continued)** _____   Company Name _____

Period   □ Six months   □ Total year

L I N E	($ in 000s)	Reference						Total
26	Purchases of productive assets							
27								
28	Payments of debt/equity							
29	instruments of other companies							
30								
31	Disbursement of loans to other							
32	entities							
33	Net cash flow from							
34	investing activities							
35								
36	CASH FLOWS FROM FINANCING							
37	ACTIVITES							
38	CASH INFLOWS							
39	Cash from sale of equity							
40	instruments							
41	Proceeds from debt sales							
42	CASH OUTFLOWS							
43	Dividend payments							
44	Acquisition of capital stock							
45	Repayment of long-term debt							
46								
47	Net cash flow from financing							
48	activities							
49								
50								

Exhibit 31.1 (continued)

Schedule __F10 (continued)__

Company Name

Period
☐ Six months ☐ Total year

LINE	($ in 000s)	Reference						Total
51	Net increase (decrease) in cash							
52								
53	Cash and cash equivalents—							
54	beginning of year							
55	Cash and cash equivalents—							
56	end of year							
57								
58								
59								
60								
61								
62								
63								
64								
65								
66								
67								
68								
69								
70								
71								
72								
73								
74								
75								

Exhibit 31.2 The Bob Corporation Estimated Statement of Earnings for the Year Ended December 31, 20X1

Revenues	$150,000
Operating expenses	(100,000)
Income before income taxes	50,000
Tax expenses	(10,000)
Net earnings	$ 40,000

Note: A dividend of $25,000 was paid during the year.

Given the above financial statements, the net cash flow from operating activities is $35,000 as computed in Exhibit 31.4.

Step 3

In step 3 the preparer determines the net cash flows from both the investing and financing activities. These are derived from the other balance sheet items to determine what accounts caused an increase (decrease) in cash.

As the comparative balance sheet in Exhibit 31.3 shows, two of the balance sheet accounts increased: Common stock increased by $10,000 due to the issuance of common stock for cash, and retained earnings increased by $15,000. The retained earnings account increased by $15,000 due to an increase in net earnings of $40,000, less $25,000 paid in cash dividends.

Exhibit 31.3 The Bob Corporation Comparative Balance Sheet

Assets	12/31/20XX	12/31/20X1	Change Inc/(Dec)
Cash	$ 75,000	$ 95,000	$20,000
Accounts receivable	45,000	60,000	15,000
Total	$120,000	$155,000	
Liabilities and Stockholders' Equity			
Accounts payable	$ 15,000	$ 25,000	$10,000
Common stock	65,000	75,000	10,000
Retained earnings	40,000	55,000	15,000
Total	$120,000	$155,000	

Exhibit 31.4   Computation of Net Cash Flow from Operating Activities

Cash received from sales		
Revenues	$150,000	
Less: Accounts receivable increase	($15,000)	$135,000
Cash disbursed for expenses		
Operating expenses	100,000	
Less: Accounts payable increase	(10,000)	(90,000)
Income before income taxes		45,000
Tax payments		(10,000)
Net cash flow from operating activities		$ 35,000

Given the above information, a statement of cash flows can be prepared as shown in Exhibit 31.5.

You will note that the increase in cash of $20,000 corresponds to the increase in cash on the comparative balance sheet (Exhibit 31.3). Therefore, we can say that the increase in cash of $20,000 from 12/31/20XX to 12/31/20X1 was due to a $35,000 increase in cash from operating activities and a negative ($15,000) cash loss from financing activities.

Exhibit 31.5   Statement of Cash Flows for the Year Ended December 31, 20X1

Cash flows from operating activities		
Net earnings		$40,000
Add (deduct) accounts not affecting cash		
Increase in accounts receivable	$(15,000)	
Increase in accounts payable	10,000	(5,000)
Net cash flow from operating activities		35,000
Cash flows from financing activities		
Common stock issued	10,000	
Cash dividend payments	(25,000)	
Cash provided by financing activities		$(15,000)
Net increase in cash		$20,000

CHAPTER THIRTY-TWO

Leasing*

In today's environment, leasing is playing a major role in acquiring assets. It is simply another way of acquiring or using assets as opposed to buying an asset. A more classical definition of leasing is a contract whereby one party (lessor) conveys the use of a capital asset to another party (lessee) for a specified rate for a specified period.

Leasing assumes "pay-as-you-use" without actually owning the asset. In inflationary times, this can be advantageous by providing payment with cheaper dollars in future years.

ADVANTAGES OF LEASING

The advantages of the leasing process are as follows:

- Conserves cash initially since large payments are not due when initially acquiring the asset.
- It protects against technological changes when the asset becomes obsolete due to technology, for example, computer equipment.
- It provides an excellent cash forecasting technique since fixed payments are outlined in the lease agreement.

---

*For further discussions on leasing, see *Handbook of Budgeting*, fourth edition, by Robert Rachlin (New York: John Wiley & Sons, 1998), Chapter 21.

- Can provide a company with the ability to test certain assets before deciding to purchase them, or to use assets for peak periods of production.
- Can provide an off-balance sheet type of financing.
- Can offer certain tax advantages.

TYPES OF LEASING ARRANGEMENTS

Most companies enter into either an operating lease or a capital lease.

In an operating lease, the lessor documents in both the short and long term the value of the asset, related depreciation, and any incurred debt. The lessee only records on the earnings statement the expenses related to leasing.

Under a capital lease arrangement, the lessee records all transactions such as the value of the asset, its related depreciation, incurred debt, and all related expense items on the earnings statement. Unlike the operating lease, the lessor does not document any transactions on the balance sheet, but does record related revenues on the earnings statement, which were generated by the lease agreement.

Where Leases Can Be Acquired

Leasing arrangements can be obtained from independent leasing companies, intermediaries such as brokers, and financial institutions (banks, finance and insurance companies). These institutions serve as a source of acquiring assets through leasing arrangements.

LEASE VERSUS CASH PURCHASE

To illustrate the financial impact of lease versus the cash purchase of assets, the following assumptions are presented.

Cost of asset—$100,000

Depreciable life—10 years

Depreciation method—straight line

No salvage/scrap value

Tax rate—40%

Lease term—10 years

Monthly rental payment—120 payments of $1,100

For purposes of simplicity, other assets associated with leasing and purchasing (state and local taxes, insurance, repairs and maintenance, interest, etc.) are not included in the calculation. (See Exhibits 32.1 and 32.2.)

Exhibit 32.1   Calculation of Net Cash Cost—Leasing

Year	Lease Payment	Tax Effect	Net Cash Cost
0	—	—	—
1	$13,200	$(5,280)	$7,920
2	13,200	(5,280)	7,920
3	13,200	(5,280)	7,920
4	13,200	(5,280)	7,920
5	13,200	(5,280)	7,920
6	13,200	(5,280)	7,920
7	13,200	(5,280)	7,920
8	13,200	(5,280)	7,920
9	13,200	(5,280)	7,920
10	13,200	(5,280)	7,920
	$132,000	$(52,800)	$79,200

Exhibit 32.2   Calculation of Net Cash Cost—Cash Purchase

Year	Cost	Depreciation	Tax Effect	Net Cash Cost
0	$100,000	—	—	$100,000
1		$ 10,000	$ (4,000)	(6,000)
2		10,000	(4,000)	(6,000)
3		10,000	(4,000)	(6,000)
4		10,000	(4,000)	(6,000)
5		10,000	(4,000)	(6,000)
6		10,000	(4,000)	(6,000)
7		10,000	(4,000)	(6,000)
8		10,000	(4,000)	(6,000)
9		10,000	(4,000)	(6,000)
10		10,000	(4,000)	(6,000)
	$100,000	$100,000	$(40,000)	$ 40,000

Exhibit 32.3   Cumulative Net Cash Costs—Lease versus Cash Purchase

Year	Lease	Cash Purchase	Available Cash Through Leasing
0	—	$100,000	$100,000
1	$ 7,920	94,000	86,080
2	15,840	88,000	72,160
3	23,760	82,000	58,240
4	31,680	76,000	44,320
5	39,600	70,000	30,400
6	47,520	64,000	16,480
7	55,440	58,000	2,560
8	63,360	52,000	(11,360)
9	71,280	46,000	(25,280)
10	$79,200	$ 40,000	$ (39,200)

The illustrations highlight the fact that leasing conserves cash during the equipment's early productive years. For example, during the first seven years (see Exhibit 32.3) the cash available through leasing is favorable by $2,560. However, for the remaining three years (years 8–10), a cash purchase is favorable. You can see that over the ten year life of the lease, additional cash ($39,200) is needed. However, it is assumed that the excess capital had been productively put to use.

APPLYING DISCOUNTED CASH FLOW TECHNIQUES

To fully analyze the cash advantages or disadvantages of leasing versus cash purchasing, it is necessary to compare both methods by applying the time value of money. This requires applying a present value factor to each year's net cash cost. The selection of a discount rate assumes that the capital conserved by the use of leasing can be reinvested into other investment opportunities, yielding at least what can be earned in today's market. The bare minimum should be at least as high as the current cost of capital. To illustrate, we will use a fifteen percent discount rate (see Exhibit 32.4).

Exhibit 32.4 Present Value of $1

							Interest Rate						
Year	1%	2%	3%	4%	5%	6%	7%	8%	9%	10%	12%	14%	15%
1	.990	.980	.971	.962	.952	.943	.935	.926	.917	.909	.893	.877	.870
2	.980	.961	.943	.925	.907	.890	.873	.857	.842	.826	.797	.769	.756
3	.971	.942	.915	.889	.864	.840	.816	.794	.772	.751	.712	.675	.658
4	.961	.924	.889	.855	.823	.792	.763	.735	.708	.683	.636	.592	.572
5	.951	.906	.863	.822	.784	.747	.713	.681	.650	.621	.567	.519	.497
6	.942	.888	.838	.790	.746	.705	.666	.630	.596	.564	.507	.456	.432
7	.933	.871	.813	.760	.711	.665	.623	.583	.547	.513	.452	.400	.376
8	.923	.853	.789	.731	.677	.627	.582	.540	.502	.467	.404	.351	.327
9	.914	.837	.766	.703	.645	.592	.544	.500	.460	.424	.361	.308	.284
10	.905	.820	.744	.676	.614	.558	.508	.463	.422	.386	.322	.270	.247
11	.896	.804	.722	.650	.585	.527	.475	.429	.388	.350	.287	.237	.215
12	.887	.788	.701	.625	.557	.497	.444	.397	.356	.319	.257	.208	.187
13	.879	.773	.681	.601	.530	.469	.415	.368	.326	.290	.229	.182	.163
14	.870	.758	.661	.577	.505	.442	.388	.340	.299	.263	.205	.160	.141
15	.861	.743	.642	.555	.481	.417	.362	.315	.275	.239	.183	.140	.123
16	.853	.728	.623	.534	.458	.394	.339	.292	.252	.218	.163	.123	.107
17	.844	.714	.605	.513	.436	.371	.317	.270	.231	.198	.146	.108	.093
18	.836	.700	.587	.494	.416	.350	.296	.250	.212	.180	.130	.095	.081
19	.828	.686	.570	.475	.396	.331	.276	.232	.194	.164	.116	.083	.070
20	.820	.673	.554	.456	.377	.319	.258	.215	.178	.149	.104	.073	.061
25	.780	.610	.478	.375	.295	.233	.184	.146	.116	.092	.059	.038	.030
30	.742	.552	.412	.308	.231	.174	.131	.099	.075	.057	.033	.020	.015

							Interest Rate *(continued)*						
Year	16%	18%	20%	24%	28%	32%	36%	40%	50%	60%	70%	80%	90%
1	.862	.847	.833	.808	.781	.758	.735	.714	.667	.625	.588	.556	.526
2	.743	.718	.694	.650	.610	.574	.541	.510	.444	.391	.346	.309	.277
3	.641	.609	.579	.524	.477	.435	.398	.364	.296	.244	.204	.171	.146
4	.552	.516	.482	.423	.373	.329	.292	.260	.198	.153	.120	.095	.077
5	.476	.437	.402	.341	.291	.250	.215	.186	.132	.095	.070	.053	.040
6	.410	.370	.335	.275	.227	.189	.158	.133	.088	.060	.041	.029	.021
7	.354	.314	.279	.222	.178	.143	.116	.095	.059	.037	.024	.016	.011
8	.305	.266	.233	.179	.139	.108	.085	.068	.039	.023	.014	.009	.006
9	.263	.226	.194	.144	.108	.082	.063	.048	.026	.015	.008	.005	.003
10	.227	.191	.162	.116	.085	.062	.046	.035	.017	.009	.005	.003	.002
11	.195	.162	.135	.094	.066	.047	.034	.025	.012	.006	.003	.002	.001
12	.168	.137	.112	.076	.052	.036	.025	.018	.008	.004	.002	.001	.001
13	.145	.116	.093	.061	.040	.027	.018	.013	.005	.002	.001	.001	.000
14	.125	.099	.078	.049	.032	.021	.014	.009	.003	.001	.001	.000	.000
15	.108	.084	.065	.040	.025	.016	.010	.006	.002	.001	.000	.000	.000
16	.093	.071	.054	.032	.019	.012	.007	.005	.002	.001	.000	.000	
17	.080	.060	.045	.026	.015	.009	.005	.003	.001	.000	.000		
18	.089	.051	.038	.021	.012	.007	.004	.002	.001	.000	.000		
19	.030	.043	.031	.017	.009	.005	.003	.002	.000	.000			
20	.051	.037	.026	.014	.007	.004	.002	.001	.000	.000			
25	.024	.016	.010	.005	.002	.001	.000	.000					
30	.012	.007	.004	.002	.001	.000	.000						

Exhibits 32.5, 32.6, and 32.7 illustrate the comparisons between lease and cash purchasing using discounted cash flow techniques.

Exhibit 32.5   Net Present Value Under a Lease Agreement

Year	Net Cash Costs	Present Value Factors @ 15%	Present Values
0	—	1.000	—
1	$ 7,920	.870	$ 6,890
2	7,920	.756	5,988
3	7,920	.658	5,211
4	7,920	.572	4,530
5	7,920	.497	3,936
6	7,920	.432	3,421
7	7,920	.376	2,978
8	7,920	.327	2,590
9	7,920	.284	2,249
10	7,920	.247	1,956
	$79,200		$39,749

Exhibit 32.6   Net Present Value Under a Cash Purchase

Year	Net Cash Costs	Present Value Factors @ 15%	Present Values
0	$100,000	1.000	$100,000
1	(6,000)	.870	(5,220)
2	(6,000)	.756	(4,536)
3	(6,000)	.658	(3,948)
4	(6,000)	.572	(3,432)
5	(6,000)	.497	(2,982)
6	(6,000)	.432	(2,592)
7	(6,000)	.376	(2,256)
8	(6,000)	.329	(1,974)
9	(6,000)	.284	(1,704)
10	(6,000)	.247	(1,482)
	$40,000		$69,874

Exhibit 32.7   Cumulative Present Value Net Cash Costs

Year	Lease	Cash Purchase	Available Cash Through Leasing
0	—	$100,000	$100,000
1	$ 6,890	94,780	87,890
2	12,878	90,244	77,366
3	18,089	86,296	68,207
4	22,619	82,864	60,245
5	26,555	79,882	53,327
6	29,976	77,290	47,314
7	32,954	75,034	42,080
8	35,544	73,060	37,516
9	37,793	71,356	33,563
10	$39,749	$69,874	$30,125

Exhibit 32.6 is a cumulative comparison of net cash costs after present value factors have been applied.

Under discounted cash flow techniques, leasing provides favorable capital throughout the life of the asset. However, it is again assumed that the available capital generated through leasing can be reinvested in other profitable investments at the current rate with at least a 15 percent after-tax return.

CHAPTER THIRTY-THREE

Monitoring and Controlling Budget Variances

Monitoring and controlling budget variances is a vital part of the budgeting process. It is the means by which management is kept informed of the extent to which the business has performed as set forth in the budget. It provides an understanding of the interrelationships between actual performance and budgetary expectations.

Budget variances must be monitored and controlled for the following reasons:

- To provide follow-up on budget commitments by each element of the company
- To evaluate management performance in relation to expectations versus actual results
- To pinpoint significant problem areas within the company
- To initiate timely corrective action on variances
- To provide the basis for developing new goals and objectives

The vehicles that communicate the information needed for monitoring and control are the various types of reports issued on a periodic basis such as weekly, monthly, quarterly, and yearly. The number and frequency of these reports must be determined by weighing the cost of production and the time the recipient needs to read and absorb the material against the value and urgency of the information. In addition, some reports require special analysis and are prepared only when needed. These reports vary according to company and circumstances.

MAJOR TYPES OF BUDGET PERFORMANCE REPORTS

The typical types of reports used to report budget variances include the following:

Accounting Financial Statement Reports. These reports reflect the variances of the items contained in the statement of earnings and the balance sheet. The items are similar to the financial statements prepared for the annual budget. Exhibit 33.1 illustrates the headings of these variance reports.

Exhibit 33.1 Illustration of Accounting Financial Statement Reports

Company Name
Statement of Earnings
As of December 31, 20XX

	Current Month			Year-to-Date		
Line Items	Actual	Budget	Variance	Actual	Budget	Variance
———	———	———	———	———	———	———
———	———	———	———	———	———	———
———	———	———	———	———	———	———
———	———	———	———	———	———	———
———	———	———	———	———	———	———
———	———	———	———	———	———	———
———	———	———	———	———	———	———
———	———	———	———	———	———	———
———	———	———	———	———	———	———
———	———	———	———	———	———	———
———	———	———	———	———	———	———

Company Name
Balance Sheet
As of December 31, 20XX

Line Items	Actual	Budget	Variance
———	———	———	———
———	———	———	———
———	———	———	———
———	———	———	———
———	———	———	———
———	———	———	———

Departmental Expense Statement Reports.   These reports reflect variations of different departments within the organization. For example, the marketing and sales function of the organization would have many sales departments within a territory. A typical sales department would report its expenses for a specific period as shown in Exhibit 33.2.

Product Cost Reports.   These reports summarize the production costs of specific products. Let us assume that Product A has to go through three production processes (priming, painting, and drying) and management wants to monitor and control the total costs of producing that product. A typical product cost report would be developed as shown in Exhibit 33.3.

Product Line Profit Contribution Reports.   These reports summarize the profit contribution for a specific product and/or product line for a specific period. This summary allows management to decide what amount of resources to allocate to the product and/or product line and whether to continue or discontinue the product and/or product line. Exhibit 33.4 illustrates such a report. A similar report would be prepared for the year ended December 31, 20XX.

Product Line Gross Margin Reports.   These reports summarize gross margins by product. They reflect data on net sales, cost of sales, and gross margin by product

Exhibit 33.2   Illustration of a Departmental Expense Statement Report

Sales Department
As of December 31, 20XX

	Month			Year-to-Date		
	Actual	Budget	Variance	Actual	Budget	Variance
Sales salaries	————	————	————	————	————	————
Sales commissions	————	————	————	————	————	————
Support staff salaries	————	————	————	————	————	————
Rent	————	————	————	————	————	————
Telephone	————	————	————	————	————	————
Utilities	————	————	————	————	————	————
Travel and entertainment	————	————	————	————	————	————
Supplies	————	————	————	————	————	————
Postage	————	————	————	————	————	————
Other: (Specify)	————	————	————	————	————	————
Total	————	————	————	————	————	————

Exhibit 33.3   Illustration of a Product Cost Report

Product AA
Cost Report
For Year Ended December 31, 20XX

	Month			Year-to-Date		
	Actual	Budget	Variance	Actual	Budget	Variance
<u>Priming Department</u>	___	___	___	___	___	___
Labor costs	___	___	___	___	___	___
Material costs	___	___	___	___	___	___
Supplies	___	___	___	___	___	___
<u>Painting Department</u>						
Labor costs	___	___	___	___	___	___
Material costs	___	___	___	___	___	___
Supplies	___	___	___	___	___	___
<u>Drying Department</u>						
Labor costs	___	___	___	___	___	___
Other costs	___	___	___	___	___	___
Total	___	___	___	___	___	___

Exhibit 33.4   Illustration of a Product Line Profit Contribution Report

Product Line A
Profit Contribution Report
For Month Ended December 31, 20XX

	Actual	Budget	Variance
Net sales	___	___	___
Cost of sales	___	___	___
Gross margin	___	___	___
Operating expenses	___	___	___
Selling expenses	___	___	___
Administrative expenses	___	___	___
Allocated expenses: (Specify)	___	___	___
Total operating expenses			
Profit Contribution	___	___	___

within a product line. Exhibit 33.5 illustrates such a report. Similar reports would be prepared for year-to-date results.

Nonfinancial Performance Reports.   These reports summarize key nonfinancial performance indicators that represent the "pulse points" of the business. These in-

Exhibit 33.5   Illustration of a Product Line Gross Margin Report

Product Line A
Gross Margin Report
For Month Ended December 31, 20XX

Net Sales

Product	Actual	Budget	Variance
Product AA	_____	_____	_____
Product BB	_____	_____	_____
Product CC	_____	_____	_____
Product DD	_____	_____	_____
Product EE	_____	_____	_____
Total	_____	_____	_____

Cost of Sales

Product	Actual	Budget	Variance
Product AA	_____	_____	_____
Product BB	_____	_____	_____
Product CC	_____	_____	_____
Product DD	_____	_____	_____
Product EE	_____	_____	_____
Total	_____	_____	_____

Gross Margin

Product	Actual	Budget	Variance
Product AA	_____	_____	_____
Product BB	_____	_____	_____
Product CC	_____	_____	_____
Product DD	_____	_____	_____
Product EE	_____	_____	_____
Total	_____	_____	_____

clude, but are not limited to, the items shown in Exhibit 33.6. A year-to-date report would also be prepared.

Financial/Nonfinancial Performance Reports.   These reports blend both financial and nonfinancial performance indicators. These also represent the "pulse points" of the business and include, but are not limited to, the items shown in Exhibit 33.7. A year-to-date report would also be prepared.

Supplemental Data Reports.   In addition to the other reports listed, these special reports may be prepared to assist in monitoring and controlling segments of the business. They may provide the following information, but requirements would vary with the nature of the company and its needs.

- Orders to be received by units, dollars, or both
- Sales in units and average selling price when units are similar
- Significant increases/(decreases) in sales volume in units, dollars, or both that are anticipated from the addition of products, new territories, and the like, or from the abandonment of old ones
- Percentage increase/(decrease) in the weighted average of sales prices from the actual current prices
- Major changes that are contemplated in methods of distributing the product/ product line
- Relationship between the total distribution cost per sales dollar
- Number of employees, employee hours, average hourly wages, and average yearly income of employees in the distribution function

Exhibit 33.6   Illustration of a Nonfinancial Performance Report

Nonfinancial Performance Report
For Month Ended December 31, 20XX

	Actual	Budget	Variance
Unit sales	———	———	———
Number of customers	———	———	———
Units/customers	———	———	———
Employee hours/units sold	———	———	———
Square feet/employee	———	———	———
KWH/unit produced	———	———	———

Exhibit 33.7   Illustration of a Financial/Nonfinancial Performance Report

---

Financial/Nonfinancial Performance Report
For Month Ended December 31, 20XX

	Actual	Budget	Variance
Net sales/employee	————	————	————
Net sales/units sold	————	————	————
Net sales/square foot	————	————	————
Employee benefit in dollars/employee	————	————	————
Payroll costs/employee	————	————	————

- Average percentage of the capacity of the plant(s) for each month of the budget period

- Major changes in the components of production costs

- Average yearly salaries of administrative employees by function

- Number of employees, employee hours, average hourly wages, and average yearly income of production employees

- Total number of employees by function

- Amount of the sales dollar to labor, materials, overhead, interest, taxes, dividends, and the remaining profits

- Book value and net earnings per share of stock by classification of stock

- Significant changes anticipated during the period in balance sheet items as cash, marketable securities, receivables, inventories, fixed assets, and current and fixed indebtedness

- Position of the industry, including share of market, technology, life cycle, and major economic and business factors

MEASURING VARIANCES IN REVENUE/GROSS MARGIN BUDGETS[1]

In measuring the impact of variances due to revenues and gross margins, it is extremely important to understand what factors affect gross margin and how to improve

---

[1]Robert Rachlin, *Successful Techniques for Higher Profits* (New York: MARR Publications, 1981), pp. 116–119.

the gross margin results. This is perhaps one the most important figures in the earnings statement. Remember that it is this amount that must pay for the costs of distributing the product, general and administrative costs, other operating costs, and taxes, yet still provide an adequate return.

Let us use the following hypothetical data to illustrate how to analyze gross margin:

	20X1	20X2	Variance
Units sold	75,000	100,000	25,000
Net sales	$500,000	$700,000	$200,000
Per unit	$6.667	$7.000	$0.333
Cost of sales	$390,000	$525,000	$135,000
Per unit	$5.200	$5.250	$0.050
Gross margin	$110,000	$175,000	$ 65,000
Percentage of net sales	22.0%	25.0%	3.0%

One of the key factors is the gross margin percentage. The illustration shows that this percentage for 20X1 was 22.0 percent and 25.0 percent for 20X2. This means that $0.22 and $0.25, respectively, are available for paying the other operating costs of the business and for providing an adequate return.

From the preceding data, note that net sales increased $200,000 as a result of the higher volume of 25,000 units and the slightly higher average selling price of $0.333. Because both sales volume and sales price are affected, we need to calculate a sales volume variance and a sales price variance.

Sales Volume Variance

Part of the change in net sales from one period to another is due to changes in the number of units sold. To reflect the impact of units sold on dollar net sales, the prior year's selling price must be kept constant, with units sold being variable. The calculation is as follows. The revenues from this year's units sold at the prior year's unit prices would be:

$$100,000 \times \$6.667 = \$666,667$$

The revenues from the prior year's units sold at the prior year's unit prices were:

$$75,000 \times \$6.667 = (\$500,000)$$

Therefore, a favorable sales volume variance would be $166,667.

Sales Price Variance

The other factor affecting net sales is price. When this year's unit sales are kept constant and unit selling price is variable, the following calculation results: The revenues of this year's units sold at this year's unit selling price would be:

$$100,000 \times \$7.00 = \$700,000$$

The revenues of this year's units sold at prior year's unit selling price would be:

$$100,000 \times \$6.667 = (\underline{\$666,667})$$

Therefore, a favorable sales price variance would be $33,333.

Note that a combination of both variances results in a total change of $200,000, the same amount of variance as shown in the original data.

Change in net sales	$\underline{\$200,000}$
Sales volume variance	$166,667
Sales price variance	$ 33,333

The cost of sales increased $135,000 because of higher unit costs of $0.50 and is referred to as the cost price variance. In addition, unit volume increased 25,000 units and is referred to as the cost volume variance. Because both volume and cost affects cost of sales, let us calculate both variances.

Cost Volume Variance.   By keeping the prior year's unit cost of sales constant and reflecting changes in unit volume, the cost volume variance is calculated as follows. The revenues from this year's units sold at the prior year's unit cost of sales would be:

$$100,000 \times \$5.200 = \$520,000$$

The revenues from the prior year's units sold at the prior year's unit cost of sales would be:

$$75,000 \times \$5.200 = \$390,000$$

Therefore, an unfavorable cost volume variance would be ($130,000).

Cost Price Variance.   This variance is used to measure changes in the cost of the product. It is calculated as follows. The revenues from this year's units sold at this year's unit cost of sales would be:

$$100,000 \times \$5.250 = \$525,000$$

The revenues from this year's units sold at the prior year's unit cost of sales would be:

$$100,000 \times \$5.200 = \$520,000$$

Therefore, an unfavorable cost price variance would be ($5,000).

Combining both cost variances results in the total cost of sales variance of $135,000, as follows:

Change in cost of sales	($135,000)
Cost volume variance	($130,000)
Cost price variance	($ 5,000)

Summary

An explanation of the $65,000 gross margin variance from period 20X1 to 20X2 is summarized in Exhibit 33.8. Note how each variance previously calculated has an impact upon the gross margin.

MEASURING VARIANCES IN EXPENSE BUDGETS[2]

Let us illustrate the process of measuring variances in expense budgets by examining the two major costs associated with the manufacturing of a product: material and labor costs.

Exhibit 33.8   Summary of Gross Margin Analysis

	Variance Calculations	Variances from Original Data
Net sales		$200,000
Sales volume variance	$166,667	
Sales price variance	33,333	
Cost of sales		(135,000)
Cost volume variance	(130,000)	
Cost price variance	(5,000)	
Gross margin		$ 65,000

[2]Robert Rachlin, *Successful Techniques for Higher Profits* (New York: MARR Publications, 1981), pp. 114–116.

How to Compute Material Cost Variance and Material Quantity Variance

Assume that the standard cost of material is $10 per unit, based on estimated costs from suppliers. Remember that these standards will have been prepared in advance of the actual purchase date. At the time of purchase, we bought 10,000 units of materials at a unit price of $11 because of an increase in the price of raw materials. Given these facts, one can conclude that there was an unfavorable variance to standard of $10,000, computed as follows:

$$10,000 \text{ units} \times \$11 \ = \ \$110,000$$
$$10,000 \text{ units} \times \$10 \ = \ (\$100,000)$$
$$\text{Unfavorable variance} \quad \$ \ 10,000$$

The material variance of $10,000 is unfavorable because it cost $1 more per unit of material as compared to the predetermined or budgeted standard of $10.

Now that we have computed the material variance, we need to reflect on the material quantity variance, which is computed at the time the raw materials are used. Assume that 8,000 units were estimated as a standard quantity for production. Actual units used were 9,000. What is the quantity variance?

$$9,000 \text{ units} \times \$10 \ = \ \$90,000$$
$$8,000 \text{ units} \times \$10 \ = \ (\$80,000)$$
$$\text{Unfavorable variance} \quad \$10,000$$

One can see that 1,000 more units of material were used, and, at the standard cost rate of $10 per unit, an unfavorable quantity variance of $10,000 arose.

The total material variance of $20,000 (material cost variance + material quantity variance) resulted because of higher raw material unit prices and more material used in the manufacturing of the product. In both cases comparison was made to a predetermined amount or a standard cost.

How to Compute Labor Variances

Labor variances include two factors: rate and efficiency. Together they form the labor variance from standards previously assigned. To illustrate, let us use the following data for both calculations:

Standards

Number of hours	5,000
Wage rate per hour	$6.00

Actual

Number of hours	5,200
Wage rate per hour	$5.50

Let use compute the labor rate variance first.

$$
\begin{aligned}
5{,}200 \text{ hours at } \$6.00 &= \$31{,}200 \\
5{,}200 \text{ hours at } \$5.50 &= (\$28{,}600) \\
\hline
\text{Favorable variance} \quad &\ \ \$\ 2{,}600
\end{aligned}
$$

This variance is favorable because of the lower wage rate of $5.50. If you multiply $0.50 (the difference) by 5,200 hours, you will arrive at the same favorable variance of $2,600.

The labor efficiency factor refers to the number of labor hours actually used versus labor hours estimated. Keeping the labor rate at standard, the variance is calculated as follows:

$$
\begin{aligned}
5{,}200 \text{ hours at } \$6.00 &= \$31{,}200 \\
5{,}000 \text{ hours at } \$6.00 &= (\$30{,}000) \\
\hline
\text{Unfavorable variance} \quad &\ \ \$\ 1{,}200
\end{aligned}
$$

The unfavorable variance of $1,200 arose because 200 more hours were worked. At a rate of $6.00 per hour, a $1,200 unfavorable labor efficiency rate resulted.

Combining both labor rate and labor efficiency variances, the total labor variances are favorable by $1,400 ($2,600 – $1,200).

SOURCES OF INFORMATION ON UNFAVORABLE VARIANCES

The following list points out sources in which a company can learn about unfavorable variances. Although this list is not definitive, it will provide the reader with a starting point:

- Sales analysis
- Production reports
- Accounting records
- Employee time records and overtime reports
- Personnel records
- Sales rep call reports
- Customer service reports
- Internal task force findings
- Internal and external audit reports

HOW TO COPE WITH UNFAVORABLE VARIANCES

There are many strategies for coping with unfavorable variances. The following list provides some suggestions and guidelines to carry out such strategies:

- Be decisive, creative, and realistic in your expectations.
- Make the task of solving a problem a team project.
- Encourage your staff to provide problem-solving suggestions.
- Be sure to establish a schedule of priorities, such as by day, week, or month.
- Call meetings periodically to review the status of priorities and targets that were established.
- Take immediate action on projects considered nonperformers.
- Communicate as soon as possible the status and approved actions within the various affected parts of the company.
- Try to give public credit to those who were involved in the problem-solving process as well as those responsible for the solution.

DEALING WITH BUDGET REVISIONS

Budget revisions often require negotiation skills and can be assisted by the following strategies:

- Try to concentrate on a few significant issues rather than ask for too much.
- Be sure that requests are fully documented.
- Use all avenues throughout the company to lobby for and promote your ideas and causes.
- When a decision is made, be sure to notify appropriate parties within the company.

TYPICAL MONTHLY MANAGEMENT REPORT

Once the variations have been determined, the final step is to prepare a monthly report to management. A typical management report is shown in Exhibit 33.9 and should be used merely as a guideline.

Exhibit 33.9   A Typical Monthly Management Report

Monthly Management Report
Bob Division
For Month of _____

Actual net sales for _____ of $X were X% of budget, but X% of actual last year. Especially good performance was accomplished with our new line of Y products. On a year-to-date basis, we are X% of budget and X% of last year.

Costs for _____ were on budget, which brings year-to-date costs of X% of budget. Slow-moving inventories are being analyzed, and special promotions are being planned to dispose of those products by the end of the quarter.

Expenses for _____ were X% over budget, primarily due to accelerating promotions for Y products that were budgeted for later periods. This brings year-to-date expenses to X% of budget. Total full-year expenses are expected to be only X% of budget as a result of planned reductions in travel and sales meetings in the second half.

Profits for _____ were X% below budget, which brings year-to-date performance to X% of budget. Full-year profitability is still expected to come in on budget.

Total human resource headcount for _____ is still X% below budget, 2% in production, and X% in the field sales force. Active recruiting is under way.

Collection of receivables is slightly behind budget, but this has been identified as a timing problem and not a collection issue. About $X of inventory has been determined to be obsolete and will be written off in the next accounting period.

Key Performance Indicators (list)

CHAPTER THIRTY-FOUR

Behavioral Implications of Budgeting

The last issue to be discussed within the budgeting process involves behavioral implications. Almost all the previous chapters of this book have dealt with the technical aspects of preparing the budget. In many cases, however, the behavioral aspects of preparing the budget play an equally important part in the budgeting process. The various aspects of outlook, accuracy, goal setting, and creativity involved in preparing budgets are direct results of behavior.

In this final chapter it is important to highlight the critical areas of behavior that affect the budgeting process. The following points are intended to assist the preparer of budgets in bringing together those critical areas that will lead to successful and workable budgets.[1]

Behavioral Judgment. The individuals responsible for the budgeting process must apply sound behavioral judgment in the development, administration, and modification of the budgeting system. The whole process must instill in all participants the three elements of success: enthusiasm, creativity, and productivity. Bringing together these three elements can be the catalyst in achieving the goals set forth by the organization.

---

[1]Robert Rachlin, *Handbook of Budgeting*, fourth edition (New York: John Wiley & Sons, 1999), pp. 34.18–34.19.

Understanding Goals. It is important to understand the goals set forth by the organization. In addition, these goals must relate to the individual's personal goals in respect to rewards, recognition, social status, and ethical standards. To be accomplished, organizational and personal goals must be in basic harmony. When they conflict, neither personal nor organizational goals will be achieved, and conflicts will develop.

Attitudes of Top Management. For the budgeting process to be successful, top management must have favorable attitudes toward the following factors: active participation, flexibility, fairness, openness, goal accomplishment, cost consciousness, productivity, and diligence. These attitudes must be transmitted to employees and supported when needed.

Understanding the Roles of Line versus Staff. Everyone in the organization must observe and understand the roles of line versus staff functions. This means that operating delineations and reporting structures must be adhered to and respected.

Aspirations. Management must continually attempt to raise the aspiration levels of individual managers and the company as a whole. These aspirations can be realized with the help of advanced technical assistance offered through professional and motivational seminars. Management itself can raise the aspiration levels of its employees by showing support and instilling confidence during both the budgeting process and the performance evaluation stage.

Pressure. An effort to minimize pressure would go a long way toward achieving budgeting goals. This does not mean that management can be lax in establishing time pressure and commitments. However, management must set realistic goals and time constraints in regard to budgeting and performance evaluation. This approach will help reduce the pressure usually associated with the budgeting process.

Overcoming Resistance to Change. Resistance to change is caused by uncertainty, lack of communication, and lack of confidence in leadership, and must be avoided. Overcoming these barriers will tend to lessen the resistance to change and result in a more cohesive organization.

Measurement Standards. Establishing unfair and irrelevant measurement standards creates an unfavorable behavioral environment. It also contributes to many of the problems mentioned above. To avoid these negative consequences, management must establish fair, relevant, and consistent measurement standards of what is good or bad.

Padding the Budget.   When lack of confidence, high stress, and poor leadership exist in an organization, managers tend to "pad the budget." This means that they allow sufficient flexibility to achieve favorable variances of actual performance versus budgetary predictions. Such padding prevents the company from investing in opportunities, because fictitious elements are contained in the budgets. These elements include higher than expected expenses and lower than expected revenues. This process of self-protection results from poor human relations and lack of confidence in management's philosophy of performance measurement, as outline above.

Approving Budgets.   Management must use a positive motivational approach in approving budgets. Too often only negatives are used. For example, rather than always criticizing the budget projections, managers should dwell on the positive aspects and deemphasize the negatives of the budget.

    This list has briefly outlined some of the behavioral considerations involved in the budgeting process. Effort should be made to avoid the negative and reinforce the positive.

    Good luck in preparing your next budget.

Worksheets and Schedules

Memorandum

TO: Budget Preparer
FROM: Author
SUBJECT: Preparation of New Year's Budget

The following are copies of the worksheets and schedules presented within the text. The exhibits should be used prior to preparing the budget schedules to support much of the company's philosophy and strategy of operating the business, which should be reflected in your budget for next year.

Refer to the text to review instructions before preparing the exhibits and schedules. These schedules and worksheets provide a basic format for preparing a budget. It will be necessary to adjust and modify budgeted accounts and strategies to meet your company's specific needs.

With that in mind, now proceed to develop a workable and realistic budget. GOOD LUCK.

ADDITIONAL WORKSHEETS AND SCHEDULES

Identification	*Title*
Exhibit 2.1	Key Overall Issues
Exhibit 2.2	Financial Impact Profile
Exhibit 3.3	Form for Determining Weighted Industry Average Return on Assets Rates
Exhibit 3.6	Ratio Profile of a Company
Exhibit 7.1	Budgeting System Checklist
Schedule A1	Unit Sales/Revenue Budget—Product
Schedule A2	Unit Sales/Revenue Budget—Territory
Schedule A3	Unit Sales/Revenue Budget—Customers
Schedule A4	Unit Sales/Revenue Budget—Salesperson
Schedule B1	Unit Production Budget
Schedule B2	Direct Labor Budget
Schedule B3	Direct Materials Budget
Schedule B4	Manufacturing Departmental Budget
Schedule B5	Product Budget
Schedule C4	Distribution Cost Budget
Schedule C1	Administrative Departmental Budget
Schedule C2	Advertising and Promotion Expenses
Schedule C5	Research and Development Budget
Schedule C3	Other Income and Expense Budget
Schedule D1	Estimated Statement of Earnings
Schedule E2	Cash Receipts Budget
Schedule E1	Cash Disbursements Budget
Schedule F1	Accounts Receivable Budget
Schedule F2	Inventory Budget
Schedule F3	Other Current Assets Budget
Exhibit 24.1	Establishing Company Priorities for Capital Spending
Exhibit 24.2	Preliminary Budget Request Form
Exhibit 24.3	Capital Budget Form
Exhibit 24.4	Capital Expenditures in Process Report
Exhibit 24.5	Plant Appropriation Request (PAR) Form
Exhibit 24.6	Capital Investment Proposal
Exhibit 24.7	Capital Expenditure Proposal—Project Schedule
Schedule F4	Fixed Assets Budget
Schedule F5	Loan Budget
Schedule F6	Accounts Payable Budget

Key Overall Issues

Company/Operating Unit

Time Span

Preparer:

Date Prepared:

Used in What Budgeting Period:

KEY ISSUE:

Factors concerning the business:

How these factors will become part of the budgeting process:

Estimate of risk:

Financial Impact Profile

					Financial Impact Profile					
Company/Operating unit										Budget period
Impact on Earnings Statement					Economic Factors	Impact on Balance Sheet				
Volume	Sales $	Price	Operating Expenses	Earnings		Working Capital	Capital Structure	EPS	ROI	Capital Expenditure
					Interest rate fluctuations					
					Changes in currency values					
					Inflation rate					
					Governmental legislation					
					Declining productivity					
					Technology					
					Political unrest					
					Mergers and acquisitions					
					Natural disaster					
					Competitive reactions					
					Strikes					
					Supplier capacity					
					Unemployment					
					Market collapse					
					Social changes					
					High labor and material costs					
					Energy shortages					
					Industry growth					
					Demographic changes					
					Weather					
					Seasonal index					
					Material shortage					

Indicate (+) for positive results; (−) for negative results; (+ −) for both

Preparer _____   Date Prepared _____

Form for Determining Weighted Industry Average Return on Assets Rates

Weighted Industry Average Return On Assets Rates

Budget Period _____   Date Prepared _____

                                        Approval _____

Calculation

Industry Segments*	Current Industry ROA Rates	Percentage of Segments of Company's Assets	Weighted Average

Comments (state relationship of weighted average rate to overall corporate objectives).

*Should coincide as closely as possible with each industry for which company operates.

Ratio Profile of a Company

Ratio Profile of a Company

Company _____

Budget Period _____

Category Standard	Prior Year's Actual	Budget Period	Industry Standard	Actions To Be Taken
Measuring Liquidity				
Working capital				
Inventory turnover				
Days' sales in receivables				
Current ratio				
Days' sales in inventory				
Accounts receivable turnover				
Evaluating Debt				
Debt to equity				
Cash flow/debt				
Times interest earned				
Debt to assets				
Measuring profit				
Earnings per share				
Return on capital				
Return on equity				
Net profit margin				
Total asset turnover				

Budgeting System Checklist

Budgeting System Checklist

Company _____

Sequence of Preparation	Responsibility	Date Required	Date Received
1. Establish overall goals and objectives			
2. Establish divisional, product, departmental goals and objectives			
3. Develop "grass roots" estimates of:	////////	////////	////////
a. Sales to new and existing customers			
b. Human resource requirements by department			
c. Additional new and replacement machinery and equipment			
d. Financial capabilities			
4. Prepare the required budgets:	////////	////////	////////
a. Sales and profit budget			
b. Production budget			
• materials budget			
• direct labor budget			
• manufacturing overhead budget			

(continued)

(continued)

Sequence of Preparation	Responsibility	Date Required	Date Received
c. Marketing expense budget			
• sales personnel budget			
• sales administration budget			
• advertising and promotion budget			
• distribution budget			
• service and parts budget			
d. Research and development budget			
e. Administration budget			
f. Capital investment budget			
g. Cash budget			
h. Balance sheet budget			
• accounts receivable budget			
• inventory budgets			
• fixed asset budget			
5. Assemble the sub-budgets and prepare the master budget			
6. Review the master budget and negotiate changes			
7. Redo sub-budgets with changes			
8. Reproduce and distribute budgets			
9. Develop monthly performance reports			
10. Conduct monthly management reviews of performance compared to budget			
11. Keep track of necessary changes for future budgets			

Unit Sales/Revenue Budget

Schedule _____ **A1**

Period

☐ Six months ☐ Total year

Product _____

Company Name

Page _____ of _____

L I N E	($ in 000s)	Reference						Total
1	PRODUCT							
2	X – number of units							
3	– unit price							
4	– sales revenue (L2xL3)							
5								
6	Y – number of units							
7	– unit price							
8	– sales revenue (L6xL7)							
9								
10	Z – number of units							
11	– unit price							
12	– sales revenue (L10xL11)							
13								
14	Total gross revenues (L4+L8+L12)							
15	Less: discounts							
16	Net sales	To D1,L2						
17								
18	Total unit sales (L2+L6+L10)	To D1,L1						
19								
20								
21								
22								
23								
24								
25								

271

Unit Sales/Revenue Budget

Schedule **A2**   Territory _____   Company Name _____   Page _____ of _____

Period ☐ Six months ☐ Total year

($ in 000s)

LINE		Reference						Total
1	TERRITORY							
2	NORTH							
3	X – number of units							
4	– unit price							
5	– sales revenue (L3xL4)							
6								
7	Y – number of units							
8	– unit price							
9	– sales revenue (L7xL8)							
10								
11	Z – number of units							
12	– unit price							
13	– sales revenue (L11xL12)							
14								
15	Total gross revenues (L5+L9+L13)							
16	Less: discounts							
17	Net sales	To D1,L2						
18								
19	Total units sales (L3+L7+L11)	To D1,L1						
20								
21								
22								
23								
24								
25								

Unit Sales/Revenue Budget

Schedule **A3**   Customers _____

Company Name _____   Page _____ of _____

Period   [ ] Six months   [ ] Total year

LINE	($ in 000s)					Reference	Total
1	CUSTOMER NAME						
2	PRODUCT						
3	x – number of units						
4	– unit price						
5	– sales revenue (L3xL4)						
6							
7	Y – number of units						
8	– unit price						
9	– sales revenue (L7xL8)						
10							
11	Z – number of units						
12	– unit price						
13	– sales revenue (L11xL12)						
14							
15	Total gross revenues (L5+L9+L13)						
16	Less: discounts						
17	Net sales					To D1,L2	
18							
19	Total unit sales (L3+L7+L11)					To D1,L1	
20							
21							
22							
23							
24							
25							

Unit Sales/Revenue Budget

Schedule __**A4**__   Salesperson _____   Page ____ of ____

Period   ☐ Six months   ☐ Total year   Company Name

LINE	($ in 000s)	Reference						Total
1	SALESPERSON							
2	E. JONES							
3	X – number of units							
4	– unit price							
5	– sales revenue (L3xL4)							
6								
7	J. SMITH							
8	X – number of units							
9	– unit price							
10	– sales revenue (L8xL9)							
11								
12	Z – number of units							
13	– unit price							
14	– sales revenue (L12xL13)							
15								
16	H.BROWN							
17	Y – number of units							
18	– unit price							
19	– sales revenue (L17xL18)							
20								
21	Total gross revenues (L5+							
22	L10+L14+L19)							
23	Less: discounts							
24	Net sales	To D1,L2						
25	Total unit sales (L3+L8+L12+L17)	To D1,L1						

Unit Production Budget

Schedule _____ **B1**

Company Name _____

Period ☐ Six months ☐ Total year

LINE	($ in 000s)	Reference							Total
1	PRODUCT X								
2	Unit sales	From A1,L2							
3	Beginning inventory								
4	Net production (L2-L3)								
5	Desired finished goods inventory								
6	Required production (L4+L5)								
7	Spoilage and waste allowance								
8	Units to be produced (L6+L7)								
9	PRODUCT Y								
10	Unit sales	From A1,L6							
11	Beginning inventory								
12	Net production (L10-L11)								
13	Desired finished goods inventory								
14	Required production (L12+L13)								
15	Spoilage and waste allowance								
16	Units to be produced (L14+L15)								
17	PRODUCT Z								
18	Unit sales	From A1,L10							
19	Beginning inventory								
20	Net production (L18-L19)								
21	Desired finished goods inventory								
22	Required production (L20+L21)								
23	Spoilage and waste allowance								
24	Units to be produced (L22+L23)								
25									

Direct Labor Budget

Schedule **B2**

Period ☐ Six months ☐ Total year

Product _____

Company Name _____

Page _____ of _____

LINE	($ in 000s)	Reference						Total
1	DEPARTMENT A							
2	Units to be produced	From B1						
3	Standard hours per unit							
4	Total hours (L2xL3)							
5	Rate per hour							
6	Total direct labor (L4xL5)							
7								
8	DEPARTMENT B							
9	Units to be produced	From B1						
10	Standard hours per unit							
11	Total hours (L9xL10)							
12	Rate per hour							
13	Total direct labor (L11xL12)							
14								
15	DEPARTMENT C							
16	Units to be produced	From B1						
17	Standard hours per unit							
18	Total hours (L16xL17)							
19	Rate per hour							
20	Total direct labor (L18xL19)							
21								
22	Total direct labor (L6+L13+L20)	To B5,L8						
23								
24								
25								

Direct Materials Budget

Schedule **B3**   Product _____   Company Name _____   Page __1__ of __2__

Period ☐ Six months ☐ Total year

L I N E	($ in 000s)	Reference								Total
1	PRODUCT X									
2	Units of material A required									
3	Unit cost									
4	Material A cost (L2xL3)									
5										
6	Units of material B required									
7	Unit cost									
8	Material B cost (L6xL7)									
9										
10	Units of material C required									
11	Unit cost									
12	Material C cost (L10xL11)									
13	Total product X (L4+L8+L12)	To B5, L7								
14										
15	PRODUCT Y									
16	Units of material A required									
17	Unit cost									
18	Material A cost (L16xL17)									
19										
20	Units of material B required									
21	Unit cost									
22	Material B cost (L20xL21)									
23	Units of material C required									
24	Units of material C required									
25	Unit cost									

277

(continued)

Schedule __B3 (continued)__

Product _____

Company Name

Period ☐ Six months ☐ Total year

LINE	($ in 000s)	Reference							Total
26	Material C cost (L24xL25)								
27	Total product Y (L18+L22+L26)	To B5, L7							
28									
29	PRODUCT Z								
30	Units of material A required								
31	Unit cost								
32	Material A cost (L30xL31)								
33									
34	Units of material B required								
35	Unit cost								
36	Material B cost (L34xL35)								
37									
38	Units of material C required								
39	Unit cost								
40	Material C cost (L38xL39)								
41	Total product Z (L32+L36+L40)	To B5, L7							
42									
43	Total direct materials (L13+L27+L41)	To D1, L5							
44									
45									
46									
47									
48									
49									
50									

Manufacturing Departmental Budget

Schedule __B4__

Department _____

Page ____ of ____

Period ☐ Six months ☐ Total year

Company Name _____

L-I-N-E	($ in 000s)	Reference							Total
1	LABOR								
2	Supervisory								
3	Indirect								
4	PAYROLL								
5	Vacations								
6	Holidays								
7	Overtime								
8	Insurance								
9	Pensions								
10	Taxes								
11	Other								
12	VARIABLE-OTHER								
13	Utilities								
14	Supplies								
15	Other								
16									
17	FIXED								
18	Training and development								
19	Depreciation								
20	Property taxes								
21	Insurance								
22	Other								
23									
24	OTHER								
25	Total	To B5,L9							

Product Budget

Schedule **B5**   Product _____   Page _____ of _____

Period _____

☐ Six months ☐ Total year

Company Name _____

LINE	($ in 000s)	Reference						Total
1	Units	From A1						
2								
3	Price per unit	From A1						
4								
5	Sales revenues (L1xL3)							
6	COST OF SALES							
7	Direct materials	From B3						
8	Direct labor	From B2, L22						
9	Manufacturing overhead	From B4, L25						
10								
11								
12	Other							
13	Total cost of sales							
14								
15	Profit contribution							
16	Percent to revenues (L5)							
17	SUPPLEMENTAL DATA							
18								
19								
20								
21								
22								
23								
24								
25								

Distribution Cost Budget

Schedule ___ **C4**

Company Name _____

Period ☐ Six months ☐ Total year

LINE	($ in 000s)	Reference							Total
1	Direct selling								
2									
3	Transportation expenses								
4	Truck								
5	Rail								
6	Air								
7	Ship								
8	Total								
9									
10	Warehousing and storage								
11									
12	Market research								
13	Other (specify)								
14									
15									
16									
17	Total other								
18									
19	Total distribution costs	To D1,L14							
20									
21									
22									
23									
24									
25									

Administrative Departmental Budget

Schedule __C1__   Department _____   Company Name _____   Page __1__ of __2__

Period ☐ Six months ☐ Total year

LINE	($ in 000s)	Reference							Total
1	HEADCOUNT								
2	Professional								
3	Clerical support								
4	Other								
5	Total								
6									
7	PAYROLL								
8	Professional								
9	Clerical support								
10	Other								
11	Overtime								
12									
13	Total								
14									
15	EMPLOYEE BENEFITS								
16	Employee taxes								
17	Insurance								
18	Pensions								
19	Vacation								
20	Other								
21	Total								
22	Office supplies								
23	Rent								
24	Telephone								
25	Cable charges								

(continued)

282

(continued)

Schedule ___C1 (continued)___

Department _____

Company Name _____

Period

☐ Six months ☐ Total year

L I N E	($ in 000s)	Reference							Total
26	Travel and entertainment								
27	Depreciation-office equipment								
28	Utilities								
29	Insurance								
30	Office expense - other								
31	Advertising and promotion	From C2,L17							
32	Taxes								
33	Bad debt losses								
34	Outside fees (specify)								
35									
36	Total	To D1,L10							
37									
38									
39									
40									
41									
42									
43									
44									
45									
46									
47									
48									
49									
50									

Advertising and Promotion Expenses

Schedule ___ **C2**

Page ___ of ___

Period ☐ Six months ☐ Total year

Company Name ___

L I N E	($ in 000s)	Reference						Total
1	Newspaper ads							
2	Shopper ads							
3	Magazine and periodical ads							
4	Telephone directories							
5	Radio							
6	Telephone							
7	Direct mail campaigns							
8	House-to-house distribution							
9	Personal demonstrations							
10	Exhibits							
11	Catalogues							
12	Samples							
13								
14								
15								
16	Total advertising and							
17	promotion expenses	To D1,L10						
18								
19								
20								
21								
22								
23								
24								
25								

Research and Development Budget

Schedule ____ **C5**

Period ☐ Six months ☐ Total year

Company Name ____

Page ____ of ____

LINE	($ in 000s)	Reference					Total
1	SALARIES AND WAGES						
2	Administrative staff						
3	Nonadministrative staff						
4	Technical staff						
5	Other						
6	Total salaries and wages						
7							
8	MATERIALS AND SUPPLIES						
9	Expendable equipment						
10	Chemical and lab supplies						
11	Repairs						
12	Other						
13	Total materials and supplies						
14							
15	OTHER DIRECT EXPENSE						
16	Taxes and insurance						
17	Periodicals						
18	Dues and memberships						
19	Depreciation						
20	Utilities						
21	Travel and entertainment						
22	Other						
23	Total other direct expenses						
24							
25	Total R&D Expenses	To D1,L9					

Other Income and Expense Budget

Schedule ___**C3**___

Company Name _____

Period _____

☐ Six months ☐ Total year

L I N E	($ in 000s)	Reference									Total
1	OTHER INCOME										
2	Gains from sale of securities										
3	Interest earned										
4	Dividends on company-owned shares										
5	Rent earned										
6	Gains from sale of plant and equipment										
7	Total other income										
8											
9	OTHER EXPENSE										
10	Interest on money borrowed										
11	Interest on notes given to creditors										
12											
13	Losses from sale of plant and equipment										
14											
15											
16	Total other expense										
17											
18	Other income (expense)	To D1,L13									
19											
20											
21											
22											
23											

Estimated Statement of Earnings

Schedule ___ **D1**

Page _____ of _____

Period ☐ Six months ☐ Total year

Company Name

LINE	($ in 000s)	Reference						Total
1	Units	From A1–A4*						
2	Net sales	From A1–A4*						
3	COST OF SALES							
4	Direct labor	From B2,L22						
5	Direct materials	From B3,L43						
6	Overhead	From B4,L25						
7	Total cost of sales							
8	Gross profit (L2–L7)							
9	Research and development	From C5,L25						
10	Selling and administrative expenses	From C1,L36;C2,L17						
11	Earnings before other income (expense) and income taxes							
12								
13	Other income (expense)	From C3,L18						
14	Distribution costs	From C4,L19						
15	Earnings before income taxes							
16								
17	Income taxes							
18								
19	Net earnings							
20								
21	*Represents units and net sales from either A1,A2,A3,or A4 depending on how units							
22	and revenues are presented							
23								
24								
25								

287

Cash Receipts Budget

Schedule __E2__

Company Name _____

Period ☐ Six months ☐ Total year

L I N E	($ in 000s)	Reference						Total
1	Net sales	From A1,L16						
2								
3	COLLECTIONS OF ACCOUNTS							
4	RECEIVABLE*							
5	Collection within current month							
6	Collection within 1 month ago							
7	Collection beyond 2 months ago							
8	Collection beyond 3 months ago							
9	Total							
10	Other cash receipts	From C3,L7						
11	Total cash receipts	To E3,L3						
12								
13								
14								
15								
16								
17								
18	* Remaining balance from line 1							
19								
20								
21								
22								
23								
24								
25								

Cash Disbursements Budget

Schedule _____ **E1**

Period ☐ Six months ☐ Total year

Company Name _____

L I N E	($ in 000s)	Reference						Total
1	Cash purchases—raw material	From B3,L43						
2								
3	PAYMENTS OF ACCOUNTS PAYABLE							
4								
5	Payment within one month							
6	Payment within second month							
7	Payment beyond second month							
8								
9	Telephone	From C1,L24						
10	Rent payments	From C1,L23						
11	Utilities	From C1,L28						
12	Office supplies	From C1,L22						
13	EMPLOYEE PAYROLL AND BENEFITS							
14	Payroll	From C1,L13						
15	Benefits	From C1,L21						
16								
17								
18	Loan repayments							
19	Tax payments	From C1,L32						
20	Purchase(s)—fixed assets	From F4,L4						
21	Cash dividends							
22	Interest payments	From C3,L10-L11						
23	Other cash disbursements	From C1						
24	Total	To E3,L8						
25								

Accounts Receivable Budget

Schedule ____**F1**____

Company Name _____

Page ____ of ____

Period _____

☐ Six months ☐ Total year

L I N E	($ in 000s)	Reference						Total
1	Beginning accounts receivable							
2	balance	Y/E balance						
3	Plus:							
4	Monthly net sales	From D1,L2						
5	Less:							
6	Collections	From E2,L9						
7	Bad debts:	Company percentage						
8	Accounts receivable—net	To F9,L6						
9								
10								
11								
12								
13								
14								
15								
16								
17								
18								
19								
20								
21								
22								
23								
24								
25								

Inventory Budget

Schedule _____ **F2**

Page _____ of _____

Period
☐ Six months ☐ Total year

Company Name

LINE	($ in 000s)	Reference						Total
1	FINISHED GOODS INVENTORY							
2	Beginning balance	Prior month						
3	Plus:							
4	Goods manufactured							
5	Less:							
6	Cost of sales	From D1,L7						
7	Total							
8	Work-in-process inventory							
9								
10	Raw material inventory	From B3,L44						
11								
12	Total ending inventory (L7,L8,L10)	To F9,L7						
13								
14								
15								
16								
17								
18								
19								
20								
21								
22								
23								
24								
25								

Other Current Assets Budget

Schedule ___ **F3** ___

Page ___ of ___

Period ___

☐ Six months ☐ Total year

Company Name

L I N E	($ in 000s)	Reference								Total
1	PREPAID EXPENSES									
2	Rent									
3	Interest									
4	Insurance									
5	Supplies									
6	Other									
7	Total									
8										
9	Other									
10	Total (L7+L9)	To F9,L8								
11										
12										
13										
14										
15										
16										
17										
18										
19										
20										
21										
22										
23										
24										
25										

Establishing Company Priorities for Capital Spending

Company

Budget Year

	Percentage of Total Budget	
	High Priority	Low Priority
Making your company a low-cost producer		
Replacing and modernizing normal plant and equipment		
Meeting required environmental standards		
Bringing in major new high technology		
Consolidating existing product lines		
Starting up new product lines		
Adding to present productive capacity		
Other: (List)		

Preliminary Budget Request Form

XYZ CORPORATION
Capital Expenditure
Preliminary Budget Request

Department _____   Number _____

Division _____   Date _____

Project Classification: Request (check one):

_____ Replacement/Cost Reduction   ☐ Original

_____ Expansion   ☐ Supplementary

_____ New

_____ Other _____

(please specify)

Description of Proposed Investment

Amount Needed: $ _____ (as shown below)

$_____ Fixed Assets + $_____ Working Capital − $_____ Net Cash Flow from Replaced Items = $_____ Net Investment

Expected Cash Flow (Benefits):

Expected Time Schedule and Priority:

Expected Benefits and Returns on Investment:

Approvals and Acknowledgements:

	Signature	Date
Project Originator	_____	_____
Department Head	_____	_____
Division Controller	_____	_____
Division Head	_____	_____
Corporate Controller	_____	_____
Director of Budgets	_____	_____
Corporate President	_____	_____

294

Capital Budget Form

Page Number _____

XYZ CORPORATION
Capital Budget
For Year 20XX

Department/Division _____

| Department | Item number | Description | Status | | Total expenditure | Expenditure this budget | Estimated R.O.I. | Priority 1, 2, or 3 | Classification | | |
			New	Cont.					Replacement cost reduction	Expansion	New	Other
Total												

Capital Expenditures in Process Report

XYZ CORPORATION
Capital Expenditures in Process Report

Item number	Description	Approval amount	Original project completion date	Spent to date	Needed for completion	Total	Expected variation	Favorable (F) Unfavorable (UF)	Expected completion date	Comments
Example X1-A-601	Replacement of casting machines	3.000.000	12/31/X1	2.000.000	1.100.000	2.100.000	100.000	UF	March 31. 20X1	Approval was obtained for 100.000 overrun

Plant Appropriation Request (PAR) Form

1. Plant appropriation request (PAR)   No. _____

       . . . . Group   Approval required

       . . . . Division

       . . . . Department   . . . .

       . . . . Product line

       . . . . Project location   (Dollar amounts in thousands)

2. Summary description of proposed project

3. Project expenditures

	This request	Previously approved	Future requests	Total project
Basis for approval				
Related expense				
Total				

4. Key financial measurements

Chart of cumulative funds flow

	Reported	Inflation-adjusted
DCRR	____%	____%
Payback period (years)	____	____

Amount

_____ Reported

. . . . . . Inflation-adjusted

0

20   20   20   20   20   20   20   20   20   20

(continued)

297

(continued)

5. Business history and forecast of .... Department/operation

Market position (a)	Reported						Inflation-adjusted (c)			
	Sales			Net income				Net income		
	Amt.	Price index (b)		Amt.	ROS	ROI	Sales	Amt.	ROS	ROI

Year

a. Last five years:
   20
   20
   20
   20
   20

b. Forecast with proposed project:
   Current year
   20
   Next five years
   20
   20
   20
   20
   20

6. Business history and forecast of ....
   .... product line

a. Last five years:
   20
   20
   20
   20
   20

b. Forecast with proposed project:
   Current year
   20
   Next five years
   20
   20
   20
   20
   20

c. Increment resulting from project:
   Current year
   20
   Next five years
   20
   20
   20
   20
   20

a- Basis -   Federal income tax rate used -
b- 20 = 100; Basis -
c- Base year -

7. Summary of project expenditures

	This request	Previously approved	Future requests	Total project
Investment expenditures...........................				
Associated deferred charges.......................				
Lease-commitments not capitalized plus lease related expenses...........................				
Subtotal – Basis for approval......................				
Patterns and tooling..............................				
All other related expense				
Grand total				
As a memo:				
All other starting costs...........................				
Trade-in value of surplus equipment				

8. Category(s):

	Total	Investment	Expense
Category (prime)			
Category (other)			
Category VII (if applicable)			
Total, this request			

Two calendar years following project completion

9. Estimated gain (loss) in net income to other G.E. Components: 20____   20____

10. Facility to be replaced

First cost.....................................
Year purchased...............................
Book value ....

Description of facility and proposed disposition

11. Starting date . . . .
month/year

Completion date . . . .
month/year

12. Utilization anticipated in first year after project completion – 20 . . . .
. . . .%

Basis . . . .

13. Number of employees
Location

	Before	After	Before	After
Manufacturing				
All other				
Total				

(continued)

(continued)

14. Performance on closed appropriations

Appropriations
past 3 years (a)

	Total expenditures	Project incremental net income	
		1st year	2nd year
Forecast (b)			
Actual			
VF% (c)			

Board appropriations
past 5 years

	Total expenditures	Project incremental net income	
		1st year	2nd year
Forecast (b)			
Actual			
VF%(c)			

(a) – CEO approval and above
(b) – In appropriation requests
(c) – Variance from forecast

15. Principal competitors

	Estimated rank or market position	
Name	This year	Last year

16. Appropriation endorsed and supporting financial data certified by

. . . .
Manager–Finance

Appropriation endorsed or approved by . . . .

. . . .

. . . .
Manager–Marketing

. . . .
Manager–Employee relations

. . . .
Manager–Engineering

. . . .
Manager–Manufacturing

. . . .
Legal Counsel

. . . .
Manager–Strategic operational planning

. . . .
Department general manager   Date

. . . .
Division general manager   Date

. . . .
Group executive   Date

. . . .

Capital Investment Proposal

Division or company: _____

1. *General description and justification.* This is, for example, the underlying situation and the solution; assets to be acquired; market profitability.

2. *Classification.* Projects are slotted for ongoing business or as new ventures. They are further classified according to objective, for example:

   a. Reduce costs.

   b. Improve quality.

   c. Increase output.

   d. Improve market position.

   e. Comply with legislation.

3. *Profitability.* The future effect on the firm or unit of the firm.

4. *Inflation.* Indexes used and their sources.

5. *Assumptions.* The main variables affecting the project, plus:

   a. Project yield sensitivity to changes in these variables.

   b. Estimated probabilities of such changes.

6. *Project risk.* Based on the analysis for (5) above, estimate the probability of a significant variance from estimated project profitability.

7. *Alternatives considered.* Include plausible options and the reasons for their rejection.

8. *Staff comments.* Include advisory and service groups and other management groups consulted, and their opinions. Explain where these opinions were not accepted.

Capital Expenditure Proposal—Project Schedule

Company/Group _____ Proposal no. _____

Title of project _____

	Years	0	1			10	11
Year-on-year general inflation rate (%)							
Fixed capital (including residual values)							
Land							
Buildings							
Plant and machinery							
Vehicles							
Other fixed assets							
	Subtotal						
Proceeds of disposals							
	Subtotal						
Working capital (including residual values)							
	Subtotal						
Repairs							
Initial expenses							
Profit before tax and depreciation							
Tax payable (see below)							
Net cash flow in current terms							
Net cash flow in constant terms							
Tax calculation in current terms							
Profit before tax and depreciation							
Depreciation							
Other allowances/adjustments—detail:							
Taxable amount							
Tax incurred, at _____ (%)							

Indicators
DCF yield in constant terms _____ (%).
DCF yield in current terms _____ (%).
Payback period in current terms_____ years

Fixed Assets Budget

Schedule _____ **F4**

Period _____

☐ Six months ☐ Total year

Company Name _____

Page _____ of _____

LINE	($ in 000s)	Reference							Total
1	Fixed assets-net beginning balance	Y/E balance							
2									
3	Plus:								
4	Additions								
5	Less:								
6	Disposals								
7	Depreciation allowance								
8									
9	Fixed assets-net ending balance	To F9,L15							
10									
11									
12									
13									
14									
15									
16									
17									
18									
19									
20									
21									
22									
23									
24									
25									

Loan Budget

Schedule ___ **F5**

Page ___ of ___

Period ☐ Six months ☐ Total year

Company Name ___

LINE	($ in 000s)	Reference					Total
1	SHORT-TERM DEBT						
2	Beginning balance	Y/E balance					
3	New loans-disbursements	From E3,L16					
4	New loans-fixed assets additions	From E1,L20					
5	New loans-other	From E3					
6	Less: repayments	From E1,L18					
7							
8	Ending balance	To F9,L30					
9							
10							
11	LONG-TERM DEBT						
12	Beginning balance						
13	Current	Y/E balance					
14	Long-term	Y/E balance					
15	Plus new loans-L3,4,5						
16	Less repayments-L6						
17							
18	Ending balance						
19	Current	To F9,L32					
20	Long-term	To F9,L38					
21							
22							
23							
24							
25							

Accounts Payable Budget

Schedule _____ **F6**

Company Name _____

Page _____ of _____

Period ___ ☐ Six months ☐ Total year

LINE	($ in 000s)	Reference							Total
1	Accounts payable—beginning balance	Y/E balance							
2	Add:								
3	Materials—manufacturing	From B5,L7							
4	Other—manufacturing	From B5,L9,L12							
5	G&A	From C1,L36							
6	Other								
7									
8	Deduct:								
9	Disbursements	From E3,L8							
10									
11	Accounts payable—ending balance	To F9,L33							
12									
13									
14									
15									
16									
17									
18									
19									
20									
21									
22									
23									
24									
25									

305

Other Liabilities Budget

Schedule _____ **F7**

Period _____

☐ Six months ☐ Total year

Page _____ of _____

Company Name _____

L I N E	($ in 000s)	Reference						Total
1	Accrued expenses	To F9,L34						
2	Income taxes	To F9,L35						
3	Deferred income taxes	To F9,L39						
4	Other noncurrent liabilities	To F9,L40						
5								
6								
7								
8								
9								
10								
11								
12								
13								
14								
15								
16								
17								
18								
19								
20								
21								
22								
23								
24								
25								

Equity Budget

Schedule _____ **F8**

Period ☐ Six months ☐ Total year

Company Name _____

Page _____ of _____

LINE	($ in 000s)	Reference						Total
1	Retained earnings-beginning balance Y/E balance							
2	Plus: net earnings	From D1,L19						
3	Less: dividends	Company policy						
4	Retained earnings-ending balance	To F9,L46						
5								
6	Capital stock	To F9,L44						
7	Paid-in capital in excess							
8	of par	To F9,L45						
9								
10								
11								
12								
13								
14								
15								
16								
17								
18								
19								
20								
21								
22								
23								
24								
25								

307

Balance Sheet Budget

Schedule ___ **F9** ___

Company Name _____

Period

☐ Six months ☐ Total year

LINE	($ in 000s)	Reference					Total
1	Assets						
2							
3	Current assets						
4	Cash	From E3,L11					
5	Short-term securities	From E3,L18					
6	Accounts receivable-net	From F1,L8					
7	Inventories	From F2,L12					
8	Other current assets	From F3,L10					
9	Total current assets	L4-L8					
10							
11	Property, plant and						
12	equipment-gross						
13	Less:accumulated depreciation						
14	Property, plant, and						
15	equipment-net	From F4,L9					
16							
17	Other noncurrent assets						
18							
19	Total assets	L9+L15+L17					
20							
21							
22							
23							
24							
25							

(continued)

Schedule ___**F9 (continued)**___

Period ⬚ Six months ⬚ Total year

Company Name _____

LINE	($ in 000s)	Reference						Total
26	LIABILITIES AND STOCKHOLDERS'							
27	EQUITY							
28								
29	Current liabilities							
30	Short-term debt	From F5,L8						
31	Current installments of							
32	long-term debt	From F5,L19						
33	Accounts payable	From F6,L11						
34	Accrued expenses	From F7,L1						
35	Income taxes	From F7,L2						
36	Total current liabilities	L30-L35						
37								
38	Long-term debt	From F5,L20						
39	Deferred income taxes	From F7,L3						
40	Other noncurrent liabilities	From F7,L4						
41	Total noncurrent liabilities	L38-L40						
42								
43	STOCKHOLDERS' EQUITY							
44	Stock (specify)	From F8,L6						
45	Capital surplus	From F8,L8						
46	Retained earnings	From F8,L4						
47	Total stockholders' equity	From F8,L4						
48								
49	Total liabilities and	L36+						
50	stockholders' equity	L41+L47						

Statement of Cash Flows

Schedule ____**F10**____

Period ☐ Six months ☐ Total year

Company Name _____

($ in 000s)	Reference					Total
1 CASH FLOWS FROM OPERATING						
2 ACTIVITIES						
3 CASH INFLOWS						
4 Cash receipts from sales						
5 Collections of receivables						
6 Interest/dividends-loans						
7 Other						
8 CASH OUTFLOWS						
9 Payments to suppliers						
10 Payments to employees						
11 Payments for taxes						
12 Payments of interest						
13 Other						
14 Net cash flow from operating						
15 activities						
16						
17 CASH FLOWS FROM INVESTING						
18 ACTIVITIES						
19 CASH INFLOWS						
20 Sale of productive assets						
21 Receipts of sales of debt or						
22 equity						
23 Other						
24 CASH OUTFLOWS						
25						

(continued)

Schedule ____ **F10 (continued)** ____

Company Name _____

Period _____

☐ Six months ☐ Total year

LINE	($ in 000s)	Reference					Total
26	Purchases of productive assets						
27							
28	Payments of debt/equity						
29	instruments of other companies						
30							
31	Disbursement of loans to other						
32	entities						
33	Net cash flow from						
34	investing activities						
35							
36	CASH FLOWS FROM FINANCING						
37	ACTIVITES						
38	CASH INFLOWS						
39	Cash from sale of equity						
40	instruments						
41	Proceeds from debt sales						
42	CASH OUTFLOWS						
43	Dividend payments						
44	Acquisition of capital stock						
45	Repayment of long-term debt						
46							
47	Net cash flow from financing						
48	activities						
49							
50							

(continued)

(continued)

Schedule ___**F10 (continued)**___

Company Name _____

Period ☐ Six months ☐ Total year

L I N E	($ in 000s)	Reference							Total
51	Net increase (decrease) in cash								
52									
53	Cash and cash equivalents-								
54	beginning of year								
55	Cash and cash equivalents-								
56	end of year								
57									
58									
59									
60									
61									
62									
63									
64									
65									
66									
67									
68									
69									
70									
71									
72									
73									
74									
75									

Index